FULLY CHARGED

Also by Heike Bruch

A Bias for Action: How Effective Managers Harness Their Willpower, Achieve Results, and Stop Wasting Time

HOW GREAT LEADERS BOOST THEIR ORGANIZATION'S ENERGY AND IGNITE HIGH PERFORMANCE

FULLY CHARGED

HEIKE BRUCH / BERND VOGEL

HARVARD BUSINESS REVIEW PRESS / BOSTON, MASSACHUSETTS

Library of Congress Cataloging-in-Publication Data

Bruch, Heike.
   Fully charged : how great leaders boost their organization's energy and
ignite high performance/Heike Bruch, Bernd Vogel.
      p. cm.
   ISBN 978-1-4221-2903-6 (hbk. : alk. paper)   1.   Employee motivation.
2. Organizational behavior.   3. Organizational effectiveness.   4. Performance.
I. Vogel, Bernd,   1970-   II. Title.
   HF5549.5.M63B79 2011
   658.3'14—dc22

                                                                    2010030908

To our families

Contents

Acknowledgments   ix

Introduction   **Leadership Is the Art of Orchestrating Energy**   1

1   **The Energy Matrix**   21

2   **Mobilizing Your Organization's Energy**   61
Escaping the Complacency Trap

3   **Rebuilding Positive Energy**   105
Escaping the Corrosion Trap

4   **Focusing Your Organization's Energy**   139
Escaping the Acceleration Trap

5   **Sustaining Energy to Rise Above Number One**   173
Getting Beyond the Traps

6   **Energizing Leaders**   225
Personal Perspectives on Boosting Energy

Appendix   **How to Assess Your Organization's Energy**   239

Notes   247
Index   257
About the Authors   271

Acknowledgments

A project like this takes a lot of energy. We are grateful to numerous institutions and individuals who helped to boost our energy and to maintain it.

We would like to emphasize the contribution of the late Sumantra Ghoshal. He was a pivotal influence on the early work on organizational energy that Heike initiated in 2001. But Sumantra was also an important source of inspiration and courage for the whole process of this research, and he still is.

Many people at the Institute for Leadership and Human Resource Management, University of St. Gallen, contributed to the agenda of organizational energy; some have moved to other institutions, but continue to work on this subject: Stephan Boehm, Michael S. Cole (Texas Christian University), Simon de Jong, Daniela Dolle, Florian Kunze, Jochen Menges (University of Cambridge), Sabine Poralla (AGCO), Anneloes Raes, and Frank Walter (University of Groningen). Their academic input but also administrative support was essential.

We are grateful to the many companies that warmed to our ideas and worked with us over the years. In particular, we would like to mention the companies that supported our early research in the consortium of the Organizational Energy Program (OEP) between 2003 and 2006: ABB, Alstom, Hilti, Lufthansa, Tata Steel, and Unaxis. With their trust and confidence in our work on energy and their readiness to collaborate with us in empirical studies, they made it possible to lay the foundation for the energy concept.

We would also like to thank the team of the energy factory, who helped us implement the energy concept in multiple organizations, learn from their experience, and further develop our knowledge on energizing leadership strategies.

We owe huge thanks to the institutions that financially supported our research: Basic Research Fund (GFF) of the University of St. Gallen, the Gebert Rüf Foundation, the Swiss Society for Organization and Management (SGO), and the Swiss National Science Foundation (SNF).

We are also grateful to those who supported the development of the manuscript: Justus Kunz, Johannes Lampert, David Maus, Rainer Sedlmayr, Christian Schudy, Slawomir Skwarek (all University of St. Gallen), and Julie Stout (Henley Business School). Lucy McCauley helped us shape this book by making the ideas sharper and more precise. Ania Wieckowski led us through the entire publishing process and helped us improve the quality and accessibility of the manuscript. We are very grateful to Lucy and Ania and their colleagues at Harvard Business Review Press who worked behind the scenes to bring this book together into its present form.

Heike Bruch, St. Gallen, Switzerland
Bernd Vogel, Henley, United Kingdom

Leadership Is the Art of Orchestrating Energy

Why do some companies buzz with energy and life, while others suffer from stagnation and complacency? Why do some organizations achieve peaks of energy and activity only to plunge into valleys of stagnant inertia? Why do still other organizations seem poisoned through and through by negative politicking and bickering, or else lost in a slough of organizational burnout?

Most leaders have experienced the ebb and flow of different states of energy in their own organizations. This energy belongs to the intangible but very powerful, so-called soft factors of human potential that lie at the core of all companies. We call this phenomenon *organizational energy* and define it as the extent to which an organization (or a division or team) has mobilized its emotional, cognitive, and behavioral potential to pursue its goals. We believe that organizational energy is measurable and therefore manageable. Much as you may have felt the symptoms of low energy in your organization—apathy, tiredness, inflexibility, cynicism—you can also deliberately boost and sustain your organization's energy so that your people are fully charged and positively energized around business goals.

1

The ability to boost energy is critical because energy is "the fuel that makes great organizations run" and therefore is a cornerstone to your people's effectiveness and your company's extraordinary performance.[1] Our research has shown that more than almost any other factor affecting a business, energy in organizations can lead to either a wellspring of corporate vitality or the destruction of its very core. Leaders need to understand organizational energy, especially in financially tense times, when executives need to find ways to engage every potential resource and advantage to its fullest. But this understanding is also key for senior executives and other leaders working in other demanding situations like turnarounds, high-speed growth, long-lasting change processes, or the introduction of innovations to the market. Leaders like Lufthansa's former CEO Juergen Weber have told us that for them, the critical question is, "How do I motivate this company in *good* times?"

The good news is that all leaders can learn to boost and leverage the positive energy of their organizations. And in this book, we will show you how.

The Case of CWT Netherlands

Carlson Wagonlit Travel (CWT) offers a good illustration of organizational energy leadership in action. A $27.8 billion firm, CWT manages business travel for more than fifty thousand companies in 150 countries worldwide. Beginning in 2000, the travel industry underwent many changes. To CWT, the ambition had been to develop long-term commitment and relationships with customers through excellent services and added value. To accomplish this, top management knew that employees on all levels needed to be highly engaged and motivated—to collectively and individually be able to identify and respond flexibly to changing customer expectations and market shifts.

But high engagement and motivation were not what Jan Willem Dekker saw when he looked around his division, CWT Netherlands, in 2007.[2] Rather than a responsive workforce, Dekker, managing director of the Netherlands and executive vice president of North Europe, saw unenthusiastic employees, reduced levels of activity, and languishing internal communication. One group of employees seemed convinced that CWT's best days were long gone; they complained about the new strategic direction of the company. Another group of employees seemed overly satisfied. Believing that things were going well and that CWT did enough for its customers, these employees did not pay full attention to individual customer needs. Still others, while appearing on the surface to do their jobs, lacked the will or readiness to take the initiative, develop new ideas, or go to the limit to pursue the ambitious strategy of CWT. Overall, most CWT employees shared a common conviction that the decade-old reorientation of the company ultimately wouldn't succeed, and they approached the new strategy implementation accordingly—detached and ineffectively.

While the company faced no dramatic declines or financial crises, Dekker wanted more out of his team: peak performance, excellence, and enthusiasm. As long as the employees' potential lay idle or continued to be consumed by internal fighting and complaining, the division would not create outstanding value for its customers and could never achieve close customer loyalty and prevail in the market.

But CWT's employee opinion surveys, which showed medium engagement scores for his area, weren't telling Dekker enough about the source of the issue. How could he objectively assess the low energy he intuitively sensed in the division? And how could he then take that information to improve the situation? We worked with Dekker to conduct an assessment that we call the Organizational Energy Questionnaire (OEQ).[3] We'll return to the OEQ later, but using the test with over 70 percent of his division—265 employees and managers—Dekker obtained a much more accurate picture of the situation.

The division's *energy profile*—the diagnostic result of the OEQ—supported Dekker's gut feeling about the level of engagement in his organization and gave him a vocabulary to talk about the problem. For one, people tended to avoid communicating with one another and in general were overly content with the status quo, rather than motivated to improve processes toward company goals. Second, the profile showed higher-than-normal levels of *resigned inertia,* which is inertia characterized by frustration, mental withdrawal, and low engagement. Finally, compared with benchmark data, the profile revealed relatively high levels of negative *corrosive energy* that manifested as aggression, internal fights, and resistance to change. What is most important, the survey also revealed a possible cause. Resignation and highly destructive energy prevailed particularly among those led by lower (third-level) management. Connecting data from CWT's earlier employee opinion surveys to the energy profile, we identified what drove this development: people across the hierarchy did not fully understand the company's overall vision and strategy.

The survey allowed Dekker to ask the questions that got to the heart of the problem at CWT Netherlands. Managers and employees at all levels affirmed that upper management had never adequately communicated the vision and strategy for the division, leaving the organization uncertain and directionless. Specifically, the participants said that they had little insight into the reasons and objectives for the company's many recent change initiatives.

Dekker then created a strategy and action plan to overcome the problem. First, through a series of decentralized workshops, he ensured that employees learned about CWT's vision, clearly understood its strategic direction, and began to define local activities. Second, Dekker started a culture development program to strengthen transparency and mutual trust—values crucial to providing exceptional services.

Within twelve months of these new initiatives, CWT Netherlands started to unleash what we call *productive energy*. The employees in Dekker's division reported back to him an evolving sense of alertness, urgency, and shared excitement for the strategy. They were much more mentally active, asked more questions, and contributed new ideas. Not only did the employee survey of 2009 show an increase of more than 20 percent in the engagement score since 2007, but the division's performance and productivity demonstrated that employees were more engaged with the core company challenges and were linking their work more closely with CWT's overall direction. As a result, Dekker and his top management team finally reported feeling positive about achieving their ambitious goals for CWT: "Although optimistic in the beginning of the productive energy approach, we were more than surprised with the positive outcome," he reported.[4]

As we learned from Dekker and hundreds of other executives like him, leaders often intuitively feel the energy in their companies and sense its impact on the productivity of their company. But they have only a limited understanding of the sources of that energy or the tools that they could use to manage it, and so they leave a key resource to languish: the company's *human* resources. By understanding how to manage organizational energy, you can learn how to ignite high performance by allowing those human resources to be energetic and productive over the long term.

What Is Organizational Energy?

At the beginning of this introduction, we defined organizational energy as the extent to which an organization, division, or team has mobilized its emotional, cognitive, and behavioral potential to pursue its goals.[5] Simply put, it is the force with which a company (or division or team) works.[6] There are different types of organizational energy, and these various types are what makes your company tick.

Note that here we're discussing a company's activated energy—not its potential energy (to borrow a physics term). To tap into the full scope and possibilities imbedded in a company's energy in motion, leaders need to understand three attributes of organizational energy. First, organizational energy comprises the organizations' activated emotional, cognitive, and behavioral potential. Second, organizational energy is a collective attribute—it comprises the shared human potential of a company (unit, or team). And third, organizational energy is malleable.

The Components of Organizational Energy

At CWT, the interplay of emotional, cognitive, and behavioral energy helped the executive group and the company to make the crucial changes it needed to succeed. Through a series of workshops, culture development, and other interventions, Dekker not only made his employees aware of the new strategic direction, but also excited them about it, and people started to share his enthusiasm for the strategy. An organization's emotional energy, therefore, becomes the degree of passion and enthusiasm its people show for company goals. Its cognitive energy translates into the degree to which its people are awake, creative, and primed to spot new opportunities or possible threats in pursuit of company goals. And the organization's behavioral energy translates into how much the employees make an effort, stretching themselves to their limits to achieve shared goals.

Leaders must be able to unleash the kind of organizational energy needed to bring a strategy or innovation idea to life, to mobilize people's creativity, to inspire them, and to foster their readiness to take action. In chapter 2, we will explore two key strategies that can help—what we call winning the princess and slaying the dragon.

Individual Energy and Organizational Energy

Organizational energy describes the human forces *shared* among executives and employees in companies or work units—not simply the energy of individuals in these companies or units. The concept of organizational energy extends those human qualities to the company's energy as a whole. Without a doubt, individual-oriented energy concepts such as emotional energy, flow, vitality, thriving, and vigor can help executives understand and encourage the full engagement of individual employees.[7] Yet executives must go beyond thinking only of the individual; by focusing on individual's energy, they risk missing out on the whole of the human forces they have at their discretion.

To appreciate the power of this kind of collective energy, let's look at an example from outside the realm of business: the fall of the Berlin Wall in 1989. The so-called Monday demonstrations that took place in East Germany during the autumn of 1989 were a key factor in the wall's eventual fall. For years, citizens had been assembling in the Church of St. Nicholas in Leipzig to pray for peace. In early September 1989, however, the mood changed and people began to demonstrate openly in the churchyard, calling for free travel to the West and pronouncing, "We are the people." In a few weeks, this cause became so infectious that on October 23, a full 320,000 people took part in the demonstration, and other cities joined in across East Germany. The collective force of these people, combined with the shifting political and economic winds throughout Europe, was too strong to stop, and this time, the military never intervened.

Though credit has been given to many individuals for the wall's fall— Pope John Paul II, Presidents Ronald Reagan and George H. W. Bush of the United States, President Mikhail Gorbachev of the Soviet Union, Chancellor Helmut Kohl and President Richard von Weizsaecker of Germany, among others—their contributions wouldn't have been enough ultimately to bring an end to Communist rule. Instead, because the idea of freedom had spread among the masses of oppressed citizens, the strong, positive, collective energy contributed the final push.

The lesson for executives is clear. Rather than relying solely on motivating the individual employee, executives must learn to unleash the company's collective human potential to create an environment where emotion, thoughts, and actions can flow and spread in the organization. Why? A company's collective dynamic force is much stronger than the sum of individual forces or motivation. And this collective power reinforces itself through interaction and group dynamics so that, as Wharton's Sigal G. Barsade and others have observed, when people interact, they actually "catch" the emotions, thoughts, and even actions of others.[8] People imitate and follow the other people around them to a certain extent, becoming inspired and infected by them. The dynamics—contagion, spillover effect, or self-reinforcing spirals—go far beyond the sum of people's individual energy.[9] People caught in these dynamics become more in sync, sharing the same energy on a more intense level. And executives who have experienced this state in their companies know it holds true also in reverse: when individuals break out of the dynamic or push back, the effect reverberates throughout the organization—for better or worse. In our experience, it is this ability to create *organizational* energy that differentiates successful organizations from those that are not so successful.

Organizational Energy Is Malleable

Unlike soft factors like organizational climate or culture, organizational energy reflects the current state of a company rather than a static condition. Where organizational culture reflects stable values, deeply internalized behavioral patterns, and basic assumptions that have built up over years, organizational energy refers to the present activation of a company's human forces.[10] This energy can change from day to day as a result of outside factors (think of the many collective actions that took place around the world in the wake of 9/11) or deliberate actions taken by internal leaders.

Unlike the case with organizational culture, therefore, leaders can swiftly and purposefully influence organizational energy. Look back at CWT's Jan Willem Dekker, who within a mere few months had turned around the way his organization engaged with its vision and strategy: a new shared excitement and enormously high levels of alertness and effort, together with well-orchestrated activities, replaced the energy that had become dormant and stale. On the downside, executives need to recognize that the reverse is also true: positive organizational energy can quickly drop or even turn negative when not properly managed.

The Energy Matrix: Four States of Organizational Energy

Leaders usually feel the dynamics and energy in their company intuitively, but they lack the frameworks and tools to assess, boost, and sustain that energy. What's more, most leaders don't know how to communicate to their people what needs to change about the company's energy and how to make those critical changes. This is where further refining our description of organizational energy can help.

At the heart of our work and this book lies a framework we call the *energy matrix*. Initially, we developed the energy matrix in 2000–2001 in a project with the American oil corporation ConocoPhillips. Since then, our journey has taken us to companies around the world. We have conducted quantitative and qualitative studies in various settings, including at a consortium of six international companies with global reach: ABB, Alstom, Hilti, Lufthansa, Unaxis, and Tata Steel. We measured energy in over seven hundred companies in fifty-five countries and conducted more than thirty case studies in European, American, and Asian companies.[11] During the course of our research and practice over the years, we refined and validated the core logic of the energy matrix, a tool we use to capture a precise picture of companies' energy.[12] Executives use this picture of the energy of their firm or work unit as a basis for understanding the dynamics in their organization and developing the right leadership strategies.

Specifically, our research shows that companies' energy can differ in two dimensions: its intensity and its quality. The *intensity* of organizational energy reflects the degree that a company has activated its emotional, cognitive, and behavioral potential: namely, the level of emotional tension, watchfulness, interaction, and communication that prevails in a company. We distinguish here between high and low intensity. While high intensity indicates a high level of emotional involvement, mental activation, and engagement, low intensity describes a reduced level of these states. A very low intensity reflects a company that is more or less in sleeping mode.

The *quality* of organizational energy describes how a company uses its energy—to what extent do emotional, cognitive, and behavioral forces align constructively with common, central company goals? We distinguish here between positive and negative energy. Positive organizational energy is characterized by a constructive use of the company's potential. People direct their emotions, mental agility, thoughtfulness, efforts, and activities to fortify their unit or company goals. Negative organizational energy reflects a lack of common orientation toward shared corporate goals. It implies a destructive use of the company's potential. In the state of negative energy, organizations show emotions such as fear, frustration, and annoyance among employees; people think and act in ways disconnected from the company's goals or even try to maximize their own personal benefit and counter the common purpose.

The combination of the two dimensions of energy—intensity and quality—maps to four types of energy states that reflect the energy of enterprises: productive energy, comfortable energy, resigned inertia, and corrosive energy (figure I-1).

FIGURE I-1

The energy matrix

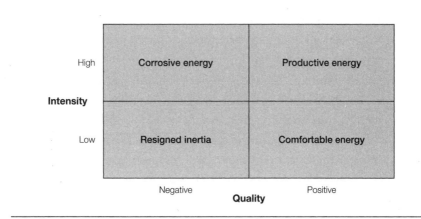

We will describe each energy type more fully in chapter 1, but here they are in a nutshell:

- **Productive energy (high positive energy):** characterized by high emotional involvement and mental alertness along with high activity levels, speed, stamina, and productivity in the organization

- **Comfortable energy (low positive energy):** characterized by high shared satisfaction and identification coupled with low activity levels, reduced mental alertness, and organizational complacency.

- **Resigned inertia (low negative energy):** characterized by high levels of frustration, mental withdrawal, and cynicism and low collective engagement in the organization

- **Corrosive energy (high negative energy):** characterized by collective aggression and destructive behavior, for example, in the form of internal politics, resistance to change, or maximizing individual benefits

These states are not mutually exclusive; they operate independently of one another. As a result, companies can experience all four energy states *simultaneously.* Indeed, no single company, division, department, or even team has only one energy state; all forces are evident at the same time. The question at the heart of our assessments, therefore, is not "Which energy state describes my company?" but rather "How strong is each different energy state in my company?" and "Which one is dominant today?"

Let's revisit CWT Netherlands as a case in point. You may recall that the results from CWT's Organizational Energy Questionnaire indicated that the organization largely experienced comfortable energy (low positive energy) as its predominant energy state. But the assessment also revealed that the company showed significant amounts of negative energy, that is, resigned inertia and corrosive energy. So even while your company exhibits largely comfortable energy, your people might be experiencing some frustration or even the first signs of burnout. For executives, this is an important distinction when they apply the energy concept: although the matrix might reveal the positive energy imbedded in an organization (in CWT's case, comfortable energy), it can also identify the weaknesses the company must overcome to mobilize and sustain its energy.

How an Organization's Energy Affects Its Performance

What, exactly, does the state of your company's energy have to do with your people's effectiveness and your company's performance? As we will show in this book, organizational energy directly affects the performance of organizations. When companies use their full potential to pursue their goals—namely, when there is a high level of passion, mental agility, effort, and activity, and this human potential is not only mobilized but also aligned to achieve joint goals—these companies prosper, are significantly more innovative, generate much more customer passion, and grow much quicker than their less-energetic competitors. When employee potential is left to languish because of poor use of organizational energy, revenues are lost, and when those people burn out because destructive, corrosive energy has completely taken over, the organization's viability is threatened.[13]

The global data we have collected over time show that all energy states are strongly predictive of several parameters, including total performance, profitability, efficiency, customer orientation, and employee satisfaction and commitment. For example, in a 2009 sample of 14,387 respondents in 104 German companies, we studied the organizations' energy and per-formance. Energy was rated by employees, and the organization's perfor-mance was assessed by key informants (the CEO or another member of the executive board) from within the company with regard to efficiency, growth, and financial results. We then transferred the ratings into a 0–100 percent scale to see how much of the positive or negative potential forces had actually been mobilized in the firms, and we identified groups of high-, average-, and low-productive-energy companies. Compared with the low-productive-energy companies, the companies with high produc-tive energy scored higher in several measurements: overall performance (14 percent higher), productivity (17 percent), efficiency (14 percent), customer satisfaction (6 percent), and customer loyalty (12 percent).[14]

On the flip side, companies with high resigned inertia scored 17 percent lower business-processes efficiency and 19 percent lower in customer loy-alty than did companies with low resigned inertia. When we compared companies with high corrosive energy with those with low corrosive en-ergy, overall performance was 20 percent lower and employee productivity was 16 percent lower. Although we cannot rule out that other factors may have influenced these companies' performance in parallel with those we examined, we see in our results a strong correlation with success. We have confirmed these findings again and again since 2002 and consistently find the same strong performance links that we found in our 2009 study.

So let's look at how this connection between organizational energy and business performance correlates specifically with all four quadrants of our energy matrix. Returning to the example of CWT, when the company regained its high *productive energy,* its people began to become more open and alert. They were much more mentally active, asked more questions, and contributed new thoughts. They also applied themselves more diligently to their daily tasks and were willing to work outside their immediate responsibilities by, for instance, assisting colleagues with challenging issues or supporting the implementation of change initiatives.

These qualities at the employee level in turn created more knowledge exchange and sharing across CWT units and generated new process solutions and products at a faster rate. A good example of a new process solution is CWT's Work@Home project. CWT was the first travel-management company that on a large scale introduced this working-at-home opportunity to its employees, and the initiative contributed to CWT's being an employer of choice. The increased enthusiasm and excitement for their work leveraged people's commitment—they displayed a marked increase in stamina and pace in their daily work and developed innovations in CWT's processes.[15] Although not every improvement in an organization's energy ultimately will translate into higher revenues, the breadth of activities, opportunities, and changes will significantly affect a company's performance and its success for the better, as our research has shown (see also the empirical results in chapter 1).[16]

Unfortunately, the opposite holds true as well. When the state of a company's energy languishes in the low-positive zone or fully in the negative zone, the organization's performance is threatened. For example, when *comfortable energy* dominates the company, then executives fail to get the organization to go the extra mile. At CWT, the OEQ revealed that people in the company consistently felt at ease, strongly liked what they were doing, and were focused primarily around efficiency in their job—which in combination with the experience of a lower level of productive energy within the company translated into a workforce that was collectively over-satisfied and wanted to protect the status quo and whose activities were characterized by routine behavior and low engagement. The impact on CWT's performance was clear, as Dekker had already observed: the customer-service innovation and quality that customers had come to expect was languishing. People coordinated with each other less efficiently, and the company as a whole was less efficient and effective in combining and creating knowledge across the units.

In the OEQ results from companies in a state of resigned inertia, people consistently answered yes to statements such as "People in my workgroup do not have much drive" and "People in my workgroup have no desire to make something happen." These kinds of answers translate into employees and units characterized by frustration, mental withdrawal, change fatigue, or burnout. People in this state become indifferent to company goals, communicate much less, and have minimal interpersonal interaction throughout the organization—to the point where some work processes within or across work units all but come to a grinding halt. These organizations have lost the discretionary human potential necessary to invest in change initiatives that go beyond daily business activities. The result? Companies languishing in such resigned inertia soon lose their best people, and the organization's overall efficiency decreases because of weakened coordination, with units not hitting their business targets or not making the urgently needed process changes.

Companies mired in *corrosive energy* tend to spend their time managing internal conflicts or micropolitical activities and have employees who mind their own individual interests at their units' expense. These attitudes show up on the OEQ in responses such as "People in my workgroup are angry in their job" and "People in my workgroup often behave in a destructive manner." These organizations use their energy for internal issues, so it is lost for the customer and markets issues as well as collaboration around processes. Our research has shown that these companies ultimately lose money at the unit level. The units' ability to leverage their joint knowledge for innovation and future products, service, and markets is all but nil—all of which threatens bottom-line results.

Getting the Most from the Organization's Energy

Leveraging your organization's energy toward its maximum potential means understanding four key aspects: how to assess organizational energy, how to decide what strategy can best help jump-start the organization, how to avoid the three common traps, and how to sustain the organization's energy.

Assessing Your Organization's Energy

As we've shown, the first step in assessing the state of an organization's energy—the key human resources of the company—is crucial for leaders. While a gut feeling of the company's energy state can well be accurate, without ways to tangibly measure energy, you may have difficulty seeing it clearly or discussing it with colleagues and employees, much less improving your organization's energy. The book's appendix includes a twelve-question version of the OEQ that we used throughout our work with companies and that you as a leader can use to create an energy profile of your organization, division, or work unit.

Deciding on the Best Strategy to Boost Organizational Energy

While chapter 1 explains each of these energy states more closely, this book as a whole will introduce ways of acting on that assessment to understand and communicate ideas about organizational energy in terms of the four states of energy. Our aim is to help leaders channel their efforts into distinct leadership activities suitable for their particular organization's energy needs. When they have a clear picture on the energy profile of their organization they can choose the adequate leadership strategy for their particular situation, be it boosting or maintaining productive energy or working off destructive energy.

Avoiding Common Traps

In attempting to manage their organization's energy, many executives find themselves confronted with one or more of three major energy traps: the complacency trap, the corrosion trap, and the acceleration trap. We'll discuss each of these and the challenge to get beyond the traps in their own chapters, but let's go over them quickly first.

The complacency trap. Highly energetic and successful companies almost inevitably become complacent or inert and lose their ability to change and reenergize. Lulled by their success, they stop questioning the status quo; lose their alertness, passion, and readiness to go the limits; and instead get overly satisfied, lazy, or even arrogant.

Assessing the organization's energy is one step; next, leaders must understand how to channel their efforts into distinct leadership activities suitable to escape complacency and inertia. We recommend two leadership strategies that help executives boost energy in organizations that lack it and to escape the complacency trap. These strategies show how executives can focus the company's emotion, attention, and behavior on either an existential threat (we call this strategy slaying the dragon) or on a compelling opportunity (a strategy we call winning the princess). In chapter 2, we will show you how to consciously choose and apply the leadership strategy that works for the energy situation your company is facing.

The corrosion trap. Why do organizations that once were thriving and engaged all of a sudden—or step by step—turn destructive? Sometimes, they fall victim to the power of corrosive energy. Take, for example, the case of Bosch-Siemens Haushaltsgeräte (BSH), the largest producer of home appliances in Europe. With about forty thousand employees in forty countries and about $10.98 billion in sales in 2008, BSH has long enjoyed a worldwide position of industry leadership.

Trouble for the company began in May 2005, when BSH management decided to close a cost-ineffective Berlin factory and move the operation to Brandenburg. Established in 1994, the Brandenburg factory was the only site where workers were not paid according to tariffs, making production at lower costs possible. Wisely expecting resistance to its plan, BSH management initially showed a willingness to negotiate with employee representatives and labor unions to achieve a solution. After a year and a half of negotiations, threatened strikes, and various threats of wage cuts and dismissals, and as the company continued to lose money at the Berlin location, BSH finally agreed to keep the factory in Berlin open with employment protection until 2010. But the workers had to accept severe cutbacks, as only 270 of the 570 affected employees could keep their jobs. A full 220 people would be dismissed, while 80 workers were guaranteed positions within other factories of BSH. Against the will of the majority of employees, the labor union IG Metall and the employee organization declared the labor dispute finished after three weeks of the strike, several protests, and numerous negotiation rounds during the previous year and a half. Ultimately, while this long period of negotiations, strikes, and fights between management and employees worked to foster internal cohesion among BSH employees, it also left a deep gap of corrosive energy and anger in the workers' relationship with management.

Any shift away from productive energy can quickly transform positive forces into corrosive energy, particularly when a company's shared focus is lost and trust abused. Internal competition, resource-allocation struggles, and conflicts about priorities can escalate. In chapter 3, we will show how to detect these elusive negative forces and how to halt any corrosive processes eating away at the organization's energy.

The acceleration trap. Another threat to sustained energy in any company is what we term the acceleration trap. Leaders often ask us, "How do we keep up the momentum of our change program while avoiding organizational burnout?" In highly energetic companies, leaders are often tempted to start too many activities simultaneously, devoting too little time to individual activities and overwhelming their employees by relentlessly pushing them past the employees' limits. What begins as a positive aspiration to attain a goal can end in an uncontrolled flood of activities if not regulated. Some CEOs follow the Olympic motto *Citius, altius, fortius* (swifter, higher, stronger) and drive their companies constantly at and beyond the edge of their capabilities. The result? Burnout, resignation, inertia, or fatigue of entire companies with the consequences we outlined earlier.

But there are companies we can learn from. For example, the Sonova Group, the Swiss world-market leader in hearing aids, has launched two new product generations each year ever since Valentin Chapero took over as CEO in October 2002.[17] And since 2003, it has enjoyed constant yearly growth rates of between 12 and 16 percent. In the recession year 2008–2009, growth dropped to 3.7 percent (organic growth to 7.8 percent), but the company still outperformed the overall market growth by a factor of two. And for the first half of the financial year 2009–2010, sales growth recovered to 18.2 percent. What's more, the products launched within the last twenty-four months generated 86 percent of the $1.1 billion company's total sales.

How does the Sonova Group maintain such momentum, continually churning out innovations that set new standards in the hearing-care industry? It does so *by deliberately orchestrating the rhythm between its high-energy phases and its regeneration phases.* Along with the company's commitment to launching two new product generations per year, therefore, Chapero deliberately embeds periods of *reduced intensity* into the company rhythm. After a high-speed product launch, employees know to expect a less intense period during which batteries are recharged, successes are celebrated, processes and plans are consolidated. In short, Sonova slows down to speed up, renewing its energy before going into overdrive again, tackling new innovation challenges. Chapter 4 will tell us more about how executives such as Chapero avoid and overcome overacceleration in their companies.

Sustaining Organizational Energy

Here's one concern we have heard from several executives of exceptionally successful or leading companies: "We have always been driven to get to the head of the pack. But how do we *sustain* the company's energy, now that we're number one?" Similarly, we cited earlier how former CEO of Lufthansa, Juergen Weber, said that despite Lufthansa's known expertise in mobilizing the company with crisis management, he was puzzled over how to prevent the company from falling into complacency. Instead of adopting strategies for maintaining energy, some managers engage in very costly yo-yo patterns, allowing the company's energy level to repeatedly drop into comfort, and then the managers use crisis-management periods to increase it again. Many executives fall into a pattern of mobilizing energy for certain key challenges, such as turnaround, crisis management, or beating key competitors. They use this lever, no matter how successful and energetic the company already is. Eventually, when the crisis lessens or the turnaround is completed, the company's energy decreases.

Executives need to acknowledge that mobilizing energy and sustaining it are two fundamentally different leadership challenges. To lead their companies beyond the energy traps, executives need to create a vitalizing management system—an energizing strategy, a climate of leadership, and an energy culture—that systematically sustains high levels of productive energy and facilitates a proactive sense of urgency among people across the company.

How This Book Can Help You Unleash and Maintain Your Organization's Energy

Who should read this book? The lessons we share here from our journey of researching and applying our knowledge about organizational energy will most benefit CEOs, senior executives, other organizational leaders, and board members. These individuals and teams are in charge of leveraging the energy, the full potential of their organizations. Understanding and working with the energy concept will enable them to boost the particular soft factors that are decisive for their company performance. But this book is also for HR executives and other HR professionals, since top management relies on this group for crucial support and facilitation.

Our research has revealed five key leadership tasks that we will map out in this book before concluding with chapter 6, our call to action for leaders throughout the organization:

1. **The energy matrix:** We begin in chapter 1 by more fully introducing the energy matrix and the four energy states. To actively manage energy, executives need to understand the status of their organization's energy and how it develops over time. Chapter 1 also illustrates how to evaluate that energy with a measurement tool (the OEQ) and guides leaders through a self-assessment. This reveals a thorough picture of the company's energy and essentially makes the relevant soft factors tangible. Once executives can identify the state of their organization's energy, we will help to channel their effort to distinct leadership activities suitable for their company's particular energy state.

2. **Mobilizing your organization's energy—escaping the complacency trap:** In chapter 2, we describe two proven leadership strategies—slaying the dragon and winning the princess—and other tools you can use to escape the complacency trap, to unleash energy in your organization, and to tackle comfortable energy and resigned

inertia. With slaying the dragon, leaders focus the company's shared emotion, mental agility, and effort on solving or overcoming an existential external threat, ultimately generating productive energy. The winning-the-princess strategy is based on the observation that productive energy can be particularly high if companies are pursuing a special opportunity. As with slaying the dragon, this kind of opportunity-driven situation doesn't automatically trigger productive energy; it requires sensitive but courageous executives who can carefully guide their organizations through it.

3. Rebuilding positive energy—escaping the corrosion trap: Chapter 3 explains how to detect elusive negative forces and how to halt any corrosive processes eating away at the organization's energy. As we saw in the example of BSH, companies fall into this trap when they lose a shared focus with their employees; this trap is often accompanied by perceived betrayal and misuse of trust. The corrosion trap transfers positive human potential into corrosive energy.

4. Focusing your organization's energy—escaping the acceleration trap: When a company is highly energetic, there is a strong temptation to start too many activities simultaneously. As a result, too little time is devoted to activities and people are overwhelmed relentlessly. This constant effort to do more leads to organizational exhaustion and, ultimately, to burnout. This is the acceleration trap. Chapter 4 describes three types of acceleration traps (involving what we call overloading, multiloading, and perpetual loading) and illustrates leadership strategies that managers can use to overcome this trap and prevent their companies from falling into it in the first place.

5. Sustaining energy to rise above number one—getting beyond the traps: We learned that highly energetic and successful companies almost inevitably fall victim to one of the traps; that is, they become complacent, develop high levels of corrosive energy, or overaccelerate up to organizational burnout. Indeed, our research shows that many managers can boost energy, but few know how

to systematically maintain it. Chapter 5 describes leadership strategies to systematically sustain productive energy through a vitalizing management system—an energizing strategy, a climate of leadership, and an energy culture. Leaders who want their organizations to rise above number one must develop a vitalizing management system that helps organizations to move beyond the traps and helps companies maintain high levels of activity, alertness, and emotional involvement to thus achieve productive energy.

6. **The courage to energize—a personal perspective of boosting energy:** Finally, we close the book in chapter 6 with a review of four pathways that executives can use to boost the energy of their companies. While a crucial message of this book is the notion of *organizational* energy, ultimately it comes down to the *individual leaders* to make the difference. What separates leaders who intellectually grasp the potential of the energy concept but don't lead accordingly, from those who engage with energizing leadership activities? Leaders who learn to deal with uncertainties can boost the energy of their people. Ultimately, however, sustaining energy requires you as a leader to step back and have the courage to open the stage to your employees—and to help them lead and create the next organizational win.

We have begun to describe in this chapter how leaders can work with organizational energy and why it is one of the decisive soft factors for high-performance organizations. In the next chapter, we present the four kinds of energy states found in organizations (the energy matrix) and explore how executives begin to transform this seemingly unmanageable and intangible soft factor into something accessible and concrete by using a practical measurement tool.

CHAPTER 1

The Energy Matrix

The tool we have developed to depict organizational energy—the energy matrix—shows that companies can differ in their energy's *intensity* (how much a company has activated its potential) and *quality* (how well a company uses its energy to pursue its goals).[1] The combination of these two dimensions of energy map to the four types of energy states in organizations.

We begin this chapter by describing these energy states. Later in the chapter, we present some specific tools to help you identify and assess the state of your organization's energy. This is a first step on the journey toward unleashing the kind of productive energy companies like CWT and Sonova have managed to do.

Productive Energy

Companies, divisions, or departments with productive energy promote success-critical core activities by mobilizing and channeling emotions, attention, and effort toward reaching common goals. Employees in these companies or units invariably experience intense positive emotions such as enthusiasm and pride; share a high level of alertness; and, at the same time, apply intensely focused effort to their work, which often collectively stretches the borders of the company's or department's competencies and capacities. This is the ideal energy state for all companies.

But one of the most distinctive characteristic of companies or units with high productive energy is their *productive urgency*—a sense of positive tension and swiftness in all that they do.[2] What's more, employee emotions, attention, and activities tend to flow together, collectively, within and across unit borders in the same direction. While companies with low energy usually suffer from differing, even competing, priorities and a lack of common focus, organizations with productive energy steer their efforts toward common goals. The shared experience of energy feeds the enthusiasm, alertness, and effort and can lead to positive spirals.[3] These companies mobilize energy quickly for make-or-break activities such as innovation and, thus, are extraordinarily effective.

The Sonova Group provides a dramatic illustration of how one company creates energy for making innovation its key activity. As we mentioned, since 2002, when Valentin Chapero took the helm as CEO, this world market leader in hearing aids has committed itself to launching two completely new product generations per year.[4] Before these product launches—one each in mid-April and early November—almost the entire company goes into overdrive. There is a buzz of enthusiasm and hard work: R&D and marketing, the technicians, and the sales force work practically around the clock to achieve the seemingly impossible—and ensure that once again, another new product makes a precision landing. Alexander Zschokke, then vice president of marketing, described the vibe for us: "It's like in the fashion business: no-show is not an option. When we are getting closer to a launch, suddenly, everything is focused on the deadline. Then, many decisions and actions need to happen simultaneously. What do we do? If necessary, we sit in a room together into the night and don't leave until the decisions are made . . . and we prioritize!" When approaching the product launch, the teams highly prioritize the target product and adjust the resources available to the tasks needed to ensure the launch.

The results of this mobilization are dramatic. "Since Chapero became CEO, we've never postponed a product launch," Markus Tomasi, then head of production, told us. "If we had lost time in the beginning of the project, pressure increased towards the launch date."

This is how Sonova generates and focuses collective energy for its core activities, across departmental borders. Only through this regular test of Sonova's limits and, when required, the company's going beyond them, can Sonova maintain its extraordinary innovation results. Products that have been on the market two years or less generate a full 86 percent of company's total sales.

Another key characteristic of companies that regularly unleash productive energy to surmount challenges is their ability to activate and focus the organization's productive forces very quickly, compared with the competition. Lufthansa, during its crisis management after September 11, 2001, offers a prime example. By this time, the company had enjoyed a decade of experience with leveraging energy for target goals such as cost-cutting during its crisis management in the early 1990s—and this experience made all the difference. While other airlines struggled to manage the drastic collapse in the market after 9/11, Lufthansa drew on proven methods and experience to quickly activate the company's productive energy for this one exceptional and threatening event. Juergen Weber, Lufthansa's CEO until June 2003, described the period after the Twin Towers were struck: "What we did in nine months at the beginning of the '90s for crisis management, we did in nine weeks after September 11th."[5] The airline immediately reviewed all routes for profitability, and the route network was reduced.[6] Twenty of Lufthansa's 236 aircraft were put out of commission, with plans made for grounding additional planes over the weeks that followed. Lufthansa also decided to expand a recently created strategic program, called D-Check, into a program the company called D-Check Acute, to generate immediate cash gains for 2002. For the particularly critical early phase, D-Check was then converted into a program for systematic cost and multiproject management for coordinating activities during the crisis. Within seventeen days of 9/11, managers had developed an action plan, presented it to the labor unions, and had it approved by the executive board.

Lufthansa's greatest challenge, however—one that many executives face during an economic downturn—was finding ways to rapidly reduce human resources costs in accordance with the law, while remaining flexible enough to quickly return the crew to full capacity when the crisis abated. Along with the hiring freeze, therefore, Lufthansa offered current employees part-time work, unpaid vacation time, and time off in lieu of overtime and vacation. And the airline came to an agreement with its labor unions to extend the current wage contract for ground and cabin crew while postponing wage increases for cockpit personnel. Moreover, all the members of the executive board waived 10 percent of their salaries, and three-quarters of the managers voluntarily waived 5 to 10 percent of their salaries.

Holger Hätty, who was then the head of strategy of the Lufthansa Group, described the process to us: "Dealing with nine-eleven went very smoothly. People knew what they had to do. It was as if we just went to a drawer and opened it, pulled out the crisis plan, and implemented it." As a result, Lufthansa was one of the only airlines, along with Air France, that did not dismiss a single employee as a result of September 11. Thanks to the D-Check Acute action plan and security surcharges on tickets and cargo goods, the airline generated a remarkable cash flow of $743 million within three and a half months. In the end, the company's community spirit and confidence were actually reinforced through the successful handling of the 9/11 crisis.

Research by Jane Dutton, professor of business administration and psychology at University of Michigan, shows that productive energy increases companies' abilities to adapt to environmental changes, supports cooperation in and between enterprise units, and has positive, long-lasting effects on a company's performance and work processes.[7] This shared enthusiasm, alertness, and effort across a company boosts cooperation, commitment, and new opportunities and accelerates the sharing of knowledge. And this sharing connects productive energy to a firm's profitability, employee satisfaction, and overall performance.

Our own empirical research underscores these findings. Companies with higher productive energy scored higher than low-energy companies on overall performance (14 percent higher), productivity (17 percent), efficiency (14 percent), customer satisfaction (6 percent), customer loyalty (12 percent), and commitment (19 percent) (figure 1-1).[8] What's more, these companies not only gain more in efficiency and performance, but also lose less money on time-consuming bureaucratic and administrative issues, conflicts, and unending negotiations.

FIGURE 1-1

High productive energy companies and performance

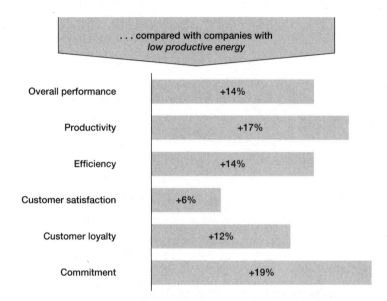

Note: Data based on subsamples of surveys from 104 German companies in 2009: 3,789 respondents for energy states, 3,886 respondents for commitment, and 225 top-management respondents for performance measures (overall performance, productivity, efficiency of business processes, customer satisfaction, and consumer loyalty).

When we delve deeper into our data, the harmful effects of low productive energy on people who have high attachment to the company (often the same level of attachment that high performers have) become even more apparent.[9] Companies with high percentages (75 percent) of strongly committed employees find those percentages dropping (to 52 percent) when the company experiences low productive energy. At the same time, the share of people satisfied with their work drops from 77 percent to 61 percent. Ultimately, these losses reflect people's disconnect to the company; on the other hand, companies gain when they experience the excitement of productive energy.

While a company's high level of productive energy drives its performance, the distribution of energy is also very important. The differences in energy between business units, divisions, or countries have implications on a company-wide scale. You should also consider, however, the distribution of energy across hierarchical levels; this has important implications for managing organizational energy. For example, in organizations with a high level of productive energy, we usually find no significant gaps between hierarchical levels, and the perception of energy is relatively homogenous. In companies with low energy, however, there are often key differences in the perception of energy between hierarchical levels. In companies with low productive energy, we find one typical gap in perception: as a rule, CEOs and their top management teams perceive very high levels of productive energy (78 and 83 percent), but the very next hierarchical level below experiences a completely different energy situation—namely, on average 20 percent less productive energy.[10] In these companies, top management seems to have become disconnected from the rest of the organization, with management's direct reports facing fundamentally different conditions to drive change, develop innovations, or implement strategies and struggling with different challenges than the top team does.

Is Your Company Enjoying Productive Energy?

- Does your company experience a constant level of healthy passion?

- Does your company regularly and constructively challenge the status quo of its strategy, products, and customer relationships?

- Do your employees continually come up with excellent ideas on how the company can avoid risks, and do they know how to take advantage of opportunities they have identified?

- Is it easy for you to implement change or new ideas in your company?

- Do you believe that your organization regularly pushes its limits to ensure its success?

- When working on tasks critical to the company's success, do your employees seem unconcerned about working overtime or on weekends, or appear prepared to do so?

- Have you lately been surprised by how quickly and effectively tasks are being accomplished?

We also find that the spread between hierarchical levels where people experience the highest productive energy and those with the lowest productive energy is generally much higher (27 percent) in low-energy companies than in high-energy companies (17 percent). In low-energy companies, the energy among hierarchical levels diverges profoundly, and thus, expectations of exceptional performance are hardly aligned. Companies with low productive energy, then, face the challenge of bridging the gaps between different hierarchical levels. These companies must find ways to mobilize the potential of people at all levels, including the organizational parts that are less connected, and get everyone engaged around the company goals.

Clearly, you need to learn to unleash collective productive energy in your organization and then understand how to sustain it. To begin your analysis of the state of your organizational energy, use the questions in "Is Your Company Enjoying Productive Energy?" to reflect on your company's or department's current situation.

Comfortable Energy

Comfortable energy is a positive energy state characterized by high satisfaction, feeling at ease, and a strong and growing sense of identification with the status quo. All companies need a certain degree of comfort and a feeling of positive energy to be sustainably successful. A company's ideal energy state combines high levels of productive and comfortable energy—that's when the company is at its most dynamic, responsive, and innovative but on a healthy and stable basis.

But on its own without the boost of productive energy, comfortable energy is a double-edged sword, because it also represents a low level of energy overall. If your company is dominated by this state, employees seem happy with the status quo but they display very low engagement with their work, even laziness. There is no productive tension to stimulate innovative thinking. That is why high levels of employee satisfaction from employee opinion surveys are misleading; companies may see diminishing performance soon after such surveys. Employees in a company that is overshadowed by comfortable energy are less mentally agile, are less active thinkers, seldom develop new solutions and creative ideas, and rarely identify possible opportunities or threats. In this energy state, your company is less likely to perceive weak signals from the environment, competitors, and customers, or even from your own organization. Finally, a sign of a reduced level of activity from companies with overly high comfort is that changes as well as routine business processes run in an unhurried, smooth fashion. Innovations are generated at a reduced rate and intensity and are primarily directed at improving the status quo rather than at going in new directions or creating breakthrough knowledge.

When there is high comfort and the company has low levels of productive energy, executives need to take action, because comfortable energy can be dangerous if it becomes the dominant energy state. Under such a state, an organization has lost its readiness and ability to change. This is what we refer to as the *complacency trap*. While our research initially hypothesized that companies should carefully limit their amount of comfortable energy, we found that comfortable energy levels cannot be too high—but productive energy can be too low.[11] As an executive, you must ensure that the level of comfortable energy is not dominant or that complacency rules your organization (high comfortable energy combined with low productive energy).

A Swiss watchmaker—representing the attitude of an entire industry—provided the textbook example for comfortable energy on the strategic level when he famously said, "A decent clock will always be mechanical, have gear wheels and clockwork. Alternatives will never really be relevant."[12] Two years later, thousands of employees of the Swiss watch- and clock-making industry lost their jobs when cheaper, quartz-based watches blitzed the market. The watchmaker industry in Switzerland only recovered twenty years later. Examples of other companies that, to varying degrees, have found their very existence suddenly threatened by complacency include Laura Ashley, IBM, Swissair, and Polaroid.[13]

Comfortable energy was not just the purview of these companies' leaders and their strategies, however. Part of the problem was that as a result of this comfortable energy, people at every level of these companies displayed high levels of calm and contentment on the job. People's comfort masked very low activity levels and reduced sensitivity to what was going on inside and outside the company.[14]

Let us look now at some of the reasons why comfortable energy can shift and become risky in organizations.

Why Do Companies Fall into a State of Dominant Comfortable Energy?

Executives face a dilemma: while succeeding is the aim of every company, often its very success gets in the way. Ongoing wins in the market and continuous market confirmation can drive a company's leaders to complacency or overly high levels of comfort. Organizations like Enron, Swissair, and WORLDCOM, all of which ranked among the most successful organizations in their industries before they encountered difficulties that threatened their very survival, buried themselves in the safety of past success formulas. These firms were therefore blind to the need for change in their own management systems.[15] That is why as an executive, you need to be vigilant against focusing on past wins, since inert companies do not foster innovation or change.[16]

When executives mired in their companies' comfortable energy are unable to unleash productive energy companywide as the dominate state, the pipeline for fresh ideas and breakthrough innovation for processes and products slowly but steadily dries up. If you have a company operating in a high state of comfort and you are in today's typical, unpredictable economic situation (i.e., *not* one of today's rare occasions in which the business environment is steady, customers are unchanging, and markets are stable), then your customers and markets will turn away quickly. A decline in performance is certain. Michael Tushman and Charles O'Reilly call this the "success syndrome."[17]

How does it work? You can find clear indicators for complacency in three key elements of your organization's management system: *strategy, leadership,* and *culture.* Over time and as a result of earlier successes, these three parts of the management system become increasingly better solidified and coordinated: the overall system runs with ever-increasing efficiency.[18] If changes in the business environment occur or the elements of the management system become largely programmed or routine, focused on protecting the status quo rather than questioning it and developing innovative ideas, then companies become complacent—and comfortable energy dominates.

Let us look at Lufthansa's financial crisis in the 1990s through the lens of its management systems—the strategy, leadership, and culture of the company. Early in that decade, Lufthansa's overly high comfortable energy revealed itself in the company's *strategy* through its long-accepted self-concept: "Lufthansa is an airline with a national mandate"—namely, that Germany without Lufthansa was inconceivable (the airline began in 1926 as a state-owned enterprise). The strategy was not questioned, and even as Lufthansa was losing the equivalent of $3.5 million each day at the beginning of the 1990s, its executives cited the business cycle and the general crisis in the airline industry at the time to convince themselves that the company's course was fine, just as it had been in the past. Similar cyclical developments had affected Lufthansa's market earlier. However, due to the German reunification, the company was actually experiencing a passenger boom at the beginning of the 1990s, and yet it was losing millions. Lufthansa's *leadership* in the early 1990s was characterized by heavy formalization, bureaucracy, standardization, and centralization. Behavior was shaped by sticking to the rules. The company valued efficiency and synergetic thinking. Top management had to be included in every detail and regularly became the bottleneck. External relationships, partnerships, and networks were given short shrift in favor of autonomy and independence.

Lufthansa's *culture* of comfort dominated in its crisis years of 1991–1992. The culture was strongly reflected in the fundamental values that the airline then stood for: the so-called German virtues of security, technical precision, punctuality, reliability, and love of order. This culture was reinforced by narrow norms and a rigid agreement with set values on confidence and loyalty. Managers were overly tolerant of their teams, shying away from giving employees valuable, honest feedback, especially if it was negative. The enterprise was very much internally focused and less aligned with the market or the customer. Juergen Weber, the CEO at the time, candidly recounted the company's prevailing attitude toward passengers: "Passengers should consider it an honor to fly with Lufthansa." Here was a company best characterized by its pride, a strong identity, and a belief in its own infallibility. What did this comfortable energy mean for Lufthansa's performance—its bottom line? While the airline was experiencing a boom in passengers in Germany, it lost money—more than $3 million every day—by postponing or ignoring necessary cost cuts and changes in the fleet or destinations.

What's the lesson here? Executives at companies with the kind of long-term success Lufthansa experienced before its crisis should seriously examine their management system to be sure they remain open to necessary changes. Specifically, you need to continuously scrutinize both your strategy and the company's underlying self-concepts to be sure they aren't outdated or based on past success formulas or a prevailing sense of security. Moreover, Lufthansa illustrates some of the most common symptoms of complacent leadership patterns to which you as an executive need to stay alert, that is, an excess of yes-men (or yes-women) and overly rules-oriented managers on all levels of the hierarchy. Thus, you should look at your leadership climate and ask yourself whether the company is too strongly centralized and bureaucratic, with labyrinthine decision-making processes that ultimately cripple innovation and energy.[19] Examine, too, your company's culture—do its values, habits, and shared basic assumptions represent a corset that limits ownership, mental agility, and proactive behavior in the organization?[20] Or does the culture encourage open feedback, questioning of the status quo, and action taking?

Unless you proactively prevent or uncompromisingly combat the kinds of forces illustrated in the Lufthansa example, your company is in danger of becoming more and more comfortable and complacent—especially if it is successful—losing the ability to change. When this happens, comfortable energy dominates the company—it has lost its ability to unleash its productive forces.

To get an idea of whether your company might be susceptible to overly strong comfortable energy, look at the questions in "Is Your Company Trapped in Overly Strong Comfortable Energy or Complacency?" either alone or with your executive team or employees. We regularly use these questions in our workshops. In chapter 2, we will offer tools to help successful companies master the complacency trap, and in chapter 5, we will describe strategies to sustain energy and generate a proactive sense of urgency in the organization.

Is Your Company Trapped in Overly Strong Comfortable Energy or Complacency?

- Is the company dominated by satisfaction with the current situation of products, services, and processes?

- Are innovations not really welcome in your organization?

- Is your company primarily engaged in optimizing the status quo?

- Has the company developed a strong culture and values that regularly bring new ideas to a halt?

- Do managers and employees highly identify with the situation in your organization as it is?

- Does the decision making in your company involve a long process?

- Do you have the impression that most of your executives and employees have few direct connections to, or contact with, your relevant markets?

Resigned Inertia

One U.S. insurance company went through long phases of change and reorganization that ultimately sent it spiraling into resigned inertia. Three and a half years into its restructuring program, which was focused on cost-cutting, employees began to exhibit signs of apathy, which put the company on the verge of paralysis. Many employees would come into work late or leave early; absenteeism rose significantly. Targets for individual units would slip by, unmet. Any new initiatives, even for social events, were nipped in the bud. When the head of key-account management attempted to foster team building through some informal gatherings, people expressed their cynicism: "We will spend quality time with our friends and family, but not with anybody related to work. Leave us out of any job–related social activity. We'd rather have the money and time you would spend on these activities for ourselves individually."

Employees at all levels resigned themselves to the roller coaster of change and simply tried to survive with the least possible harm or personal engagement. They could be overheard making cynical comments—a common response in such situations since it allows people to mentally and emotionally handle negative experiences without taking any action or initiative.[21] Over time, as employees lost hope that the company would ever stabilize, the energy in the organization dropped to an all-time low. High levels of resignation dominated, and work processes all but came to a grinding halt.

Whereas comfortable energy still retains some positive qualities, resigned inertia falls squarely in the negative, low-intensity quadrant, as was clearly the case at this insurance company. Executives who sense their company is drifting into resigned inertia should assess whether their firms exhibit certain attributes. First, the companies may experience low activity levels with greatly reduced communication or interpersonal interaction throughout the organization. Second, large parts of the company may be mentally withdrawing and openly showing indifference to company goals, and employees typically experience feelings of frustration, disappointment, and sorrow. Third, and perhaps the biggest problem with companies in a state of resigned inertia, is their weakened ability for change and innovation. Even substantial pressure to change often fails, because the prevailing resignation, lack of hope, and internal dissociation is simply too great—all of which constitute a serious threat to efficiency and performance.

Our empirical research reveals that companies high in resigned inertia are significantly less successful on several measures than companies with low resigned inertia. For example, employees' intention to leave the company is on average 17 percent higher in high-resigned-inertia companies, while commitment to the organization is 16 percent lower. Customer loyalty was lower by 19 percent, and customer satisfaction was lower by 13 percent. Efficiency levels of internal business processes in high-resigned-inertia companies are lower by 17 percent, growth by 9 percent, and employee productivity by 16 percent. Finally, these companies' overall performance was 20 percent weaker than low-resignation companies.[22]

Let us also look at how your people are affected individually when they experience resignation. If you are in charge of a company that faces high levels of resignation, such as in our insurance company example, you could expect that only 46 percent of your people are highly committed to your organization, compared with 81 percent of the employees in organizations with low resignation. That is a considerably low share of your population and makes for a huge difference of 35 percent. The number of people who respond that they are "often-to-always thinking about quitting" the organization jumps from 2 percent to 13 percent for high-resignation companies. Furthermore, if you consider satisfaction in companies with high resigned inertia, only 60 percent of the people are highly satisfied with their work (compared with 82 percent for companies with low resigned inertia). What's more, only 64 percent are highly satisfied with their colleagues (compared with 90 percent), and just 49 percent of the employees are highly satisfied with their supervisor (compared with 83 percent). Let's face it: executives in these organizations must deal with a huge number of people with low or mediocre attachment to the company—and the leaders miss out on the people who are highly convinced to work in the right place because employees have unlearned to experience productive energy or they have already left the company. Not a situation that you want to be in.

Why Do Companies Fall into a State of Resigned Inertia?

Let's look at the case of ABB, a vivid example of a company that was driven into resigned inertia—with dramatic implications for the performance of a formerly highly energetic, successful company. In a series of changes at the CEO level and repeated restructuring, the company lost first its guiding orientation, reacted with overacceleration, and then lost its self-confidence as an organization before it was finally able to rebound.

Founded in 1987 through a merger of the Swedish Asea Group and the Swiss Brown Boveri Group, ABB became one of the largest industrial groups of its time, with 170,000 employees.[23] Under the leadership of CEO Percy Barnevik, the company's revenues grew from $17.8 billion to $36.2 billion between 1988 and 1995, while its operating income leaped from $854 million to $3.2 billion. In the first two years alone, Barnevik bought out fifty-five more companies—moves that were then considered indicators of the company's success, but later would be seen as signs of excessive growth and incessant change.

At first, ABB's matrix structure, which consisted of various business areas and countries, permitted a largely seamless integration of the newly acquired companies. ABB was celebrated as a "dancing giant," and Barnevik was highly admired.[24] But after eight years of permanent growth, ABB began to lose its strategic focus—and the first negative signs of the company's excessive complexity emerged. The healthy tension in the ABB matrix began to degenerate into intense rivalries that distracted from the markets and threatened effectiveness and performance.

Barnevik's next two successors, Göran Lindahl and then Jörgan Centerman, tried restructuring in various ways between 1997 and 2002, in an effort to fix the problems associated with the matrix. But the expected success never came, and sales and profits continued to plummet. Soon various stakeholder groups became ever more critical of ABB, and employees, customers, analysts, and shareholders alike trusted the company less and less. In 2001, the company reported losses of $691 million, and its debt level grew to a record-breaking $5.2 billion by mid-2002. ABB had become a classic case of a company mired in resigned inertia. Employees also expressed mental and emotional withdrawal, frustration, disappointment, and sorrow. As one middle manager told us, "I just feel worn down and heavy. Even the smallest things seem almost insurmountable. And the rest of the organization cannot bolster me, because they're in the same situation."

We will continue the story of ABB later in the book and will show how the company eventually emerged from its downward spiral. But for now, we can clearly extract from the story the three core drivers of resigned inertia that you need to watch closely: change processes that never seem to end, or frequent changes among top management; lack of clear and positive perspectives; and overacceleration.

Unending or unsuccessful change processes and frequent changes among top management. As was the case at ABB, employees at companies that are lost in a state of resigned inertia typically tell us they see no light at the end of the tunnel of change. Or, as one manager at a company mired in resigned inertia told us, "We would be glad if we knew that we were in a tunnel at all." Employees at these companies eventually become disillusioned and emotionally exhausted.

Change processes that never seem to end are often the result of frequent changes among top management, especially CEOs, which was the case at ABB. Executives at such companies must monitor whether their company is sliding into a chronic state of resignation and whether employees are developing a fundamental skepticism against every kind of change. One manager of a midsize French company told us, "I've had my job for six years. During this time, this company was renamed three times, my boss changed five times, and the CEO four times." Instead of thinking about developing ideas for business improvements, people in this company became highly creative in their cynicism. Jokes circulated in the company, such as how the new CEO's office chair contained an ejection button, making it easier to kick him out quickly.

Lack of a clear-cut or positive direction. A second driver for resigned inertia that warrants top-management attention is when a company shows little or no clear-cut or positive direction, even when there are no real change initiatives in the offing. This can be the case when companies undergo long phases of uncertainty about the company's future or face unsatisfactory corporate development through recessions in sales, market share losses, or failed or only moderately successful innovation. The series of CEOs at ABB, for example, first tried changing the entire organization from a technology-driven, heavily decentralized matrix company to a division-based knowledge company routed in e-commerce and Internet-based processes. Then, three years later, leaders changed ABB toward a customer-centric organization. Over time, such loss of orientation and series of broken commitments can trigger a downward spiral of employee apathy and resignation.

Overacceleration. A third driver of resigned inertia is what we call the *acceleration trap*. Like an overworked machine, the organization's efficiency becomes deeply impaired when the organization's resources and human potential are constantly overloaded. This was a key mistake that Barnevik made—growing ABB at an astounding rate and acquiring fifty-five companies in a very short period.[25] And it's a pervasive problem today: faced with market pressures and financial shortfalls, well-run companies slash innovation cycles, increase the number and speed of activities, raise performance goals, and introduce new management technologies or organizational systems. The companies often succeed brilliantly at doing more with less. But then, having seen what the company can achieve by working at full capacity, misguided executives assume that the furious pace can become the new normal. They call for yet more acceleration. As other executives join the cry, what began as an exceptional burst of achievement becomes an uncontrolled flood of activities.

Just as burnout among individual employees has been shown to hinder their achievement, burnout at the collective level or even burnout of entire organizations also similarly hurts companies' performance as a whole.[26] In their study of the burnout syndrome, Gilbert Probst and Sebastian Raisch describe the magnitude of excessive growth or incessant change.[27] For example, before its demise, Enron profits had risen by 2,000 percent in the years 1997–2001. WORLDCOM, during its four-year hyperactive phase, acquired seventy-five companies. And at the conglomerate Tyco, new-company acquisitions topped more than two hundred per year. At all of these companies, failure came close on the heels of such exponential growth and change. The resulting lack of corporate focus confuses customers, threatening the brand. The pace saps the motivation of the employees who had helped get the company through the crisis in the first place. Error rates rise, customer complaints increase, and company performance sinks. Managers respond by further increasing the pressure, which only strengthens the acceleration trap's hold. Exhaustion and resignation begin to blanket the company, and the best employees defect.

To assess the level of resigned inertia in your organization, answer the questions presented in the box "Is Your Company Caught in Resigned Inertia?" Chapter 3 will describe strategies and instruments to keep a positive perspective. Chapter 4 will offer tools to help successful companies master the acceleration trap, and in chapter 5, we will describe strategies to sustain energy and generate a proactive sense of urgency in the organization.

Is Your Company Caught in Resigned Inertia?

- Is your company engaged in a change process that has already lasted so long that your employees complain of being unable to see the light at the end of the tunnel?

- Do you have the impression that your employees no longer care about the well-being of the company?

- Do most people in your organization express negativity about the viability of new initiatives and change?

- Does it seem as if your people only communicate or interact with one another when it is absolutely necessary?

- Have your employees openly expressed feelings such as frustration, disappointment, and sorrow?

- Is the humor in your organization cynical?

- Is it difficult for executives and managers to create excitement among employees, because so many change activities have failed in the past?

- Do you sense that the departments and teams in your organization seem fatigued or are showing other signs of burnout?

Corrosive Energy

In contrast to the energy states of comfortable energy and resigned inertia, corrosive energy is characterized by high intensity—a high level of activity, alertness, and emotional involvement. But the quality of that energy is negatively targeted, misaligned with or specifically set against the company and its goals. Employees feel strong negative emotions such as annoyance, fear, or rage about, for example, a comprehensive change project, interdepartmental squabbles, or interpersonal issues with colleagues. Recall the massive strikes at BSH recounted in the introduction of this book. Over several years, BSH employees resisted the closing of the company's Berlin factory. At one point, employee representatives even announced a lawsuit against the BSH management as a possible way to fight through their position. When corrosive energy permeates a company, people are using their energy in a destructive way to prevent change or innovation or to weaken others, for their own personal benefit.

The energy at one German industrial company, for example, quickly turned corrosive because of management's actions when the company hit a financial downturn. Top management told employees that the situation was critical, with an urgent need for change. The employees believed management's vivid descriptions and stood ready to make the needed sacrifices to overcome the crisis. During the collective bargaining taking place at that time, employees were prepared to accept moderate salary increases. Even the traditional Christmas celebration was canceled for economic reasons. But the situation took a turn for the worse when employees discovered that the board members had given themselves a 14 percent salary increase. The company's energy quickly transformed from high productive energy to negative energy, characterized by annoyance and aggression.

The result was a hard internal struggle, with employees demanding a 17 percent salary increase, and the most radical negotiations the enterprise had ever experienced. Continuous strikes over weeks and a crisis in the company's business process forced out top management within six months. Three years later, the company was still struggling with the financial effects of the destructive energy that erupted. More important, with the employees' impaired confidence in top management and a continued rift between management and employees, the foundation for future cooperation was in tatters.

Had the executives at this German company detected the signs of corrosive energy brewing in their midst, they might have been able to turn around a negative situation. You can identify corrosive energy as it's occurring by the following core attributes: high levels of anger and fury; high alertness and creativity in seeking opportunities to harm and weaken others internally; and destructive internal conflicts, micropolitical activities, or active resistance to change. In other words, any tendencies of your unit's weakening another in favor of maximizing individual interests ultimately robs the organization of its vitality and stamina and creates corrosive energy.

Why Do Companies Fall into a State of Corrosive Energy?

We've identified three main drivers of corrosive energy to which you as a top manager need to stay alert. Let's look at these three drivers in detail.

Negative competition among internal units. Internal competition can often yield positive results, such as unleashing productive energy in a sporting way, especially when all competing units are rewarded somehow. At the very least, it can often offer lower-performing units access to bench learning about managing energy from "winners" if the lower performers are not stigmatized as losers. But too often in our research, we have seen the unhealthy side of internal competition, which you should be aware of and work to prevent.

Specifically, implicit or explicit competition among units is likely to trigger corrosive energy if there are winners and losers in the game. Consider what happened with a recent restructuring of a Swedish industrial enterprise, which resulted in the formation of three divisions that top management declared equal, both in terms of resources and in strategic priority. But the way that expenses were handled in each division soon proved that the divisions were not equal at all and that management was favoring one division. Without any comprehensible reason, the newly suggested pay scale for employees in this division started well above that of all other divisions—for similar work and functions. As word of these facts spread around the company, employees grew more certain that the purported equality was actually a farce, and corrosive energy ate away at the company morale.

Fortunately, there is a better way to use internal competition so that it doesn't degenerate into corrosive energy. Martin Strobel, CEO of Baloise Group since January 2009, did just that.[28] He created a modified remuneration system for field representatives of the insurance company when he was CEO of Baloise Switzerland. Specifically, he introduced a competitive dimension to the variable-reward system, which formerly was solely dependent on the achievement of objectives of each individual employee. The variable remuneration now partly depended on how well everybody performed individually compared with other employees. At the same time, Strobel encouraged internal knowledge exchange and cooperation among employees. So as not to jeopardize knowledge exchange within the corporation but rather to exploit the positive effects of internal competition, Strobel decided on a combination solution: competition of the sales force was limited to within separate regions, while there was knowledge exchange but no competition between all the regions.

Egoistic behavior of individual groups, managers, and employees. As in the German industrial company described earlier, whose board members gave themselves a 14 percent salary increase while asking employees to tighten their belts during a financial downturn, egoistic or unfair behavior of individuals can be the source of corrosive energy. The same is true for the behavior of a subgroup in the organization, for example, a certain occupation group or a project team. The 2001 pilots' strike at Lufthansa illustrates the immense amount of destructive power that negative behavior of a small group can unleash.[29] When the pilots' labor union demanded an increase in salary of approximately 30 percent, the union decided to underscore its demands with a warning strike. After an effort by the executive board to preserve Lufthansa's consensus-oriented approach (one board member met informally with the pilots to try to resolve the problem), the union felt its demands still weren't satisfied. Lufthansa's management then refused to make any voluntary concessions whatsoever. The discord came to a head when, during a public demonstration by the pilots in the airport in Frankfurt on the Main, the ground crew decided to form its own counterdemonstration to communicate how the pilots' strike was causing unrest within Lufthansa. The encounter of the two groups in the airport set off an aggressive argument that came close to a physical fight.

The barriers between the pilots' labor union and Lufthansa management grew to such heights that after thirteen days and seven unsuccessful negotiation rounds, the two parties had still failed to come to an agreement on their own. At that point, Hans-Dietrich Genscher, the former German secretary of state, was asked to arbitrate. With his help, a new wage agreement was finally concluded—a full eight months after the pilots' initial demand.

The pilots' strike had a far-reaching impact on Lufthansa. Aside from the onetime cost of $103 million caused by the $2\frac{1}{2}$-day strike and the additional permanent annual staff costs totaling about $170 million, the company's culture, especially its community spirit and "we" feeling, suffered great damage. The pilots' unwillingness to compromise ultimately ended up further widening the gap that had historically existed between the pilots and ground crew. The episode left scars in the organization—scars that were visible years later.

Interestingly, the escalation of the pilots' strike was based primarily on emotional reasons. Perhaps if the pilots had felt more appreciated in the organization and had believed that their concerns were taken seriously, the strike and its massively negative outcome could have been avoided. Corrosive energy, we have found, is closely coupled with a negative emotional charge: entire units share short-term, eruptive anger or aggression. Because people tend to remember negative incidents best, these events guide people's behavior for a long time. Even after overcoming the most serious crisis Lufthansa had ever faced—the emotional and economic shockwaves of 9/11—the old shared feelings of anger, pain, humiliation, irritation, and the desire for revenge returned among employees, and the damage from the strike could still be sensed for years.

Corrosive energy within top management teams. In many cases, corrosive energy starts at the top—and you must begin to fight and avoid corrosive energy in your own team. Toxic behavior, negative competition, or micropolitics in the executive suite lay the groundwork for anger, fights, and destructive engagement in the organization. Employees who observe a lack of alignment, trust, and behavioral integration in the executive board will often respond with destructive behavior and aggressiveness against their colleagues as well.[30]

Hard discussions to the point of true conflict are no surprise in top management teams—and are, to a certain degree, even a necessary ingredient in any top management team that makes good decisions. Tension will be particularly high if management is confronted with what Amy C. Edmonson and Diana McLain Smith call "hot topics."[31] Hot topics emerge when executives face highly uncertain and ambiguous issues, when differing individual viewpoints are based on the members' values and beliefs, and when stakes are high. Every top management team that makes strategic, long-term decisions bumps up against these very circumstances again and again. It makes a huge difference, however, whether executives approach these hot topics constructively or in a corrosive manner. Productive energy implies engagement in constructive discussions, while corrosive energy has an undermining, negative quality focused on damaging individuals or misusing power, rather than making progress around the matter at hand.

Corrosive top management teams we've observed show high levels of activity, alertness, and emotional involvement, but the teams' full engagement is directed against the ideas and initiatives of others in the team. Members do indeed mobilize their full potential, but not to jointly solve the company's common challenges. Instead, they destructively fight for their own individual agendas and against others' achievements that threaten their position and ambitions—with dramatic effects on the results of their organization.

In our research, we found that 15 percent of the top management teams had increased levels of corrosive energy. On average these teams experienced 47 percent corrosive energy while low corrosive top teams showed on average 24 percent corrosive energy.[32] Companies with top management teams entrenched in corrosive energy showed performance rates that were 20 percent below the performance of companies with low corrosive energy. Moreover, growth at those companies was 16 percent, trust was 16 percent, and efficiency was 21 percent below average. All these observations underscore the need for top executives to act swiftly and firmly when they identify early signs of corrosive energy in their team of top managers.

When plotting a destructive battle in the boardroom, board members need to remind themselves that corrosive energy is highly contagious and even more so because of the top management team's high visibility. Usually, any fighting in the team will simply unleash more conflicts and negative dynamics between silos and units throughout the company. And we find strong support in our data. Companies whose top management teams score high in corrosive energy also show significantly higher average levels of corrosive energy (40 percent) than companies whose top management teams score low on corrosive energy (18 percent).[33]

Why Is Corrosive Energy So Dangerous?

Corrosive energy poses dangers for two reasons: it escalates rapidly and destroys trust and value. We have often seen how what started as relatively small corrosive events, such as the ones we mentioned above, can escalate dangerously, transforming positive processes into negative events. Companies should quickly overcome this destructive energy; otherwise, they find themselves caught in a downward spiral, with ever more aggression and destruction directed at the organization.[34] Managers and employees typically react with negative behavior to protect themselves or gain individual advantages. To make matters worse, employees tend to adopt or even exaggerate the perceived emotional reactions of their colleagues and supervisors.[35] With this added sense of unity, commonly experienced events within a group (such as employees) can lead to strongly shared collective emotions and attitudes against other groups (such as management or other internal departments).[36]

Most dangerously for executives, the continuous effects of corrosive forces, as Peter Frost points out in his book *Toxic Emotions at Work,* is a blow to the basic foundations of the company and can rapidly impair corporate values, culture, and mutual support, causing long-term damage.[37] Our research shows that companies with high corrosive energy, as compared to companies with low levels of corrosive energy, showed a significantly reduced sense of identity among their employees—i.e. their sense of belonging and striving for shared goals was seriously weakened.[38] Even goodwill that's been nurtured over many years can quickly crumble in the face of such negative energy. Companies usually need years to recover from this damage.

All of this is to say that you should fight corrosive energy early and decisively to avoid ill effects on performance. Poisonous emotions and energy, as Frost shows, increase the chance that employees will burn out and that corporate productivity will suffer. Our research shows that the destructive impact of corrosive energy on performance significantly surmounts the positive performance effects of high productive energy. One of our studies compared low-corrosive-energy companies with high-corrosive-energy ones (figure 1-2). The high-corrosive-energy companies in the study showed more emotional exhaustion and higher turnover rates. Moreover, these companies showed lower levels of overall performance, employee productivity, efficiency of business processes, customer satisfaction, customer loyalty, job satisfaction, and commitment to the organization. High corrosive energy also constrains internal coordination and process improvement. More important, these organizations lose sight of customer-related issues, innovations, and improvements of products and services. In our experience, the organizations also spend significantly more time on bureaucratic and administrative issues as well as on conflicts and negotiations than do organizations or units characterized by high productive energy. The extra time, of course, costs real money to the companies we have worked with.

FIGURE 1-2

High corrosive energy companies and performance

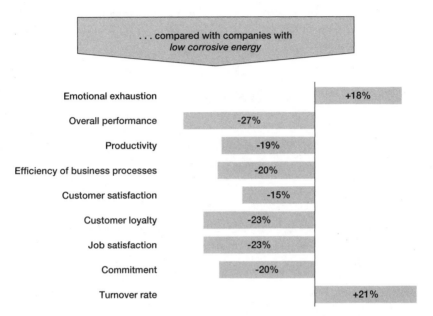

... compared with companies with *low corrosive energy*

Emotional exhaustion	+18%
Overall performance	-27%
Productivity	-19%
Efficiency of business processes	-20%
Customer satisfaction	-15%
Customer loyalty	-23%
Job satisfaction	-23%
Commitment	-20%
Turnover rate	+21%

Note: Data based on subsamples of surveys from 104 German companies in 2009: 3,789 respondents for energy states, 3,555 respondents for emotional exhaustion, 3,893 respondents for satisfaction, 3,886 respondents for commitment, 3,673 respondents for turnover intention, and 225 top-management respondents for performance measures (overall performance, productivity, efficiency of business processes, customer satisfaction, and consumer loyalty).

Let's look again at the people who really feel connected to their company. In companies with high corrosive energy (as compared with those with low corrosive energy), the number of people committed to the company drops from 88 percent to a mere 51 percent.[39] For highly corrosive companies, the number of people who are "often to always thinking about quitting" the organization is 10 percent, compared with 2 percent for low-corrosive-energy companies. Regarding job satisfaction in highly corrosive companies, only 65 percent of the people are highly satisfied with their work (compared with 82 percent for companies with low corrosive energy), 69 percent are highly satisfied with their colleagues (compared with 92 percent), and 56 percent are highly satisfied with their supervisor (compared with 84 percent). In all cases, the number of people attached to and satisfied with their company drops precipitously, which should be a concern and challenge for every executive.

Is Your Company Showing Signs of Corrosive Energy?

- Do you have the impression that many employees are not working toward the company goals, but rather are trying to maximize their own benefits?

- Is silo thinking prevalent in many of your units?

- Is it impossible for you to pursue new ideas or processes because at least one group of employees is actively working against you?

- Are conflicts a dominant feature of the work in top management?

- Do you have the impression that certain groups of employees annoy one another, no longer trust one another, or even hate one another?

- Do questions about management integrity and "walking the talk" play a secondary role in your organization?

- Have you seen a decline in your employees' mutual support?

In chapter 3, we'll offer some hands-on tools for dealing with corrosive energy. For now, some guiding questions in "Is Your Company Showing Signs of Corrosive Energy?" will help you begin analyzing potential corrosive energy in your organization or department.

Measuring Organizational Energy

Thus far in this chapter, we have described the four energy states that we have found in our research at companies. We emphasized that you as an executive should monitor your organizations for distinct attributes of these energy states to get a handle on the status of your company's human forces. Now we will look at ways that companies can more specifically and tangibly measure the energy state of their organization, division, or team.

Why should you measure organizational energy, that is, the extent to which your company has mobilized its human potential in pursuit of its goals? Our experience is that most executives already have a gut feeling about the state of their company's energy. But unlike the concrete evaluations that leaders conduct for finance or market share, executives' knowledge about the use of the organization's *human* potential often lacks precision, clarity, and a shared language. Moreover, executives find it difficult to articulate their gut feeling to systematically improve the organization's energy. For these reasons and more, you should regularly take the pulse of the organization or unit by measuring energy.

Recall the example of CWT Netherlands in the introduction of this book. Once Jan Dekker, the company's executive vice president for North Europe, gained clarity about the true state of his unit's energy, he and his executive team could act more decisively to turn things around.[40] This new clarity also increased the team's sensitivity to, and awareness of, different energy states in the organization, which allowed them to better focus their leadership efforts on the vision and strategy implementation. How can you as an executive or a team leader similarly discover which of the four organizational energy states your company embodies and then leverage that information (your company's *energy profile*) to help the organization succeed? Along with observing and describing these energy states, there are different ways to make the energy of your company tangible. We'll begin by explaining how to work with our core method of energy measurement, the OEQ (Organizational Energy Questionnaire). We will also present different ways to measure organizational energy (employee surveys, energy pulse checks, workshops, and audits) and describe how executives can benefit from such applications.

The Organizational Energy Questionnaire (OEQ)

The Organizational Energy Questionnaire (OEQ) is a standardized survey instrument that we use to measure and analyze companies' energy profile (including the energy profiles of the company's units, departments, and teams). In most cases, we also assess the major energy drivers, such as inspirational leadership climate, top-management-team integration, strategy commitment in the organization, and a vitalized culture, as well as common energy killers, such as the acceleration trap, a lack of cooperation in the value chain, or insufficient cohesion in top management teams. The OEQ makes leaders' vague beliefs and instincts about the highly elusive element of energy tangible and manageable.

By mid-2010, more than 250,000 people in over seven hundred companies have participated in the energy questionnaire, which we have administered in fifty-five countries and twenty-four languages. We work in companies with two versions of the questionnaire. A highly detailed version of the OEQ consists of thirty-six questions (the OEQ 36)[41] and often takes weeks for us to assess large companies entirely. But we also often administer a more compact version that is equally useful for companies and that we will present here in this book: the OEQ 12.[42] This energy self-assessment consists of twelve questions—three questions for each of the four energy states. Of the three questions, one is emotional, one cognitive, and one behavioral to capture the different facets of the respective energy states (figure 1-3). The full OEQ 12 and an implementation guide is provided in detail in the appendix to this book, so you can use it with your own organization and while reading this book.

The result of a company's OE measurement—what we call a company's OE Index[43]—contains a precise picture of its four energy states, illustrating the degree of intensity and interplay among them. Because *all four* energy states are present simultaneously, we don't ask executives to position their company (or unit or department) in a single energy quadrant. Rather, we ask, "How strong is each of the four energy states individually?" And this is what this measurement shows—a differentiated picture of the productive and the counterproductive forces in the organization. Armed with this picture, you can take leadership actions to improve your organizations' energy profile. For example, equipped with your organization's OEQ results, you might decide to mobilize productive energy, remove the sources of resignation, or work on reducing aggression or destructive behavior in the organization—actions that are all very different but that might need to be addressed simultaneously, depending on the organization's energy profile.

When we measure the energy of entire companies, we present the result—the OE Index—of the company as a whole. The index precisely reflects the four energy states and usually shows one or two that are dominant. The company's OE Index offers a first strong indication of the energy situation and suggests initial leadership moves. In a second step, we drill down and analyze the energy profiles of the units, departments, and teams in the organization and the patterns of the energy states across hierarchical levels and across collaborating departments. This multifaceted

FIGURE 1-3

Questions in the OEQ 12©

	People in my _____ (please fill in "company," "department," "unit" or "team") . . .
1.	. . . like what they are doing.
2.	. . . do not have much drive.
3.	. . . feel relaxed in their jobs.
4.	. . . are angry in their jobs.
5.	. . . feel enthusiastic in their jobs.
6.	. . . have no desire to make something happen.
7.	. . . often speculate about the real intentions of our management.
8.	. . . really care about the fate of this company.
9.	. . . are efficient in how they conduct their work.
10.	. . . often behave in a destructive manner.
11.	. . . go out of their way to ensure the company succeeds.
12.	. . . feel discouraged in their jobs.

(To view the complete version of the OEQ 12©, scoring instructions, and ways to interpret the results, please see the appendix of this book.)

approach allows top and line managers to monitor energy, indicating how strongly a company's positive energy potential has been activated in pursuit of the company goals, where unused potential lies dormant, and where the destructive engagement in the organization is prominent.

Analyzing and Visualizing Organizational Energy with the OE Index

While the results of the OEQ show how much of the company's human potential and energy is activated in different ways, the OE Index allows you to visualize how energy plays out in your company. Figure 1-4, for example, shows an OE Index that we calculated for a large international

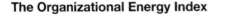

FIGURE 1-4

The Organizational Energy Index

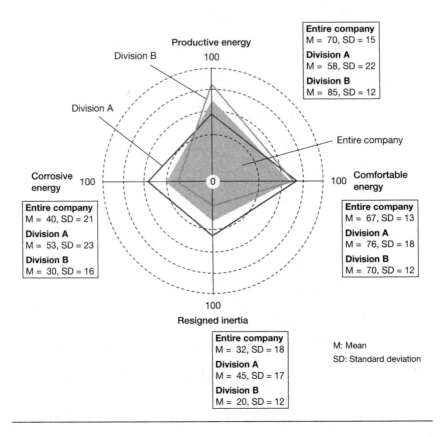

organization. The gray-filled shape indicates to what extent each energy state is present in the organization; the darker lines indicate the same for two divisions within the company.

There are several things to keep in mind when you are looking at OE Indexes. First, the degree of each of the four energy states is captured on a scale from 0 to 100 percent, with 0 percent being the minimum and 100 percent being the maximum degree of each energy state. Since we can generally say that the best organizations are like geniuses, who use a larger percentage of their brains than the average person does, companies falling in the *productive energy* zone tap into almost 80 percent of their potential while they usually score low on negative energy.

Second, keep in mind that the energy states are independent of each other, and the OE Index will reflect this. Therefore, the percentages like those in figure 1-4 and in most OE Indexes do not add up to 100 percent. For example, your company might have mobilized as much as 70 percent of its productive energy, but your people might also experience high levels of comfortable energy (67 percent), feeling very satisfied and at ease or enjoying their work.

Let's look at figure 1-4 in detail and the large international company that it depicts. Although the degree of *productive energy* (with a score of 70 percent) seems average, at large organizations such as this one, this score is actually relatively high. This does not mean that large companies cannot unleash most of their productive forces, but as a rule, large organizations have more-dynamic and less-dynamic areas. At the same time, a 70 percent productive-energy score means that the company is shy of its full (100 percent) potential and there is still some room for improvement. A large international organization's good-practice benchmark is 77 percent, while smaller companies should compare themselves against a benchmark of 81 percent and beyond.[44] In the same benchmark study, the bottom 10 percent of companies in the sample experienced only 55 percent productive energy.

Continuing with our analysis, remember that the score for *comfortable energy* cannot be interpreted in isolation. This is what makes working with the results of employee satisfaction surveys so difficult. And in general, executives have a hard time answering the question "How satisfied should our people ideally be?" It is impossible to judge whether the level of comfort is high because there is a high level of intense work and enthusiasm in the organization, or if the comfortable energy is dominant because employees enjoy the slow pace of the organization. Thus, with comfortable energy, you should look not only at the absolute level, but more importantly, at how that level relates to the level of productive energy. In our example, the company scored 70 percent in productive energy and 67 percent in comfortable energy. In this case, comfort is not too high; executives should focus leadership activities toward mobilizing even more productive energy. The leaders should also ensure that the activities discourage an emphasis on the status quo or a change-adverse atmosphere in the organization. This explains why some companies refrain from using satisfaction as the core criteria for employee surveys, since comfort by it-self does not give the whole story of the human forces in an organization. On the other hand, our research reveals that companies do suffer when they fall below a certain level of comfort. Companies with low comfort-able energy compared with those with high comfortable energy scored lower on overall performance (–16 percent), employee productivity (–14 percent), efficiency of business processes (–11 percent), customer satisfac-tion (–7 percent), and customer loyalty (–15 percent).[45] In addition, in companies with low comfortable energy, employees expressed an inten-tion to leave the firm at a 16 percent higher rate and expressed a 15 per-cent lower commitment to the organization, compared with those companies with high comfortable energy.

In light of these statistics, then, there is no absolute best-practice benchmark for comfortable energy. Rather, it is important that comfort-able energy not be the dominant energy state and that productive energy be at least equally high. For the organization in our example, the level of productive and comfortable energy works. We encouraged executives to keep an eye on the level of productive energy to ensure that it didn't drop and, better yet, to raise it higher. The level of comfort itself was not con-sidered critical or alarming.

Ideally, the index for both negative energy states should be close to zero. It is unrealistic to find an organization or even a single work unit or department that does not have any degree of frustration or aggression. However, when the degree of negativity in organizations goes beyond the normal noise, you should give this topic top priority. Why? Negative en-ergy works directly against organizational goals. Corrosive energy is highly counterproductive, and resigned energy pulls people down, destroys their morale, and works as a constant headwind against whatever the organization is trying to accomplish. That is why you need to address increased levels of negative energy promptly and forcefully.

According to our benchmark studies, the score should not be higher than 20–25 percent for both resigned inertia and corrosive energy. A higher score indicates a need for action; consider it a challenge, something for the organization to aspire to. Benchmark studies showed that the top 10 percent of companies in the sample had on average 12 percent resigned inertia and

18 percent corrosive energy. The energy profile of the example company depicted in figure 1-4 shows high levels of negative energy, including slightly elevated resigned inertia, indicating that executives should take action to identify and remove the sources of frustration in the organization.

More alarming, however, is the level of aggression and destructive forces in the company. With a level of corrosive energy of 40 percent, there is much more than the normal noise in this organization. These executives quickly need to find ways to neutralize the company's corrosive energy. Too often, though, executives are uncertain whether to address such negativity; many hope that the corrosive engagement will disappear on its own. Others feel paralyzed because they do not know whether they should intervene or how to tackle the problem.

But leaders need to remember that these negative forces work directly against their goals. As an effective leader, therefore, you must remove both corrosive energy and resigned inertia quickly and forcefully. Corrosive energy is destructive; people actively thwart the achievement of goals. Resigned inertia pulls people down, sapping the morale in your organization. Both negative forms of energy are highly infectious. They will not go away on their own—rather, they tend to grow, infect others, and often become negative spirals. That is why swift action is paramount. In chapter 2, we describe how to overcome resigned inertia, and chapter 3 describes strategies for neutralizing corrosive energy.

Sometimes, fundamentally different energy profiles can coexist within one organization. For example, in large, decentralized companies with independent company units, great differences in energy states are comparatively unimportant and can be used as a means for benchmarking and bench learning within the organization. Pronounced differences between the divisions make such an internal benchmarking useful indeed. By breaking the energy measurement down into an organization's different units, centers of productive energy and best-practice approaches can be identified, as can feelings of resignation, pockets of corrosive energy, and complacency tendencies. Meanwhile, the foundation can be laid for the divisions to systematically learn from each other. As an executive, you can identify possible change agents who can take a leading position in a company-wide change, and you can identify possible bottlenecks or other particularly difficult parts of the organization that may need support or more intense change management.

When monitoring change processes, strategy implementation, or even turnaround processes, you may find it particularly interesting to compare measurements over time, at intervals of, say, twelve, eighteen, or twenty-four months or as a pulse check in a much shorter time frame. Additionally, cross-company benchmarks can be very informative, especially as measures that systematically access soft factors and permit benchmarking within a certain branch or against best-in-class companies.

Using and Applying the OEQ

As a leader, you can use the OEQ in three ways: as a periodic employee survey in organizations, as an organizational energy pulse-check (for example, to monitor change processes), and as an instant energy check to use in workshops for top management. In the following sections, we describe examples of how we've worked with various companies in these three ways—and the lessons you can draw in applying the OEQ to your own company.

The OEQ as an employee survey. When used in employee surveys, the OEQ can uncover not only energy states (as was the case at CWT Netherlands, recounted in the introduction), but also the most relevant drivers of energy, its "killers," and beneficial and harmful consequences. As a leader, you can use employee feedback to gain detailed insights into questions such as, Where are the dynamic key groups, and where do we show tendencies of inertia and symptoms of exhaustion? How good are we compared with best-practice companies in our industry, size, or region? Are we on track with our strategy implementation? Is there silo thinking in the organization, or is there a fruitful collaboration in the value chain? Is the energy focused on the right things? How strong is our sense of passion for customer issues in the organization? What are the relationships between our company's energy states, energy drivers, and performance? And which levers can we use to improve energy and performance? Once you've administered the OEQ, you can begin to answer these kinds of questions using the results.

For more than six years, Alstom Power Service (APS), a Switzerland-based business division of the French Alstom Group, has included the energy concept in the company's employee survey as part of its efforts to strengthen a sense of shared identity at the company.[46] To facilitate working with the survey results, APS nominated so-called identity champions for each of the five regional divisions.[47] Organization-wide, the identity champions facilitated workshops in divisions, business units, and country organizations, where they tackled the respective survey findings. As a result of the workshops, every unit identified issues regarding its energy state and defined action plans that addressed the results and the two overarching topics—engagement and alignment—which top management had set as underlying strategic topics for the identity process.

In this way, local line management actively started to implement strategy, develop an organizational identity, and improve the group's energy level. By integrating these activities, managers could address their group's specific issues, such as high-speed growth in some countries and downsizing in others. And the OEQ eventually allowed top management to see where units were behind, but also how APS's identity became stronger overall, supporting the company's business ambitions. One identity champion said, "The repeated OEQ results over time sent a clear and tangible signal to managers and the organization that the identity process provided a way forward for APS."

After the initial period and capability build-up through 2005, APS continued to conduct an annual energy measurement as part of its employee opinion survey. What's more, the company tied the energy measurement even tighter to the management systems in place. Targets for energy levels, survey results, and delineated activities became part of the annual management audit for the individual line manager, with defined activities such as leadership training specific for line managers, standardizing between-country business processes toward approaches with one level of quality process, and improving how good performance is recognized in the organization.

As a leader of your organization, you, too, can use the OEQ as an employee survey to dig deeper into the quality of your organization's energy. Conduct the survey on a regular basis, and be sure to visibly monitor improvement in a number of key projects. This promotes a feeling of progress in the organization, channeling organizational energy toward relevant activities and preserving the enthusiasm that normally exists only at the start of the process. Moreover, results need to align closely with the company's strategy and planned business activities; the OE Index is not relevant or effective in a parallel world, but only as an integral component of the company's business activities. That is how the energy concept becomes part of the corporate language, culture, and way of doing business in these organizations, as it did at APS.

The OEQ as an organizational energy pulse-check. Pulse-checks can be powerful for tracking the implementation of change initiatives or strategies at early stages. So, instead of using the OEQ at 12-, 18-, or 24-month intervals, you can administer it more often, even on a yearly basis.

Especially in times of change, firms need to build up and preserve productive energy while preventing or reducing negative energy, namely, corrosive energy and resigned inertia, which both directly impede the success of the change. Fundamental organizational change often triggers uncertainties for employees: "How will the change work?" "What does this mean to me as an employee?" Employees view these uncertain situations as stressful, and negative energy in the form of resistance, aggression, or frustration is likely to rise.[48] In certain phases of a change, people's attitudes, emotions, and actions will fluctuate, and these important variations in energy can be monitored with the help of OEQ pulse-checks.

Executives are often concerned that during times of change, morale usually drops anyway—why reveal this negativity in numbers? This is also the reason why employee opinion surveys are often put on hold during change processes. But it's never wise to ignore or postpone actively dealing with fluctuations in energy as they emerge. It takes courage to use a pulse-check during painful or critical changes, but doing so has an enormously engaging effect. A pulse-check demonstrates, first, that you as a leader care about your people's opinions and energy states in hard times as well as good. And second, particularly in tough times, it is important that you demonstrate professional and systematic management of the human energy in your organization. We'll say more about this in chapter 2, but this kind of systematic survey supports an active coping mechanism that will allow employees to understand the energy shifts during times of change while giving them the opportunity to express their feelings and concerns.

That was the case with Deutsche Annington Immobilien Group (DAIG), one of the leading residential property companies, when it underwent its strategy process. It used the OEQ as a pulse-check to support a major structural change. The German company employs more than one thousand people and offers approximately 217,000 apartments to rent and buy across Germany, complemented by customer-oriented services. In 2009, this company started to transform itself into a modern, full-service organization with innovative customer offerings and quality control, which involved big, structural changes, from the structuring and geographic placement of major functions to the composition of individual work groups and job descriptions.

DAIG used the OEQ in two ways: first, as a tool to evaluate how the employees' identification with the change initiative developed over time and, second, to identify levers (e.g., transparency, role clarity, and transformational leadership) for successfully implementing the change project. The recognition of these levers was especially relevant for the daily behavior of top and middle management.

A target group of about 150 people, including top and middle management as well as selected employees, was invited to answer the online survey both at the beginning of the change project and again half a year later, when the main structural changes began to be implemented. The results told company leaders which aspects were well managed and which would probably jeopardize the change's success. As one middle manager told us, "It is good to see that my team has understood why we started this program, and that they're willing to change. It is not always easy for managers to have so much transparency, but in the end, it helps." Further measurements with the OEQ followed during the course of the change in 2010 to evaluate its success.

Typically, you can conduct such a pulse-check relatively frequently, such as every quarter or at least every six months. Because emotional, mental, and behavioral resistance to change corresponds with corrosive energy, pulse-checks are sometimes done weekly, especially in very dynamic phases of change. Sometimes, the OEQ in the format of a pulse-check is used in the change task force itself to help members express their attitudes and feelings about how the change is going. But no matter how the questionnaire is employed, the main benefit is that you as a leader can intervene quickly to counteract problems, thus substantially increasing the likelihood that a change process will succeed.

The OEQ as an instant energy check in workshops for top managers. A final way you can use the OEQ is as an instant energy check in a workshop format. The purpose is to get a quick picture of the energy perception of the participants in the room; this snapshot serves as a basis for a joint analysis and strategy planning for improvement. Often these workshops are part of a strategy meeting. The number of participants is flexible, ranging from six to twelve senior executives during a strategy meeting to large groups of two hundred or three hundred at strategic management conferences. (See "Seven Steps to an Instant Energy Check.")

We've seen again and again the positive results that such instant energy checks can yield in companies, helping them to maintain high levels of productive energy and overcome tendencies of inertia or overly strong comfortable energy. Energy workshops are also particularly effective whenever there is strong negative tension, resignation, or a destructive climate in organizations. In early phases of change processes, these workshops can be invaluable for triggering change and creating awareness for the need to take action.

In this chapter, we've seen that every company has its own particular energy profile that is identifiable and measurable, and this organizational energy differs according to its intensity and quality. Those of you who are willing to identify and understand your company's specific energy profile have taken a first step in managing your organization's soft factors. Over the next several chapters, we'll illustrate what you can do to actively direct the shared emotional, cognitive, and behavioral potential of your organization toward the company's main goals in order to sustain productive energy.

Let's turn now to chapter 2, where we can begin to answer a key question: How can you mobilize and orchestrate your organization's energy potential?

Seven Steps to an Instant Energy Check

Here is how you can instantly check the energy of your teams, units, or companies, either in a targeted workshop for this purpose or as part of a regular company strategy meeting:

1. Familiarize the participants of the workshop with the energy concept and leadership strategies. Executives must establish a shared language to interpret results and draw conclusions.

2. Measure the energy of the organization among the workshop participants with the OEQ 12. In large groups of 50 to 250 people, also measure the energy of the various units represented in the workshop—and provide separate energy profiles.

3. Either the executives themselves or the facilitators should present the OEQ results and then kick off the conversation to interpret the results.

4. If you have large groups of more than twelve people, divide the audience into small groups to interpret the results and to identify causes for the existing strengths and weaknesses in the energy profile. If you have measured the energy of the various units represented in the workshop provide time for two discussions: one for the units and one for the organization overall, facilitating step 5 for each discussion.

5. Ask the group(s) to identify concrete activities to improve the energy profile or individual energy states such as corrosive energy.

6. Reconvene in the large group to present and discuss the findings and recommendations. In our experience, workshops quickly achieve a shared understanding of the situation and the crucial activities to be taken. Facilitators need to challenge buzzwords and clichés such as "Leaders have to be role models" and uncover what the real issue is beneath. Push for a concrete set of activities that can be assigned with accountability and a time line.

7. For smaller groups, spend at least three hours in the workshop; for larger groups, you need at least half a day or a day, depending on how thorough the discussion, conclusions, and concrete activities should be.

CHAPTER 2

Mobilizing Your Organization's Energy

Escaping the Complacency Trap

What can you do when you find that your company lies in a low-energy zone? Two proven strategies we have identified for unleashing the emotional, cognitive, and behavioral potential of almost any company are what we call *slaying the dragon* and *winning the princess.*[1] Both strategies emphasize the mobilization of a higher level of productive energy and, in so doing, represent the primary tools for combating the complacency trap, when your company is languishing in a cycle of low positive energy. These two strategies are also effective in fighting resigned inertia and can be used in a variety of situations and combinations, as we'll show in more detail in this chapter.

To jump-start the company toward productive energy, you as a leader must help your organization identify either a major threat or challenge (the dragon) or a promising opportunity (the princess)—and then help the organization overcome or take advantage of it.[2] Both of these strategies activate organizational energy by requiring a level of intensity in both engagement and commitment—a level that routine activities do not ignite. These strategies can be particularly powerful when used in tandem; toward the end of this chapter, we will discuss how the sequencing works.

Each strategy comes with its own set of initiatives and change processes. Let's begin with a look at how you can use outside threats to energize the organization.

Slaying the Dragon: Using Outside Challenges to Mobilize Your Company

When your company is mired in the complacency trap or in resigned inertia, your organization's ability to identify a threat and support its employees through that challenge can increase levels of productive energy for an intense, short-term spurt. Although slaying the dragon can increase the energy of a company in a crisis situation, the strategy works even when the company is in good shape. In that case, the challenge for you to create awareness of a possible threat or danger is even greater. In these situations, where there is no obvious and immediately tangible threat, the key leadership task is to frame the concern as a possible threat and arouse people's awareness around it—even while the business continues to run smoothly. Used in this way, slaying-the-dragon strategy focuses on preventing a threat or challenge before it emerges.

Lidl, a German-based international chain of discounters, entered the Swiss market in March 2009. CEO Andreas Pohl wasn't taking any risks. As well as the company was doing, he knew he had to prepare his staff for a possible negative reception from the Swiss market. He launched a dragon strategy both to foster staff cohesion and commitment and to stave off any kind of confusion or uncertainty during the transition. He knew that entering a new market would be a strenuous process that would require the full energy of the entire newly hired staff, and he wanted the employees to be fully charged as the operation began.

Although Pohl might have instead framed the Swiss market as a princess—emphasizing the opportunity for Lidl in a new country—a scandal at Lidl Germany in 2008 had become public, and there was a risk that the bad public relations could affect Lidl Switzerland. The Swiss management team, sensing this risk, wanted to do what it could to deal with any perceived threat to the new stores' success. For example, staff might have to respond to negative questions or comments from customers, their friends, or the public. It would be far better, the managers decided, if Lidl's new Swiss staff were prepared to handle these issues *before* the store openings. As Silja Drack, head of human resources for Lidl Switzerland, explained, "We needed to take proactive measures to protect our new employees and calm their fears."

In the same vein, Pohl organized a management workshop with the top Swiss team to identify all concerns with which the future sales team might be confronted. Three main issues emerged during the workshop:

- **"Germans again!"** Another German discounter chain had already entered the Swiss market in 2005, posing an enormous threat to local Swiss grocery chains. Lidl represented yet another German corporation that would threaten the viability of regional Swiss brands and products.

- **Perception of bad working conditions:** Again, after the market entry the other German discounter chain had been heavily criticized for its bad working conditions, i.e. offering Swiss locals primarily part-time work, to save costs. Locals feared that working conditions would be similar at Lidl Switzerland, which raised insecurity among prospective employees.

- **Public scandal:** In 2008, Lidl suffered from bad publicity in Germany when management was accused of spying on employees with hidden surveillance cameras. This scandal resulted in a general climate of insecurity among employees and a public perception that Lidl exploited labor. Therefore, even before Lidl had entered Switzerland, the company had to contend with these perceptions.

Once these issues were on the table, the team was able to develop measures to counteract them. During the weeks before Lidl's Swiss stores opened, for example, new local employees received an intensive training both to prepare them for the opening and to address their concerns about the three potential threats that the management team had uncovered. To begin with, Swiss employment contracts and social security packages were refined to ensure that part-time employees would receive social security on par with full-time workers. Then, to avoid accusations by employees, no cameras were placed in the inner zones of any store (even though this is common practice in most retail stores to prevent stealing). Finally, to ensure that all store policies would conform to local regulations and expectations without posing an undue threat to regional markets, all policy details were approved by local Swiss authorities. Additionally, the management team started negotiations with Swiss labor unions to ensure backup in case any accusations surfaced.

As a second step, in February 2009 (one month before the opening of the Swiss stores), Lidl started a media campaign featuring established employees who voluntarily agreed to demonstrate their commitment and pride to be part of the new team of Lidl Switzerland. Photos of these employees appeared in posters and brochures, along with their personal statements addressed both to prospective customers and to future employees. For example, a married employee couple said, "We enjoy Lidl's work climate and its benefits!" And a Swiss Lidl manager addressed customers directly: "My time is at your disposal!" In the summer of 2009, Lidl kicked off another media campaign—this time it was based on the aforementioned topics of possible concern, such as spying on employees, working conditions, why part-time work is used at Lidl Switzerland, and the fear of another German discounter chain. The main objective? To convey to new and future employees the impression that working conditions would be sound and that management would stand behind every worker should he or she be accused or otherwise attacked by local consumers or competitor grocers.

Both campaigns proved to be an overwhelming success, raising confidence, pride, and cohesion among all employees. Through the advertisements, Lidl Switzerland also became more familiar to locals, making it easier for consumers to connect with the discounter. As a result, all employees of Lidl Switzerland could fully focus on the stores' grand opening—a crucial time for market entry success—and could continue to work hard during the extended period of Lidl's entrance into the Swiss market.

In the end, the effort of the management team to proactively strengthen the employees' confidence—by helping them to slay the dragon of bad publicity—made all the difference. Twenty-nine stores were opened, which exceeded Lidl's initial plan by three, and thirty more openings were scheduled for 2010. The stores performed better than planned in 2009, with financial goals met and exceeded. Because the company identified the threat early on and worked with all of its employees to solve the problem, those employees were highly energized to take on the challenge.

To be clear, we are not advocating the invention or escalation of a threat to serve the end goal of boosting organizational energy. Some business thinkers recommend jolting overly self-satisfied organizations with a quasi-crisis.[3] This strategy can be highly effective if applied openly. However, creating imaginary dragons to slay can damage management's integrity and be an unreliable tactic if used in a manipulative way. If people are not aware of the fact that the threat is imaginary, such a quasi-crisis might mobilize the organizational energy the first time it happens, but it won't lead to long-term productive energy. Rather, disillusionment sets in once employees realize that the crisis has been artificially produced—and passion, alertness, and effort quickly decline. What's more, when a real crisis does eventually emerge, gaining enough of people's trust to act on it becomes nearly impossible.

That is why we reject the idea of inventing potential dragons or even disproportionately dramatizing existing ones. The threat itself as well as the interpretation of the threat should always be authentic. But this is all the more reason that you must therefore be vigilant in identifying and prioritizing threats even when there is no acute crisis situation.

In our research and practice, we've seen again and again how companies respond positively to authentic threats in the way that Lidl responded. But even if the threat is a real one, a positive response by the team is not a guaranteed or default reaction. You've probably seen it before: at many companies, external threats are stress triggers that can become contagious.[4] In some environments, employees can develop a kind of collective stress that may actually lead to increased resigned inertia, which manifests as heightened levels of uncertainty, reduced engagement, burnout, or even paralysis in the organization. Because of this, we do not recommend using the slay-the-dragon strategy for a company with already high levels of resigned inertia. Instead, those companies should turn to the winning-the-princess strategy.

No matter how you slay the dragon—be it to jump-start your organization out of inertia or for crisis management—the key to the success of this strategy is your leadership and the way you involve your team. Unleashing productive energy requires more than just uncovering existing or possible threats and articulating them. Rather, you must then also involve people across the company in solving the problem or preventing the threat. You must foster a shared belief that you and they will master the challenge together, and you must make the challenge a key aspect of peoples' work. This approach raises emotional engagement and mental alertness and makes people go beyond their own perceived limits. It's what eliminates the status quo and shakes up mind-sets, procedures, beliefs, and behavior. Implementing the strategy of slaying the dragon, therefore, involves three tasks, each with several steps (figure 2-1). The box "Summary of Tasks for Slaying the Dragon" outlines these tasks.

FIGURE 2-1

The slaying-the-dragon strategy

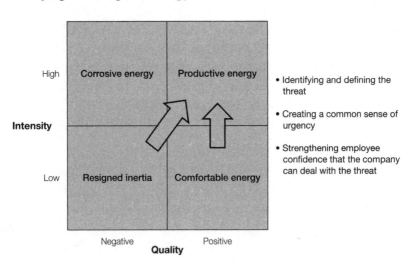

- Identifying and defining the threat

- Creating a common sense of urgency

- Strengthening employee confidence that the company can deal with the threat

Summary of Tasks for Slaying the Dragon

Identifying, Interpreting, and Defining a Threat to the Company

1. Take your time to identify potential dangers and to fully understand them.

2. Dig deep to understand the threat and its roots, and interpret these.

3. Paint a vivid picture of the dragon.

4. Get the management team and other staff involved in interpreting and defining the threat.

Mobilizing Communication to Create Awareness of a Common Problem

1. Make the danger realistic and relevant.

2. Appeal to employees' emotions.

Strengthening Collective Confidence That the Company Can Deal with the Threat

1. Present the threat as a challenge.

2. Provide challenging practice, creating role models based on past successes.

3. Offer emotional encouragement.

Identifying, Interpreting, and Defining a Threat

For leaders who need to jump-start their companies by slaying the dragon, the first major task is to identify and thoroughly understand outside threats. This a core challenge for you as a member of management because it is here where you either catch the gravity and the logic of the imminent threat—or not. So you must engage fully with the following tasks to ensure that the threat to your organization becomes the vehicle that boosts your organization's energy.

Identifying the Dragon in Good Times: Lufthansa's D-Check Program

Lidl had a clear dragon to fight as it entered the Swiss market. But what can you do as a leader in relatively good times to provide a needed jump start to an organization that isn't facing an obvious threat? Ask your managers to design realistic worst-case-scenarios for their departments and to develop potential solutions and backup plans. Lufthansa did just that with its D-Check program, which, as you may recall from chapter 1, the airline expanded in the wake of 9/11.[5]

D-Check was initiated in early 2001. Derived from an industry term referring to the comprehensive technical overhaul of a plane, Lufthansa's D-Check was a strategic change program to completely take apart, examine, and upgrade the organization's functional capability. But when CEO Juergen Weber decided to launch D-Check, Lufthansa had just experienced its best year yet (in 2000), with record pretax profits of around $1.7 billion. Why did Weber see a need to launch D-Check? His management team had noticed the faint signals of the impending airline industry crisis. It was a threat that, if handled well, could jump-start the company to the head of the pack.

The first task for Weber and his business-unit heads was to meticulously define the threat. They invested significant time researching and understanding all the possible issues that could arise. Then, in a workshop, Weber involved his top managers in discussing and estimating the risks posed to the company's survival. Specifically, he asked all the business unit heads to estimate, in a worst-case scenario, the greatest realistic risk within the next three years for their business units (e.g., price fluctuations, sudden drops in load capacity, and infrastructure bottlenecks). By considering all these risks together, across the business units, the managers then developed a worst-case scenario and determined that Lufthansa would have to generate a combined €1 billion (around $1.4 billion) additional cash flow over a projected period of three years to prepare the airline for future risks. D-Check thus mobilized a great deal of energy—a total of 1,320 D-Check cost-saving projects in all—in order to meet, and eventually far exceed, its financial goal.

Take time to identify potential dangers. It isn't always obvious which dangers are truly relevant; threats in the market often emit weak signals and can therefore be easily overlooked. That is why you as a leader must begin by thoroughly analyzing and interpreting the organization's situation and searching for signs of possible trouble. Since danger signals can be so subtle, rarely can you interpret their implications right from the start. As a rule, the picture is diffuse and complex, requiring time and attention to paint a clear and focused image of the most relevant possible threat and what it means for the company.

Often the threat is an encroaching competitor. The simplicity of this approach is appealing; it's easy to see how you can effectively activate the spirit of competition by concentrating on another corporation. But you should also consider other approaches to mobilizing energy, for example presenting employees with a threat such as international competition, impending bankruptcy, or a disruptive technology that could make the company's products or services obsolete.

Identifying an underlying danger or other challenges to the organization is especially demanding for companies that are doing very well in the market or are otherwise exceptionally successful. But those dangers are always there: you may be facing a growing competitor, or you might be number two in the market and want to attack number one—or, like Lidl, you might be facing the challenges that come along with new growth opportunities. Don't allow yourself or your team to become so self-satisfied as to ignore these potential threats. The box "Identifying the Dragon in Good Times: Lufthansa's D-Check Program" offers a good example of how a company avoided the pitfall of too much complacency.

Unfortunately, planning a strategy to meet an impending threat is the exception rather than the rule in most organizations. Many leaders and managers tend to downplay or ignore potential problems altogether, even when they notice subtle signs of trouble. Donald B. Bibeault calls this syndrome *defensive avoidance*: instead of identifying a potential threat accurately, managers actively reinterpret it in a reassuring way, making themselves believe that their current strategy is correct and that the threat doesn't exist.[6] In fact, Lufthansa itself almost went down that path of defensive avoidance. Until CEO Juergen Weber took the helm in time to recognize the crisis and begin a turnaround 1991, Lufthansa's management had been explaining and excusing its performance to itself (and employees and stockholders) as simply part of "normal airline-market fluctuation," although during this period the company made several million dollars losses every day.

Why do so many leaders succumb to defensive avoidance or otherwise fail to react to danger signals? Weak signals appear initially as a low priority, and interpreting them is challenging and time-consuming: the signals usually get lost among day-to-day business demands. Especially in times of crisis, then, systematically identifying, analyzing, and interpreting threats is indispensible. As Weber told us, "The bigger the time pressure, the more discipline is needed to analyze carefully and to plan accurately." You must pick up on weak signals for potential threats or other challenges and then give those signals the highest priority—even when the threat isn't yet urgent.

Dig deep to understand the threat and its roots, and interpret it. Managers often pay inadequate attention to analyzing potential threats or consistently interpreting developments in the market and environment to design possible scenarios for their company. Why? There are two reasons. Companies often lack sufficient systems to systematically identify weak signals, much less to thoroughly and regularly analyze the signals' effects on specific processes. Or leaders feel time pressure, which then results in superficial or inadequate analysis, which overlooks the root causes of the danger. In either case, the company leaders usually end up attacking only the symptoms rather than the real reasons for the threat, thereby wasting precious time.

To overcome the first problem—a lack of identification systems—you should focus on anticipating threats and interpreting their effects by regular market analysis. Involve your employees in identifying the weak signals, or seek out external experts, who don't have the typical company blinders in strategy discussions. Obtaining others' opinions and knowledge early on allows for a considerably more proactive coping, and you can mobilize productive energy much earlier and for a much wider array of possible challenges. To deal with the second problem—the pressure of an urgent threat—you must dig all the more deeply into what is going on in the company. Your analysis must be detailed and readily actionable if the organization has any hope of attacking the threat before it becomes unmanageable.

The challenge is to avoid superficiality and instead to dig deep, thoroughly analyzing and understanding the dimensions of the problem and its root causes. Primarily, you should ensure careful reflection by creating certain processes or platforms whereby strategic issues, possible threats, or relevant trends are discussed. It is crucial that you reserve enough time, create an atmosphere where participants can distance themselves from daily business, and ensure an open, thoughtful discussion.

That is what we saw at Lufthansa with the D-Check program. Weber made it a point to research his industry carefully and to include his managers in the process *before* the industry's downturn. By doing so, he identified the threat early and was able to attack it.

But even impending threats that are not external or industry-wide need to be researched carefully. In 1995, Pius Baschera, CEO of Hilti from 1994 to 2006, noticed that something had changed in the way the company was going after its strategic goals. The company, a construction and building-maintenance market leader based in Liechtenstein, was unable to achieve its goal of double-digit growth in sales; nor did it attain expected increases in profitability and productivity.

With its 6.6 percent growth rate, Hilti was objectively still quite successful. Management, however, had the impression that although Hilti got the machinery to go faster, the company had to spend more and more energy just to get the same results as before. As nebulous as the threat was, Baschera took it seriously, undertaking intense dialogue and far-reaching searches within the company to find the answer. He gave the research top priority, later calling it "difficult and enormously important." In 1996, each of the four executive board members alone had invested approximately fifty full days into the problem. Led by top management together with market region heads from Europe, Asia, and the United States, the company conducted thousands of customer interviews and researched industry trends, going as far as holding an international conference on the topic.

As a result of this intensive process, Hilti confirmed that while the strategy the company had been pursuing for about a decade was essentially the one, misaligned incentives had encouraged the sales force to sell combinations of products that made little sense, driving down first sales margins and then innovation levels. By identifying the roots of the problem and then interpreting it, Baschera and his management team were able to reinforce the strengths of the existing strategy and course-correct by diverging away from sales growth to sustainable profitable growth.

With these measures in place, the company's operating profit rose from $127 million in 1996 to $258 million in 2000.

Paint a vivid picture of the dragon. The slaying-the-dragon strategy works only when leaders draw the attention of the organization and channel the energy toward one particular challenge. You as a leader, therefore, need to do two things. First, you must focus on the one decisive threat or challenge—the dragon—and articulate this as a clear, imminent threat. It is not enough to simply identify all possible threats; you must also narrow them down, ideally to define the one challenge. And then, second, you have to paint a vivid picture of this most relevant, troubling, and dangerous threat.

Too often, leaders don't do the latter. In our research, we've seen again and again how executives, in trying to vividly portray the threat, instead develop and communicate a picture that is too complex, overly analytical, and too detailed. The big picture of the actual problem and the key challenge gets lost. Abstract presentations of problems are hard for employees to connect with emotionally.

To release energy means to seize your people on an emotional level, in a way that gets their adrenaline going and ready to attack the dragon. You need to help employees grasp the predicament emotionally, while inspiring them to think creatively about how to deal with the problem. Head-centered, overly abstract, complex, or purely numbers-driven information about possible threats works against this kind of passionate engagement. That's why you need to summon the courage to focus on the crucial challenge that is relevant in the future.

Why is this so hard for executives to do? Fearing that smaller but important challenges will be overlooked, executives often present a comprehensive list of dragons to employees instead of helping them to focus on just one. Although we understand this impulse, we have seen that when priorities aren't set, leaders risk diffusing their own focus and that of their people.

As a leader, therefore, you need to set a focus and ideally create a vivid illustration of the crucial challenge. If a visual picture of the dragon can be created successfully, the direction can be shown clearly and employees will be able to identify the numerous smaller problem components that have to be considered and addressed.

One way you can present a dragon very concretely, and in a way that triggers strong emotions with employees, is to identify a key competitor as the major threat—and make it the dragon that employees picture in their minds. Ryoichi Kawai, then-CEO of Komatsu, the Japanese earth-moving equipment company, faced the challenge of Caterpillar's entry into its until-then protected home market by popularizing the slogan *Maru-C* (encircle Caterpillar) among all employees. Kawai leveraged this competition with Caterpillar into a highly disciplined and effective process of building up Komatsu's strengths and market positions. The single slogan reveals the company's focus on its primary threat.

Get the entire management team involved. Although containing and interpreting threats is primarily a leadership task, top executives nevertheless should find ways to involve middle management and other staff members. By deliberately gathering information, perceptions, and interpretations from various organizational levels and other sources, you can get a more complete picture of the company and any underlying threats.

In the course of our research, we often hear very different statements from various managers regarding the same change initiatives. This lack of both clarity and mutual agreement is critical because management's behavior, interpretations, and attitudes substantially affect how the organization's energy gets channeled. Executives remain the starting point for how the company's situation is interpreted down the line; the more uncertain the situation, the more employees look toward upper management for guidance. That is why top management has to invest in developing a clear, unmistakable picture concerning the interpretation of the situation and to involve other managers and employees in this process. This kind of shared involvement is not just a "nice-to-have"; it's key to the strategy's success. First-line employees observe much in the company that you as a leader cannot—particularly the behavior of higher level management itself.

The Schneider Weisse brewery in Bavaria deliberately involves middle management in trend analysis to identify and contain potential threats. This sixth-generation brewery, currently headed by Georg Schneider VI, operates in a dynamic, international market for beer. To capture important changes, each manager receives a standard form in which he or she can fill in relevant trends in different segments (e.g., market, society, competitors, legislation). During the annual strategy workshop, the information from those forms is evaluated, prioritized, and interpreted. The result? A razor-sharp image of the organizational landscape—as well as a shared understanding among the managers who created it. For example, one such trend analysis revealed that mixed drinks such as beer flavored with grapefruit or soft drinks were entering the beer market—a trend that affected Schneider's business. In response, the company deliberately decided to stick to its tradition of making and selling pure Weisse. Another development that was identified through Schneider's trend monitor was the deterioration of the beer market's image. Because of recent adolescent behavioral patterns such as flat-rate drinking (wherein participants pay one price at an event to drink as much as they want), binge drinking, and other forms of alcohol misuse, beer's image was seriously damaged. After the managers' collective analysis during a strategy workshop, Schneider Weisse decided to invest in developing a "beer culture" in Germany— comparable to the existing wine culture—which would help position the traditional beer as a delicacy more than a particular type of alcohol. The entire sales force, Schneider decided, would be trained as beer sommeliers. This step was so innovative and far-reaching that he would never have made it—and managers would never have been able to understand and internalize it—without the trend monitoring, which involved all of them.

Aside from the added advantage that such a broad view provides, proactively involving managers is itself the best way to stave off negative energy. When you don't make the time and effort to involve your managers and staff members, you risk alienating people throughout the company, or at the very least, your employees will feel a certain detachment from even the organization's most threatening situation. When top management excludes others in the company from its information gathering and analysis, a company's high performers are often the first to abandon ship during a change process.

Mobilizing Communication to Create Awareness of a Common Problem

The second leadership activity you need when slaying the dragon is to communicate the threat or danger in a way that creates a true and deeply felt awareness of the problem plaguing the organization.[7] Communication is critical for spurring action, assert Ronald A. Heifetz and Donald L. Laurie: "Rather than protecting people from outside threats, leaders should let the pinch of reality stimulate them to adapt."[8] Thus you can involve employees in solving the problem—employees who have a lot of insight and wisdom from their experience on the company front lines.

Too often, leaders don't work to communicate the threat throughout the company. They fail to make it relevant to employees and don't involve them. Why not? Some executives fear being seen as weak if they talk about an organizational threat, even more so if they involve staff members in the problem-solving process rather than tidying up the problem alone. Other managers fear that they would make their staff members anxious— or make people panic and even quit their jobs—if they revealed the unvarnished truth about potential organizational problems.

But even well-intentioned attempts to keep problems away from employees usually have the opposite effect. Employees sense that operations are not running smoothly, that customers are turning away, or that markets are collapsing. Or they learn the truth of the organizational situation from some other source, which makes them lose confidence and trust in the company leadership. Instead, you must make the danger realistic and relevant to your people.

Make the danger realistic and relevant. Managers often underestimate the depths of communication it takes to get employees personally concerned enough about a problem to want to do something about it.[9] Instead, the executives themselves go through a very long process of analyzing, understanding, and interpreting the current situation until they fully penetrate a problem. Only when the dragon is absolutely clear and obvious to them do leaders then communicate the challenge throughout the organization. The problem is that by then, they've lost sight of the long process they themselves went through to come to this conclusion. They have just undergone a truly catalyzing process around the threat to the organization—but then they only communicate the threat briefly, sometimes as a one-off communications to their people. No wonder their employees don't fully grasp the gravity of the danger!

As a rule, then, you should communicate possible threats to your people at an early stage, when you sense the first weak signals that a problem may emerge. That way, the threat becomes tangibly realistic to *everyone*—not just to you and your team—and together, employees can examine the threat and create a plan of action.

The simplicity of Komatsu's aforementioned *Maru-C* approach to slaying the dragon is appealing: it's easy to see how leaders can effectively activate an awareness of a threat. Our experience has shown that the spirit of competition is easily energized by concentrating on a major competitor. It is more difficult, however, to realize and concretize other challenges such as international competition, financial problems, loss of customers, or disruptive technology that could make the company's products or services obsolete. Especially in corporations without an obvious crisis or ones that are experiencing a boom, the biggest challenge is to find a dragon that is plausible, not too theoretical or abstract, and close enough to contribute to quickly mobilize employees.

The SKF Group, a global leading supplier of products, solutions, and services in ball bearings, seals, mechatronics, and lubrication systems, and headquartered in Goteborg, Sweden, successfully engaged with intense communication to make a potential dragon significant. Between 2004 and 2005, amid a long track record of success, SKF organized a leadership development workshop called Step Up for its 170 top executives. The workshops were designed to foster the company's continued success by strengthening and energizing leadership throughout the company. Tom Johnstone, SKF's CEO, visited each of the fifteen workshop sessions personally and discussed strategic issues as well as major challenges with the groups. To sensitize the executives to potential problems that SKF could soon face, Johnstone showed a graph comparing international salaries. Average salaries in Sweden and Germany, it showed, were about thirty times higher than in China. He told his executives, "We want to stay in the European market. We want to keep our headquarters in Goteborg, and we want to produce globally, even in Sweden and Germany. Why shouldn't I hire thirty Chinese people instead of one of you?" This concrete illustration of a possible threat proved to be the starting point for numerous productive discussions about the company's finances and strategy.

Appeal to employees' emotions. You should communicate the threat or a dragon through personal appeals to people's emotions. Emotions are a particularly effective lever for you to use, and negative emotions don't always cause damaging stress: under certain circumstances, these emotions can cause *eustress*—a positive form of stress that produces extraordinary effort and persistence that would not have been activated without the negative impulses.[10]

Heinrich Huber, the head of a medium-sized German technology company, used the element of surprise to create emotional concern for an impending threat to his people. When his company had been in its start-up phase, it was vital and alive and his people were continually engaged in their work. But now that the company had successfully managed its start-up, Huber's once-strong people were starting to show signs of complacency. Huber struggled with how to inject a renewed awareness and urgency into his managers. His initial attempts to inject these qualities failed, given that the start-up's financial figures appeared solid enough.

Then, on a trip to China, Huber found a way. He purchased a boxful of Chinese products that his company manufactured as well. At the next management meeting, he poured the contents of the box onto the table. "All of that costs twenty-five dollars," he told his managers. "You all know what it costs when we produce it." Everybody knew that it cost nearly $2,000. "What does that mean for us?" Huber asked. "How can we feel proud about our start-up success when our costs have become so high?" Huber's directness shocked the managers in the room awake—and they subsequently insisted on taking action before the threat became urgent.

Other companies create emotional concern through vivid customer feedback. Busch-Jaeger's CEO, Hans-Georg Krabbe, used the element of surprise to create concern around an impending threat to this ABB subsidiary that employs about one thousand people in Lüdenscheid and Aue,

Germany. Krabbe had noticed that after decades as the technological leader in the field of electrical installation technology, the company was developing an increasing number of technologically sophisticated products that were too complicated from the customer's point of view. In 2002, Krabbe received a customer complaint letter together with a broken control switch for window blinds. The client had smashed the control panel in anger because it was too complicated to use. At the next company meeting, Krabbe put the destroyed product on the desk and said, "Our customer smashed our product in rage." Again, as a reaction to the tangible object in front of them, employees and managers alike expressed strong concern about the threat and began to brainstorm about how to simplify their designs for customers.

Following through is also important. Krabbe kept the smashed control panel on his desk, mentioned it in every meeting, and confronted the employees continuously with the problem. The concern in the company was so big that people felt strongly motivated to develop a product that would be much simpler to operate. Nine months later, the new control panel was finished, and the employees introduced it to the marketplace with pride.

To achieve a true shake-up, then, you must appeal to people's emotions while communicating a rational argument. Your people need to feel not only the emotional shake-up, but also a strong, common concern about the changes that are necessary—thus creating a collective readiness for action throughout the company.

Strengthening People's Shared Confidence That the Company Can Deal with the Threat

Finally, to mobilize a company through the slaying-the-dragon strategy, you must as a leader help employees believe that as an organization, all of you can successfully overcome the danger together—that the company's strengths and abilities are up to the challenge.[11] This confidence can make the difference between simply stirring up confusion, fear, and resigned inertia and actually inspiring employees toward positive, productive energy.

You can use four strategies for building a shared confidence in the face of a potential threat. First and most important, you must present the threat as a positive challenge. Thereafter and throughout the process of slaying the dragon, you should provide challenging practice, create role models based on past successes, and offer emotional encouragement.[12]

Present the threat as a challenge. Although we have described the dragon as a potential *threat*, research shows that leaders best motivate their people by instead framing an impending danger as a *challenge*. This does not mean sugar-coating the situation. To the contrary, you must share with employees all the details you have gathered and paint a clear picture of the situation. It means that you must strengthen people's confidence that they can solve the problem—that as a company, all of you can stretch yourselves to meet the challenge together. One way of doing this is to outline specific, tangible actions that the organization can take to overcome the challenge.

In the chaos following 9/11, for example, Lufthansa's leaders reminded its people that they had faced crises before (for example, the financial, political, and industry-wide changes of the 1990s) and had overcome them. Problem-solving strategies included proven reaction mechanisms such as grounding part of the airplane fleet and voluntary salary waivers or immediate reduction of overtime and vacation. Since Lufthansa had relied on these and other coping mechanisms in the past, they did not come as a shock to employees, who well understood their necessity and effectiveness. One senior manager later described this post-9/11 period: "We had developed well-proven instruments, techniques, and competencies for effective crisis management, and we knew it. People at this company, therefore, had a certain self-confidence: if anyone knew how to overcome critical situations, we did." Lufthansa's leadership framed the company's message to employees with this candidness and certainty, and by framing the threat as an opportunity, executives were able to energize their people to face it.

You should not underestimate (and indeed can take advantage of) your employees' ability to develop a very precise, subjective picture of how competently and powerfully your company can or cannot deal with a danger. For example, a company that estimates a danger as exceeding the company's abilities to overcome it, such as a market collapse that company leaders perceive as insurmountable, will find its employees naturally falling into resigned inertia, with attendant feelings of frustration or cynicism. Fortunately, you can change your company's energy fundamentally. Doing so requires you to instill a generally accepted impression that through the company's strengths and abilities, it can and will meet challenge.[13]

Provide challenging practice, creating role models based on past successes. Too often, executives only look forward and point to future goals while neglecting to acknowledge the long and mostly successful road an organization has already traveled. But past success is the best confidence booster. When people experience success, they build their confidence in their own ability to deal with challenges.[14] As we saw in the Lufthansa example, the same applies to teams, business units, and entire companies: success produces an immediate, positive response about the groups' shared ability to perform and overcome problems.

Positive comparisons with the past can take on an almost contagious quality that spreads throughout the ranks, catalyzing people's faith that even difficult goals will be attained and that overwhelming threats can be met.[15] Painting a precise picture of an organizational success story means homing in on the specific activities that were needed to overcome the threat. As a leader, you should highlight effective examples of how employees made a difference, what competencies they possessed, what actions they took to cope with challenges, and which resources they used.

This means that when there isn't a threat present, companies need to seize the opportunity to take on challenging tasks nevertheless. As Bo Risberg, the CEO of the Hilti Group, advises managers, "Take the hard way. Look for experiences with difficult challenges. They will make you strong." But for challenging tasks to lead to increased confidence, managers must ensure that employees attribute the success to themselves and to their shared effort and not to outside factors such as top management, the environment, or other outside influences in the company. Only then can employees build the necessary trust in their own ability to perform for future challenges.

Other sources of potential success stories are performance reviews and conferences. At German software producer CAS, for example, challenging projects are presented regularly at internal manager conferences. "After these conferences," CEO Martin Hubschneider explained, "others, too, want to be on stage, and [everyone] says to themselves, 'What he can do, I can do as well.'" Phoenix Contact, a Germany-based leading developer and manufacturer of industrial electrical and electronic technology, uses a formal, internal application process to collect its people's success stories. The company chooses only the most sophisticated projects. Then the person responsible for the project presents progress and results at an annual conference. The selection process highlights the chosen projects as all the more special, encouraging imitation throughout the company.

All of this is to say that especially in very demanding periods, such as in a slaying-the-dragon phase, you should regularly pause, look back at the organization, and draw your employees' attention to achievements to demonstrate that the organization will have the competence to achieve even more. Looking back in this way boosts employee confidence that future challenges can be surmounted as well.

Outside role models—even competitors—can also inspire and ignite employees' passion for overcoming a threat. Chapter 5 describes how CEO Martin Strobel acted as a role model at Baloise Switzerland to good effect when his company was facing a financial crisis.

Offer emotional encouragement. The final way to strengthen trust in the organization's shared ability to manage challenges successfully is to create a positive emotional climate in the company or individual units.

When ABB was near bankruptcy in 2002, CEO Juergen Dormann supported his staff by circulating "Friday letters," weekly newsletters that strengthened employees' shared identity. While keeping employees informed about the financial situation of the company, the letters also boosted people's confidence in their ability to overcome the challenges. "I would like to reassure you that I am confident we will meet our business targets this year," he wrote in one letter, following it up two weeks later with, "There is great pride in our company, and a great sense of resolve. This strengthens my conviction that we will master and overcome the tough challenges facing us."[16]

As a leader, you can similarly strengthen employee confidence by sharing your perception of the company's ability to master the challenge or by pointing explicitly to company strengths. But you can also pay very specific attention to individual team members who show particularly high self-confidence or to those people affected most directly by the challenge; these people can serve as messengers and catalyzers, who affect others within the company or unit with their confidence and energy. In any case, choose a venue (be it e-mail, video, or company-wide meetings) that allows you to communicate directly with your teams or units, and encourage them to believe in their strengths. That way, you ensure that your very personal message doesn't become diluted or that only parts of it actually reach people on the front lines.

There are other ways you can offer emotional encouragement to your organization when dealing with a threat. Communicate openly with your people, and show direct interest in their ideas.[17]

Phoenix Contact did just that as part of its effort to galvanize energy and foster trust during the worldwide economic crisis beginning in 2008. In 2008, Phoenix, which had earned $1.5 billion that year, faced an alarming forecast. The company had conducted several worldwide surveys of its biggest customers to get an idea about future demand, and the news was not good. Gunther Olesch, executive vice president and member of the board, communicated with Phoenix employees openly, directly, and promptly about the survey results—each survey more dire than the last. Ultimately, declining monthly earnings starting in November 2008 resulted in a 19 percent loss for 2009—the strongest decline in a single year, more, even, than the sum of all percentage losses since World War II.

Even though the decline was tremendous, employees remained confident. "Because of the realistic picture employees received during the crisis, along with a strong culture and high degree of energy before the downturn, the employees stuck together during the bad times," said Klaus Eisert, executive partner. "An existing healthy environment and a high degree of trust cushioned the shock."

From the start, Phoenix assured its employees that no dismissals would occur. Although short-time work (a usually across-the-board reduction in employees' full-time hours to prevent the necessity of layoffs) had been introduced as an adaptation to the weak economic situation and to provide liquidity, no additional budget cuts occurred within human resources. Members of the board of executives also accepted a wage reduction of 8.7 percent (the equivalent of what the employees lost through short-time work) to declare solidarity with the workforce and to send a positive signal. The scenario was that Phoenix needed to save $123 million. Through the engagement and proactive cost reduction activities of the employees Phoenix Contact saved $183 million in 2009.

An important focus besides cost-cutting during the crisis was to foster confidence in the organization by explicitly stimulating innovation. Despite cost-cutting in all other areas, the budget for innovation stayed the same—the management team maintained the same volume of investments in that area, as it had been planned with a 9 percent revenue increase.

Phoenix already held an annual internal best-practice workshop, in which employees presented their ideas in front of the management team and coworkers. In 2009, the company conducted the workshop twice. Giving employees the opportunity to express their ideas in such public ways not only stimulated innovation, but also sent a message of emotional support to employees themselves: that their ideas mattered. As a result, in 2009 the company presented 2,600 innovations at the critically important annual Hannover trade show in Germany, where exhibiting companies show their new products. Even in the midst of the crisis, Phoenix presented more new products at the show than ever before. This was clearly a positive sign to the public, to the company's competitors, and, most important, to the company staff. It demonstrated that Phoenix was seriously committed and confident of getting out of the recession as soon and as strong as possible.

The company's continued success since then has depended on the willingness of its people to work with all their energy and effort, fueled by the pride they took from overcoming this crisis so successfully. And in the first quarter of 2010, incoming orders increased by 33 percent, actual turnover grew by 22 percent, and Phoenix hired 290 new people.

Before You Slay the Dragon . . .

Dragons, like threats, are powerful phenomena and can become quite dangerous if not handled properly. You should therefore be aware of three risks that come with this strategy:[18]

- **Overwhelming the company:** Mobilizing inert companies requires breaking through strongly encrusted layers of status quo. But our work with companies shows that some organizations—those that have experienced exceptionally long phases of inertia or comfort—have often lost the competencies needed to activate their potential. Panic, activism, or paralysis typically sets in. You must therefore find ways to incite the needed shake-up while not overwhelming the company or pushing it into complete paralysis—a delicate balance many executives face.

- **Insufficiently channeling the company's energy:** Even when companies are somehow jump-started into action, sometimes there still isn't enough joint understanding between leaders and employees about how to channel the newfound energy toward common goals, projects, and activities. As a result, activated energy can turn negative, spiraling down into the corrosive energy zone. That's why you have to find a common organizational focus for this kind of energy work. Productive energy emerges not only by activating a company's potential, but also by purposefully channeling the unleashed forces.

- **Overestimating how long and how often a threat can mobilize people:** When managers try to use the slaying-the-dragon strategy for years or repeatedly apply it, it can begin to backfire. The strategy is therefore effective only in the short run or mid-run. When energy mobilizes around a relevant threat or crisis, this energy can quickly diminish when the danger has been averted.[19] Productive energy, then, diminishes rapidly—sometimes back to the previous low level. Companies that are repeatedly slaying the dragon face the same problem; what's more, the threat has to be bigger, more dangerous, or more dramatic every time it's unleashed, and over time, management needs more and more pressure to mobilize additional energy. In the long run, this process can drive a company into a state of burnout. As a leader, you therefore have to beware not to overuse this strategy and not to use it for too long a time.

One way to avoid the above three pitfalls is to alternate a slaying-the-dragon strategy with an effective complementary strategy, one that alternates the dragon's quick discipline and decisiveness with a longer-term look at future opportunities and organizational vision. This complementary approach is the winning-the-princess strategy. We'll explore that strategy in the next section.

Winning the Princess: Using Opportunities to Mobilize Your Company

While the challenge of a dangerous "dragon" can very effectively mobilize organizational energy, leaders will sometimes do better to apply a more positive approach: inciting the organization to pursue a promising opportunity. This strategy works better over the long haul, as positive energy can be built slowly over time. A tantalizing innovation, a new developing market, new kinds of customers, or a new organizational vision or mission all can represent a future opportunity that could release substantial potential within a company. In fact, the more detailed and concrete the vision of the desired future, the better it is for creating fundamental organizational change.[20]

As we've described earlier, this leadership strategy is called *winning the princess*. Like slaying the dragon, this strategy can effectively move companies out of resigned inertia and the complacency trap into productive energy (figure 2-2). The princess and dragon strategies share many other similarities as well and in fact can be viewed as different sides of the same coin. For example, both require courageous leadership, a strong communications strategy, and attention to the emotions of employees. As an executive, therefore, you have to work closely with people in the company to consciously define, communicate, and apply an "object of longing."[21]

But unlike slaying the dragon, winning the princess works particularly well at companies floundering in resigned inertia. When resignation, internal dissociation, and frustration prevails, it usually suggests a discrepancy between what top management says is possible in the company and what is actually happening. In these companies, employees are loath to initiate change, since they had little success—perhaps even failed—in previous change projects. If top management were to introduce an overarching threat strategy here (i.e., slaying the dragon), the

FIGURE 2-2

The winning-the-princess strategy

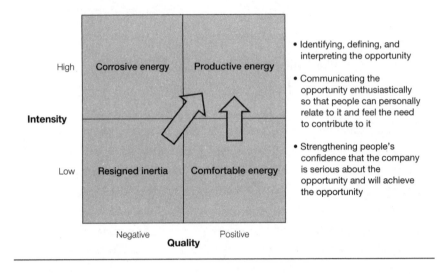

strategy would probably not activate the organization and would probably create more resignation as employees anticipated yet another failure. Winning the princess leverages the positive tension that management creates with a very clear picture of a possible future, one that feels worthwhile for employees to pursue. Activating organizational energy through an attractive opportunity builds positive emotional tension and enthusiasm and encourages employees to intensify their activities. When people feel closely connected to pursuing a dream or a deeply desired goal, they naturally work more effectively and with greater commitment and focus.

A promising opportunity alone, however, is not enough to mobilize a company's energy. As with the dragon strategy, pursuing a princess either can unleash enormous productive energy or can lead a company to cynicism, frustration, or negative stress. Just as with the slaying the dragon strategy, everything depends on execution. For you as a leader, that means finding a way to transfer your vision of a salient opportunity to your managers and employees, nurturing in them the dream, and building their confidence that it can be achieved.

Summary of Tasks for Winning the Princess

Identifying, Interpreting, and Defining an Opportunity

1. Develop a clear and vivid picture of the future, a vision that is unique for your company.

2. Inspire your employees to work toward a collective goal.

Passionately Communicating the Opportunity

1. Create enthusiasm for the vision, making it emotionally appealing for your employees.

2. Develop a clear branding of the vision.

3. Monitor the company's progress in pursuing the vision.

Strengthening Collective Confidence in the Opportunity

1. Participate personally and visibly in the pursuit of the vision or opportunity.

2. Deal consequentially but fairly with employees who do not support the vision.

3. Align reward systems closely with pursuing the vision or opportunity.

You can apply the winning-the-princess strategy by engaging in three crucial tasks that parallel those in the dragon strategy. The box "Summary of Tasks for Winning the Princess" summarizes these three tasks and their substeps.

Identifying, Interpreting, and Defining an Opportunity

Winning the princess begins with identifying which "princess" the company will pursue—and clearly interpreting and defining that opportunity or vision. This is your most important and most difficult task as a member of management, especially since initial ideas tend to be relatively abstract.

Because of the abstract nature of these long-term visions or opportunities, management frequently fails with this strategy: if you cannot clearly identify a vision in the first place and it remains in the realm of vague generalities, how can you hope to communicate it throughout the company? You therefore need to develop a clear and vivid picture of the future—a vision that is unique for the company—and inspire your employees to work toward a collective goal.

Develop a clear, vivid, and unique picture of the future. As a leader, you need to help employees literally see a picture of the desired future or special opportunity that the company, unit, or department hopes to pursue.[22] The vision should be as simple as possible so that it can be explained in few sentences, and it should be intuitively plausible, clear, and convincing.[23] With a simple, but vivid picture of the desired future visions, you and the rest of management can help release positive excitement and increased commitment among people throughout the organization.[24] Such a vision will naturally be concrete and emotionally appealing while not so precise and detailed that it overwhelms employees.

As a general rule, then, any vision or opportunity you develop as an executive should (1) be clearly distinguishable from other company visions, with details that are very specific to the company; (2) include concrete, vivid, positive, and ambitious imagery; (3) go beyond the scope of a simple strategy or business plan and instead offer a big picture, or a comprehensive idea of the future; and (4) be as simple as possible, intuitively plausible, clear, and convincing.

So, for example, making the opportunity or vision *specific* to the company is crucial. You don't want to find yourself in the position of one U.S. consulting firm, which held a seminar for its top managers and asked them to identify, out of five visions presented, the one pursued by their own company. Only 10 percent of the managers named the correct vision, while almost 70 percent identified the vision of their strongest competitor as that of their own company. It turned out that the leadership hadn't taken the time to refine and sharpen the vision to make it company-specific—and instead had leaped directly to trying to communicate a rather nebulous plan.

Similarly, visions need to include concrete, vivid, and ambitious imagery that is primarily *positive*. Another tale of warning here, this from an information technology (IT) division of a French supermarket chain. The division head, a dedicated manager who used every up-to-date management instrument available to lead his team, took six months to develop and enthusiastically explain a new vision to his team. But his staff members did not buy into it; the division head could easily see that there was no real discussion about it in the hallways and no action being taken in meetings, and most importantly, his managers weren't even sharing the vision with their teams. The problem? The vision itself: "We want to be the supporter." Although the message made sense—the IT team did, after all, provide support to other units in the company—ultimately, it was a bit of a yawn. Who wants to be the "supporter"? This was not a vision that would inspire people to dream big. By June 2008, the division head gave up his vision and started the process again.

Inspire your employees to work toward a collective goal. That previous example also highlights the importance of crafting a vision that addresses not only a small fraction of employees, but also people across the organization, emphasizing that the goal is a collective one. (For examples of inspiring visions, see the box "Some Famous Effective Visions.") For example, it is a mistake to use a vision synonymously with strategy or business plans. Those kinds of visions simply describe what market position a company is aiming at or how much the company wants to cut its costs (e.g., "We want to be number one," or "We want to be the leading supplier in our industry"). In contrast, a useful vision should help people picture special opportunities that are relevant and attractive for all company divisions. If the vision covers only the interests of some employees and excludes others, then it will cause resignation or even corrosive behavior rather than mobilizing the organization's energy. A good vision, therefore, emotionally addresses substantial parts of the enterprise and energizes them for cooperation, unleashing the critical mass of the company's potential.[25]

Passionately Communicating the Opportunity

Successfully defining and communicating the opportunity creates a high level of vision awareness in your organization. People know, understand, and feel attached to the organizations' specific vision or opportunity. Our

Some Famous Effective Visions

- **John F. Kennedy:** We will land a man on the moon and return him safely to the earth.

- **AT&T:** Our service is universal—we will provide every house in the United States with standard telephone service.

- **Ford:** Mass-producing automobiles is our business.

- **McDonald's:** We are the world's leading fast-food vendor.

- **Domino's Pizza:** We guarantee your pizza will be delivered within thirty minutes, no matter where you live.

- **Nokia:** We are the world's leading cellular phone provider and a leading service provider of wireless and fixed telephone networks.

- **Nike:** Everyone who has body is an athlete. We help athletes become winners.

- **Tata Motors:** We will produce a $2,500 car (the Rs 1-Lakh) in January 2008.

research shows that organizations where people are highly aware of the vision, compared with those who are not, have 13.5 percent more productive energy and 18.8 percent less corrosive energy.

At the same time, in companies with high vision awareness and subsequently a higher level of productive energy, we found elevated crucial performance indicators. Companies where the vision was more present showed 17 percent higher overall performance, 22 percent higher employee productivity, and 125 percent more growth. Let's look at how you can improve your people's awareness of and attachment to the organization's vision.

Create enthusiasm for the vision, making it emotionally appealing for your employees. Communicating the princess strategy effectively requires that you as a leader, especially if you're the CEO, *sell* your vision.[26] It is not enough to make the vision known; you and your team have to make it emotionally appealing for your people.[27] Think of ways to emotionally involve people in the vision process instead of trying to use purely rational appeals or trying to otherwise persuade them to pursue the vision.

The German automaker Audi did this in a highly energizing and authentic way when, after strong growth between 2000 and 2008, the company faced a decline in sales in 2009. As a result of the global financial crisis, sales fell from $42.8 billion in 2008 to $37.3 billion in 2009, with 950,000 fewer deliveries. That's when Peter Kössler, head of the Audi production plant in Ingolstadt (nicknamed PI), and Sieglinde Wolter, an internal consultant for soft skill and change processes, decided to lead the company through a change process, called Imagine, with the vision "We create enthusiasm for Audi." In practice, this meant blurring the lines between divisions at the plant and instilling a team spirit in which every employee would feel motivated to pursue new opportunities for PI's success.

The first step was to engage the management team. Kössler and Wolter therefore initiated an activity called the Children-Managers' Conference. Before the management conference began, the top 125 managers of PI were asked to write down their personal success story at Audi in the format of a fairy tale—how they overcame challenges on their way to meeting their goals so far, important situations for them or their team, and successes that made them feel proud. They were provided with sample tales and prompts such as "What was your assignment? What did you do then? What problems or challenges came up on the way to success? Did you reach the required goal, and was your success permanent?"

As the conference itself began, all participating managers also received a "vision book" that included the manager's personal success story, PI's visionary concept, and questions for reflection on this vision, such as "Where are we today? How do I want to influence PI and my division according to the vision? What is needed to create enthusiasm at Audi?" The managers were asked to link their own personal story at PI with the vision of the team. After the short presentation of Audi and Imagine's vision, the managers divided into smaller storytelling groups of ten, in which each manager presented his or her own story and listened to the story of the others. The group then selected one success story that fit the best with Audi's vision.

Then, the event took a surprising turn for the managers that day, when 125 "children managers"—local schoolchildren enlisted for the purpose—entered the factory building. "We thought that if we could get children enthusiastic about our successes, then we would be able to extend this enthusiasm to our employees and customers," said Kössler.

The already-formed manager story-teams were assigned ten children each, and in these new teams of twenty, the groups had to come up with a way that the *children* could present the chosen success stories to the other managers, the other children, and the PI executive management board, the last of which acted as jury of the conference. The children each received a shirt and a tie (to make them look like professional mini-managers), and they were given two hours to prepare for the presentations with the help of their manager teammates. The result? An array of imaginative short theater plays, role playing, and stand-up comedy routines that presented each hero's story. As each group waited in the hallway at the Audi plant before making its presentation, the area soon transformed into a loud and animated stage energized by the students' and managers' joint creative powers. Their enthusiasm was infecting everyone in both the hallway and the meeting room.

One participating manager, Christian Fritsche, described the event: "I use lots of technical terms in my daily business, and here this was about communicating on a kid's level. It was a great experience." Using the motto "PI is creating enthusiasm for Audi," the children-managers performed their team hero's story. Right after the performances, the managers and children had one hour for feedback, self-reflection, and a discussion about PI's vision together with their line managers, before the Children-Managers' Conference ended. The event was deemed a success by all participants, including the children, who enjoyed the creative time outside school. The innovative method of presenting the new vision to management made it easier for the managers to think and actively work on the concept—and then to pass on the vision to employees and "infect" the whole production plant in Ingolstadt.

But communicating an opportunity for the organization isn't solely a matter of creating enthusiasm; as a leader, you must also help your people interpret and understand the vision concisely and clearly. Otherwise, employees are left to speculate about what it means for them and their work.

The executives at Tata Steel provide a good example of how you can help individuals in your organization relate personally to the vision and how you can adjust individual tasks so that employees can contribute to it (see "Tata Steel: Implementing a Vision by Creating the Desire for Action Among Employees").

Tata Steel: Implementing a Vision by Creating the Desire for Action Among Employees

Tata Steel focused on its employees in three ways during a restatement of the company's vision. First, it engaged its employees in the creation of the vision. Then, it launched a comprehensive communications campaign. Finally, the company followed up with a full-blown initiative to increase employees' commitment to the vision.[28]

As a first step, Tata Steel's forty top executives developed basic ideas on the vision during a two-day discussion round. But CEO B. Muthuraman encouraged the whole workforce of Tata Steel to participate in the vision's creation. Via the corporate intranet, employees could comment on the first ideas for the vision, express their opinion, or give their own ideas; more than eight thousand workers used the opportunity to express their opinion. After collecting all ideas regarding the vision, an internal working group, together with external specialists, defined two main goals out of the many ideas the employees had.

Once the vision was defined, the next step was to realize the vision and communicate it broadly throughout the company. The Vision 2007 project was launched in May 2002, and various communication channels from posters to mouse pads were used to spread the vision among Tata Steel's employees. Furthermore, the vision was a key topic of regular large-group meetings like the Senior Dialogue, which involved five hundred senior executives. Muthuraman also used the company paper and electronic newsletters to internalize the visionary concept even more.

A further initiative was launched to increase employees' commitment to the vision and their desire to act upon it. Called ASPIRE (ASPirational Initiatives to Retain Excellence), its motto was "Vision without action is just a dream . . . Vision along with action can change the world." Muthuraman described the reason behind the launch of ASPIRE. The goal was now to follow up on the simple explanation of

(continued)

the vision in 2002 by involving each team and everybody else in a disciplined and passionate enactment of Vision 2007.

For that purpose, the motto *Lakshya 2007: Ek Chunauti* (Vision 2007: One Challenge) was created. Over 1,500 workshops in small groups of twenty to twenty-five people were held to help the employees identify their individual and team goals with Vision 2007. An ASPIRE diary was issued to every participant to help break the whole vision down into each employee's individual tasks. The employees were asked to write down what they were doing during their working day. This way, people started to connect the vision to their daily work, associating what was new in the company with their own activities. Because the diary was in written form, it furthermore presented a concrete and compulsory personal commitment to Vision 2007.

Develop a clear branding of the vision. A second key principle for communicating the winning-the-princess strategy is effective branding. That is, you need to develop a simple, easily recognizable, and thematically appropriate wording of the central opportunity.

When Ratan Tata, head of the Tata Group and CEO of Tata Motors, first announced his plan to produce a very small, very inexpensive car—the Tata Nano—he explained his vision: "I observed families riding on two-wheelers—the father driving the scooter, his young kid standing in front of him, his wife seated behind him holding a little baby. It led me to wonder whether one could conceive of a safe, affordable, all-weather form of transport for such a family. We are happy to present the People's Car to India and we hope it brings the joy, pride and utility of owning a car to many families who need personal mobility."[29] There was a big gap between the cost of the average two-wheeler [motorcycle] and entry-level cars such as the Maruti 800, which retails for about $5,000, and Tata planned to fill it.[30] However, Ratan Tata's dream only became tangible when it was branded. By calling it the "one-lakh car" (one lakh equals about $2,250), the company made the idea of the car immediately obvious: it would be a people's car. It would be affordable for everybody.

After crafting the right language, you must beware not to overuse it. Too often, clever catchphrases and logos become mundane—and forgettable—when organizations include them on every official communication or in every speech and management talk. Branding works best when used sparingly and in a concentrated way, thematically supporting the organization's core objective.

Monitor the company's progress in pursuing the vision. Once you have communicated the vision or opportunity as effectively as possible, you need to ensure that people stay focused on it. Vision processes are usually long marches that often entail long-term strain for companies and their employees.[31] Change fails when people become uncertain about how close they are to their goal or even if they're moving in the right direction—and they soon lose their energy around a process.[32] That is why you should carefully monitor how the company is progressing toward its goals and communicate first successes as early as possible—taking care not to give the all-clear signal too early and thereby diminish energy around the change.

For example, TeamBank, a Germany-based bank with about 1,200 employees, monitors its vision "to be number one in its market segment through 2012" in the form of an acrylic model of a city named Easy Town.[33] The model sits in the bank's headquarters, so that anyone walking through the atrium can easily see the plastic city. Every element of Easy Town is a symbol of a future building block of TeamBank: trains to Europe are a symbol of new markets; the "credit factory," out of which small rolls of paper emerge, symbolizes standardized and slim transactions; streets are called "alleys of growth"; and in one part of the model, a tiny, smiling woman walks along a red carpet with a "best employer" award in her hands. When milestones on the way to achieve the vision are completed, the acrylic model is filled with building blocks in these sections, and they are lit up. Everyone at headquarters can easily follow the company's current progress by walking through the atrium, and other employees can see the model through photographs on the company intranet—which also appear in headquarters meeting rooms.

Strengthening People's Confidence in the Opportunity

To successfully pursue a princess, you need to help your people believe they can attain the opportunity—so that the group is collectively confident that it can, over time, bridge the gap between where it is now as a company and the challenging vision in the distance. Clearly, if you as an organization's leader cannot make your people believe that the princess can actually be won, you lose your credibility, and the change program or vision cannot succeed (see "Losing the Princess in France" for an example). Let's first walk through the three elements of this step, and then look more closely at an example of all three in action.

Losing the Princess in France

Mobility Technologics (MT), a large French international technology company, had for decades successfully worked in a decentralized structure with many divisions. Management had made big investments in this structure, with accountability and reward systems that encouraged entrepreneurial responsibility for profit and growth in every division. But with the increasingly globalized marketplace and growing customer demand, paired with increased competition from low-cost Asian vendors, MT's old, decentralized business model was beginning to look obsolete. "Full service from a single source" became the vision for the future, one that CEO Philipp Malkowich developed and introduced enthusiastically through a series of workshops with three hundred top managers across the divisions.

Although this new direction made sense for most of the participating managers, and even though Malkowich had created some enthusiasm for MT's new direction, many employees remained skeptical. It quickly became apparent that top management was not following up with the decisions to support the vision and simultaneously foster the existing business. Managers did not change the reward systems or incentives to promote cross-divisional cooperation. The division heads, already lacking enough staff to fill existing orders, were not given the human resources for their chronically understaffed divisions to make way for new, integrated projects. The same heads also had a long history of acting alone and independently; moreover, the order books were filled, with capacities fully booked three years out. How would the company fulfill these orders through a new, centralized system? Once the division heads realized the hesitation in top management to tackle the issues around the vision, they became rather detached from the idea. In the face of these realities and people's inability to truly imagine how the company could accomplish the CEO's new vision, it ultimately failed.

Participate personally and visibly in the pursuit of the vision or opportunity. As we will discuss more fully in chapter 6, leaders' own actions and behavior in pursuit of the vision lie at the heart of mobilizing the company's energy around it. As we saw in "Losing the Princess in France," once the managers at Mobility Technologics realized that the company ultimately wasn't willing to support the proclaimed vision with the additional resources needed to fulfill it, the vision failed. In general, people in organizations intensely observe the behavior of top management and use it as an indicator of how committed the company is to the vision or new opportunity.[34]

As a member of top management, you therefore need to take a few high-impact steps to support your cause, such as investing in highly visible, successful projects that pave the way for the vision or opportunity to become feasible. In fact, you can use a variety of symbolic activities to boost people's confidence in the vision. For example, you should visibly shift resources away from other activities in the organization to the new projects that work toward the vision. Additionally, you could emphasize the vision in the organizational structure with your own business unit early on for a new technology or product if that is the way into the future. Also, every major communication should refer to the vision and underline its importance to the organization. Making the reallocation strongly visible sends a powerful message across the organization, making clear that management is serious about pursuing the new opportunity.

Deal with employees who do not support the vision. You need to be willing to separate yourself from (and dismiss, if necessary) senior people in the company who don't support the vision. Certainly, you should first make an honest attempt to win naysayers to the vision, but a vision cannot succeed if some members of the management team are working against it.[35] If you hesitate to act forcefully against people who adhere strongly to old strategies and visions, employees will lose confidence in any new opportunities the company is trying to pursue.

Align reward systems closely with pursuing the vision or opportunity. To help strengthen employee confidence in a new pursuit, you can tie the reward system to the opportunity or vision. Money itself is a powerful symbol as well as a tangible incentive in and of itself.[36] By offering monetary rewards and bonuses, for example, you can visibly reinforce behavior that supports the vision. Ultimately, any vision whose pursuit isn't well rewarded will lose meaning over time—as we saw in the example of France's Mobility Technologics.

Leaders in many companies have set up bonuses that have nothing to do with the vision the company is trying to pursue. This sends exactly the opposite message and discourages people. Again, if employees hear that the vision matters on the one hand, but they observe that other behaviors are rewarded on the other hand, management loses all credibility around the vision.

Let's look at how CEO Hubertus von Gruenberg implemented all three of these elements to bolster employee confidence—and his organization's energy—while implementing a new vision at Continental AG, the German manufacturer of automotive systems and tires. At the time, market share within the tire market was firmly distributed among the various providers. The product was highly developed and therefore unsuitable as the basis for innovation or a leap in technology. The automobile industry, meanwhile, had greatly reduced the number of suppliers needed, and so Continental AG was in danger of becoming a secondary supplier. Instead of acting on the dragon strategy, von Gruenberg chose to identify a princess and set his company out to win this goal. He proclaimed a strategic reorientation away from supplying individual tires to becoming a global automotive-systems provider to the automobile industry to both reduce Continental's dependence on the tire business and to foster innovation.

But some Continental executives were not convinced; the break away from making tires as a central product and gaining technological competence in the other needed areas would take a number of years. Because of management's reticence, the new strategic orientation, therefore, was only mildly visible in the company.

Through a series of consistent, clear, and symbolic actions, however, von Gruenberg repeatedly underlined his commitment to his vision for the company's new opportunity, for instance, creating a division called Automotive Systems. Established initially as a supplier of preassembled wheel and tire systems, the division was also charged with developing a series of innovative product ideas for the chassis. In two years, the division had increased the sale of tires that were already premounted on rims from 10,000 pieces to 3 million.

Equally important, von Gruenberg used the company's internal newspaper to ensure that these successes became widely known throughout the company. He also highlighted the division's achievements when he made presentations to managers or analysts and in many informal settings.

At the same time, von Gruenberg invested intensively in new product ideas for a car chassis that used the existing and acquired competencies in tire technology. Although these product ideas clearly could not immediately contribute to the company's bottom line, they nevertheless visibly symbolized the company's path to becoming a full systems provider. With the acquisition of Teves, the brake and chassis division of ITT, a few years later, Continental completed the execution of its vision and became the worldwide leading technological authority on antilock brake systems and electronic stability programs that further improved these systems.

Von Gruenberg made one additional move that, although difficult, sent an important message that he was serious about his vision. As Continental AG's chairman of the board, he dismissed an executive committee colleague who did not buy into Continental's new vision and who continuously raised concerns about the new vision and Continental's strategic positioning. For both management and employees, the dismissal was a drastic signal that the status quo at the company was changing. Even if not everyone agreed with the dismissal, from this point forward no one at Continental doubted that implementing the new vision was a top priority that would be pursued on all company levels.

The result? In 2008, the Automotive Systems division contributed $18.8 billion (or 62 percent) to Continental's overall sales of $30.3 billion, and has increased sales and profits for the sixth consecutive year.

Before You Win the Princess . . .

Winning the princess is a powerful strategy, but, like slaying the dragon, it comes with its own set of risks:

- **Overfocusing on the long-term opportunity:** Although the future vision or opportunity should be the key focal point for mobilizing energy, you must also ensure that in the process, you don't neglect the many other activities that are vital to the company's success. This is a delicate balance. You must find the right equilibrium between long-term vision and future-oriented activities on the one hand and the requirements of the current day-to-day business on the other hand.[37] You and your team must therefore create the basic conditions under which your employees can perform their daily business. At the same time, you need to create space for quite the opposite orientation, one that animates people to pursue an opportunity and, if necessary, to initiate extensive changes in their business practices and processes.

- **Increased demands for continuity of leadership:** The winning-the-princess strategy, by its very nature, demands long-term pursuit and, therefore, continuity. Think of it as running a marathon, rather than doing a short sprint to the finish line. Since it is you, the company leader, who generally articulates and shapes the vision or dream of an opportunity, employees usually associate the dream with you; only rarely can you successfully transfer such a vision into the hands of a successor who will continue its implementation unabated. (Some of these exceptions include Continental AG, Volkswagen, and IBM.) Usually, the vision dies or becomes stunted when you (the role model) leave the company. The demands for continuity in management, therefore, are especially high with this strategy, because vision processes are normally characterized by a long-term horizon spanning at least three to five years, depending on complexity, content, and market situation. In companies using the winning-the-princess strategy, employees typically engage emotionally with the process: they let themselves get excited, they trust their leaders, and they are willing to expend their energy and put their hearts and souls into the vision or desired opportunity. If the process then comes to a halt because you, as the key leadership figure, depart, not only will the princess probably remain unknown, but the people left behind will also probably suffer and be scarred emotionally. At the very least, they will be reluctant to follow your successor's vision again. As a leader, you must consider this risk carefully before pursuing a winning-the-princess strategy. It is your sole responsibility to realistically estimate how long you expect to stay with the company as its guiding force.

- **Neglecting the time limitation of an opportunity:** As an energy-mobilizing strategy, winning the princess is unsuitable for maintaining high levels of productive energy over extended periods. If you wish to apply this leadership strategy, therefore, don't overestimate the impact of your vision or assume that pursuing any particular opportunity will mobilize your company's energy endlessly. As Knut Bleicher, an emeritus professor at the University of St. Gallen, says, visions are "dreams with an expiration date"— and that is exactly what they are supposed to be. As a dream for a certain period, a vision is a very suitable and powerful instrument to mobilize energy. After too long, however, the inherent tension in any future opportunity or vision begins to decrease. That is why you should consider setting an "expiration date" for your vision, such as Ratan Tata of Tata Motors did when he dreamed up the new Rs 1-lakh car, revolutionary for its low price tag (one Indian lakh—or 100,000 Rs, or rupees—equals about $2,250). He set a launch date of January 2008, five years after he introduced the vision to his organization. Tata's vision triggered enormous creative tension throughout the company—in part because it was so clearly time-limited: the 1-lakh car, the Tata Nano, was launched by the Tata group in an auto exposition in Delhi on January 10, 2008.

These risks aside, winning the princess is a strategy that builds on your company's sense of pride, strength, and effervescent excitement at a new opportunity. Used wisely, it can propel your company toward long-term growth and productivity.

Orchestrating Your Use of the Dragon and Princess Strategies

As we've discussed, both of the strategies for focusing organizational energy have their limitations. Slaying the dragon relies on mobilizing negative emotions and transforming them into productive energy for short-term problem solving—which risks neglecting long-term development. Winning the princess focuses on unleashing and leveraging energy in pursuit of a joint vision for the future, but can detract needed attention from short-term problems such as efficiency and productivity.

Ideally, you could combine the immediacy, decisiveness, and discipline of slaying the dragon with the lightheartedness, joy, and pride of winning the princess. In practice, however, it is difficult to combine the two strategies simultaneously, because the focus that is vital to mobilize energy gets lost. Confusion about priorities can plunge your company deeper into resigned inertia or comfortable energy, and you get the worst of each strategy, without the benefits. When we asked Juergen Dormann about his vision for ABB in the midst of his company's crisis, he rightly answered, "I may have a vision for ABB but I will not talk about it now. We have to solve a problem and we need all our energy for this. I will not start irritating people with visions or other longer-term perspectives before we are out of this turnaround."

Fortunately, there are some useful ways to orchestrate your use of the dragon and princess strategies and gain the benefits of each. You can sequence the dragon with a princess or slay small dragons on your way to winning the princess. Let's now look at how you can do this.

Sequencing the Dragon with a Princess

After a dragon strategy has been completed successfully, the renewed energy in the organization can be used to achieve more with it, to go on to pursue new opportunities. But if your organization has followed the dragon strategy for too long, continually focused on stemming possible losses, it is likely to have difficulties switching to the princess strategy. You therefore need to explicitly introduce an end-of-the-dragon period to signal that a new, fundamentally different period has begun. At the same time, the princess period should be approached with different means and should be completely marked off from the dragon phase in how the strategy gets communicated. After ABB completed its turnaround successfully, Dormann explicitly declared the end of the fight for survival of the company in one of his weekly letters. He asked the employees to celebrate, look back with pride, and dedicate a similar degree of engagement to other challenges, such as innovation and sustainable growth, from that point forward. In addition, ABB conducted a survey to get an idea of whether the employees were ready to pursue a vision. With an overwhelming majority of 80 percent, the ABB workforce responded that it was looking to a new challenge and a vision for the future, and the organization began to pursue its princess.

Slaying Small Dragons on Your Way to Winning the Princess

The only effective way to simultaneously combine a slaying-the-dragon strategy with winning the princess is to create a path to the long-term vision that would inevitably include dealing with some short-term threats and problems. This is precisely what von Gruenberg did when he transformed Continental AG from a tire producer into a provider of complete systems to the automotive industry. Even during the quest for this princess, all employees knew that the vision could only be reached if the company's operating problems could be solved. Von Gruenberg battled small dragons such as high costs by developing production in lower-salaried areas of Eastern Europe, close to the automotive industry. By 1998, when von Gruenberg moved on to become head of the company's board of directors, the corporation had achieved an annual net profit of $183.7 million and had managed a fundamental transformation from a tire producer to a global supplier for the automobile industry.

The simultaneous pursuit of both strategies is at its best during a financial crisis, in which companies that have already started down the road of a vision process are forced to ask themselves, "Should we abandon the vision or ignore the crisis?" If you don't inform your employees about how you will handle the crisis, they will greet any statement of a vision cynically. On the other hand, if you abandon the pursuit of a vision in order to deal with the crisis, you will have a hard time building up commitment and confidence later for long-term processes. In fact, you need to hold on to the vision while actively managing the crisis, focusing on it and mobilizing energy to solve it. The only way to achieve this is through a common language and a common message across both the vision and the short-term crisis.

Take, for example, a large industrial corporation that since 2007 has followed a vision called Premium. The vision—to be number one in the market—had been widely communicated within the corporation and pursued until late autumn 2008, when the company faced severe financial problems in the global financial crisis. The story is familiar: although the executive board wanted to continue fostering the focus of Premium, there was a growing restlessness, insecurity, and concern among employees about their leaders' inaction in response to the crisis. The connection they felt between the vision and their experiences, the challenge they used to feel, and their everyday life disappeared.

And so, after intensive talks with managers of various levels and workshops with executives, the consensus was this: start a dragon process while continuing with Premium at the same time. The crisis-management program was called Premium Sprint, and its goals were to achieve the vision explicitly, despite the crisis. Premium Sprint became a complete success. There were no dismissals, and employees were fully engaged in overcoming the crisis. Costs saved and additional cash flow that was generated massively exceeded the targets of the Premium Sprint program. An employee survey showed even stronger commitment to the strategy than before the crisis.

Although both the dragon and the princess strategies can be connected in a meaningful way in some situations, remember that they are primarily strategies to mobilize energy, and energy will likely plummet once the acute danger is over or the opportunity is achieved. Other strategies are better suited to overcoming corrosive energy, avoiding burnout, and sustaining energy over the long term, as we will see in the next three chapters.

CHAPTER 3

Rebuilding Positive Energy

Escaping the Corrosion Trap

In the last chapter, we described two strategies you can use to jump-start your organization if it has become mired in a low-energy zone. But sometimes, you find yourself as a leader confronting even more serious problems. Recall our examples from Lufthansa, BSH, and other companies whose energy became corrosive; clearly, corrosive energy represents the most destructive way of using the company's potential. Yet it can be deceptive, since this trap manifests in an energetic way: an organization with corrosive energy will *appear* highly emotionally involved, creative, and active—but for all the wrong reasons and with a misguided focus, because these forces are invested largely in interpersonal aggression, infighting, and internal rivalries.

You will need to act quickly when faced with short-term, corrosive energy. Fights and other conflicts and the damages they cause rapidly accelerate, destroy trust, and put future collaboration at risk. Because of its dynamic and contagious nature, corrosive energy makes problems grow rather than diminish over time.[1] Leaders who do not intervene forcefully will soon risk a downward spiral of negative energies in the company—and the longer these leaders wait to refocus the organization's energy, the worse the consequences.[2]

Let's begin with an explanation of why leaders fail to notice these elusive negative forces and how you can detect them. Then we'll look at how you can deal with these forces hands-on to avoid the corrosion trap or, if the organization has already fallen into this trap, to eliminate any corrosive processes already eating away at your organization's energy. Finally, we show you how to prevent destructive energy from coming back; the key is systematic investment in the company's organizational identity.

Detecting Corrosive Forces

Your company could be trapped in corrosion without your even realizing it. The organization can appear highly active, fully alert, and emotionally involved—all while the underlying energy gets misdirected and misused. Corrosive energy damages companies and works against company goals while weakening units or maximizing individual personal benefits at the cost of the organization as a whole. For example, we know the CEO of a global American industrial corporation who landed the biggest contract in company history—while competing with another business unit in his own company without its knowledge and severely undercutting that unit's prices. This one brief incident destroyed all attempts to increase cooperation among the three independent businesses and instead quickly created intense internal rivalry.

Or recall the 2001 pilots' strike at Lufthansa recounted in chapter 1. The strike illustrates how ignoring early indicators of mounting tension can lead to short outburst of corrosive energy with immense destructive power. The pilots had felt for quite a while that they were unfairly treated.[3] But the information never really surfaced to a level where executives could identify it and act on it. As we suggested in chapter 1, the resultant, disastrous pilots' strike might have been averted if the essential emotional core of corrosive energy had been addressed up front.

To keep corrosive forces from eating away at the organizational fabric of trust, mutual support, and identity, you need to have a clear picture of the company situation and its corrosive energy. You first must recognize that you're caught in the corrosion trap; then you need to deal with the corrosion head-on; and finally, you must learn to measure negative energy in its earliest stages.

Look for the Trap

Although we have worked with companies whose executives actually caused the corrosive energy in their organizations, executives often simply fail to detect the corrosive forces piling up around them. Executives either *overlook and neglect,* or even *consciously deny,* the negative forces at work.

First, as a leader you might not realize that people feel disconnected from the company or top management. Or you might deliberately distance yourself from the events that affect lower-level employees. Often, leaders also create an atmosphere in the organization that makes people actively filter or polish bad news before it reaches top management. Research by management scholars Elizabeth Wolfe Morrison and Frances J. Milliken shows that many executives live in a dream world that has little to do with reality, a situation that amounts to a kind of organizational silence.[4] Like the fabled courtiers surrounding the emperor, no one wants to be the one to point out the deficiencies in the "new clothes."

Our research confirms empirically this tendency to sugarcoat bad news about the organization's energy state. As described earlier, in most companies, there can be a significant difference between top management and the other management levels regarding the perception of the company's predominant energy state; this is especially true for corrosive energy. This dichotomy not only keeps leaders from combating corrosion right away, but is also observed by employees, who then lose faith in the top management's judgment.

To prevent such perception gaps, you should foster cultures that encourage feedback and other forms of extensive communication. We have seen that in such an open environment, executives at different hierarchical levels in the organization will share similar perceptions regarding the energy in the company. Not only do these corporations tend to score better in their energy profiles, but they are also significantly more successful than others. As described in chapter 1, companies with low levels of corrosive energy had 27 percent higher overall performance levels than did companies with high corrosive energy. Moreover, employee productivity in those low-corrosive energy companies was 19 percent higher, and efficiency of business processes 20 percent higher.[5] What's more, the foundation for successful cooperation was far better: people's commitment to the organization was 20 percent higher, and their intention to leave the company was 21 percent lower. Trust levels, too, were 39 percent higher among companies with low corrosive energy.

Second, executives sometimes actively deny evidence of corrosive energy and do not want to see destructive dynamics, either because they aren't sure that their past proven leadership can fix the problem or because they fear that acknowledging negative forces in the company will reflect badly back on themselves, as a sign of personal weakness. Furthermore, they lack the courage to confront people with negative feedback and are afraid of uncomfortable consequences and uncontrollable reactions.

That's why you need to actively work to avoid sweeping negative energy under the carpet, in hopes that conflicts or sources of aggression will get resolved on their own or just go away. Rather, actively look for and confront this energy head-on.

The trouble is, when it comes to dealing with corrosive energy, individual executives often possess little positive experience in handling conflicts and in overcoming negative dynamics. Two first steps that are especially useful when it comes to detecting corrosive forces in companies are facing conflict directly and measuring the amount of corrosion in the organization.

Face Conflict Head-On

Leaders who deal directly and quickly with conflict are best able to detect the corrosion trap. Though it may seem reminiscent of the chicken-and-egg quandary, facing even small conflicts in this way will help you to get a clear picture of the negative energy dynamics, in their earliest stages, throughout your organization. Early detection is particularly critical for executives in companies with highly autonomous business units that need to collaborate around the company's products and services. One CEO of a large European automation technology company has it right: "I always listen carefully when I hear about conflicts between units, when I sense lip service in board meetings, when people report permanent fights at the interfaces between units. Also when I meet people across our company and they indicate that they do not see the overall direction. If they have the impression that everyone in the company concentrates on their own business without acknowledging the bigger picture of the company— then I am alert. To me these are strong signals."

This CEO's method points to a second crucial task for you as an executive, once negative behavior has been detected: uncompromisingly address that behavior, making evidence of corrosive forces tangible for the people involved. That means that you must point out the destructive tendencies and dynamics you see your people engaging in, and describe how these harm the organization. Make your impressions and observations as concrete as possible, and link them to specific incidents.

For example, in one company we studied, executives invited input from external customers, who saw the competition between two internal business units. The executives were then able to show employees directly how harmful this behavior was. Other executives we've worked with share specific examples of corrosion they've seen at work in the company and connect these examples to hard facts, such as dropping quality measures and decreasing rates of cross-unit innovation. The box "Early Warning Signs of the Corrosion Trap" shows some key indicators of the corrosion trap.

Measure Corrosion in the Organization

Once you have used general observation to understand the qualitative dynamics of the corrosion trap and the nascent corrosive forces in the company, take a quantitative measurement of your organization's energy. This will help you precisely locate the negative forces in specific departments or business units and will give you a more robust report of the emotions and experiences of all managers and employees involved. What's more, the anonymity of a survey can eliminate people's fears about openly raising issues about destructive tendencies in the company. This measurement can be based on the Organizational Energy Questionnaire (OEQ), which we introduced in chapter 1 and which is more fully explained in the appendix.

Anonymity is critical, to be sure. As a leader, you need to make clear to your people that identifying and measuring corrosion isn't about finger pointing or looking for a scapegoat. Rather, it means systematically searching for the causes of corrosive energy and jointly developing measures to

Early Warning Signs of the Corrosion Trap

Answer each question and add up the score. (Up to 5 "yes" responses: virtually no signs of an emerging corrosion trap; 6–10 "yes" responses: beware—some early warning signals of corrosion present; more than 11 "yes" responses: danger zone—the company is likely to be trapped in corrosive energy.)

Polished Communication Versus Real Dialog

- Do executives in your organization appear to feel disconnected, distancing themselves from events that affect lower-level employees?

- Do people in your organization create an atmosphere that makes people filter or polish bad news before it reaches top management?

- Do meetings in your organization seem to contain benign discussions while the real issues have already been discussed earlier outside the meeting?

- Do people in your organization tend to pay lip service in direct communication but criticize and complain behind the back of their managers or colleagues?

- Is feedback (especially on negative issues) not fully honest?

Denial of, Versus Proactive Dealing with, Corrosive Tendencies

- Do employees overlook, neglect, or even actively push away evidence of corrosive energy, such as conflicts between teams or power struggles and micropolitics?

- Do employees appear to believe that open expressions of anger, aggression, hostility, and rivalry will get resolved on their own somehow, without targeted leadership efforts?

Lack of Alignment

- Does your organization have highly autonomous business units that sometimes approach overlapping customer bases?

- Has trust suddenly decreased between your organization's top executives and the heads of its business units?

- Is your organization gradually losing the aligning effect of an overall focus and strategy?

- Are different parts of the organization fiercely competing for resources, attention, or power?

Lack of Trust

- Do members of your company completely trust their supervisors?

- Were there certain incidents in which employees' trust of management was shaken (e.g., strikes, change processes perceived as unfair, or layoffs)?

- Is the trust in the fair procedures (promotions, compensation, investments, or other critical decisions) in your company not 100 percent?

Weak Organizational Identity

- Is your company missing a shared sense of pride?

- Do different units of your organization optimize their subgoals, even at the cost of the shared company goals?

- Is the focus in your organization often to be better than another unit in the company, rather than to be better than external competition?

---

overcome it—even if it turns out that it was the company's leaders themselves who were the root cause.

For example, in a workshop we conducted with upper management at a global nonprofit organization, an energy measurement revealed that the executives in the room showed an exceptional amount of negative energy; resigned inertia and corrosive energy were significantly elevated. While the managers themselves were not surprised about the result—it simply confirmed their own gut feelings—the CEO of the organization, David Miller, was astonished.[6] Until that day, he had not sensed any destructive powers in the company. But our analysis of the energy profile showed, among other things, that managers felt frustrated by what they perceived as a lack of communication combined with deep uncertainty about the company direction, especially concerning the realignment of the organization—a process that Miller admitted was confusing even to himself. Decisions had been delayed and due dates had been rescheduled, which would have been tolerable on their own if Miller had done a better job of communicating the process. Instead, the members of management knew only that in the works was a fundamental change that would affect them, most likely with layoffs on all levels. The organization's focus was lost, distrust and uncertainty would spread, and micropolitical actions and speculations would absorb more and more work time.

All of this came as a surprise to Miller. The workshop allowed him to restore the lines of communication by telling his managers what the real problem was: that he himself had little information from the advisory board about the impending organizational change, and that no final decisions had been made about positions or particular employees. As a result, the participants agreed on rules on how the realignment would be handled, and they committed themselves to open communication, including regular workshops during the upcoming transition period to take the pulse of the upper management and to agree on how to the lead their people.

Cleaning Up a Corrosive Atmosphere

Now let's explore the next step after you've detected corrosive forces in your organization: cleaning them up. Once negative forces are revealed, you then need to address any misconduct that could harm the organization in the short or long term—and to make clear that such corrosive action cannot be tolerated. As one HR director from a large utilities company told us, "Negativity is either on the table or under it, but it cannot be neglected. Once we decided to put the negatives squarely on the table and deal with them, that made our lives much easier."

Can corrosive energy easily be rechanneled into high positive energy? The simple answer is no. So why won't the dragon and princess strategies work for a company ensnared in the corrosion trap? When a company is in a corrosive state, it is already more engaged than if it were in a state of resigned inertia or comfortable energy. Corrosive energy as a rule cannot simply be redirected and turned into productive energy. Corrosive energy and productive energy come from different sources; corrosive energy is often related to power struggle, perceived unfairness, and egoistic tendencies, while productive energy is related to the organization's goals, tasks, and shared initiatives. Employees mired in anger, conflict, and personal revenge cannot quickly or easily return to trusting each other and cooperating. It is unrealistic for you to try creating passion for your company's collective goals or initiatives while negative forces like distrust, hurt feelings, or feelings of revenge dominate. You must deal with those negative emotions before the dragon or princess strategies could apply.

Instead of translating corrosive energy directly into productive energy, you need to engage in a two-step process that we call *energetic refocusing* to overcome the corrosion trap: first, you must phase down negativity, and then, second, you positively charge up the company again by building a strong organizational identity (figure 3-1).[7]

If you phase down the negativity in the company without then leading your people to embrace an exciting, new joint outlook, your company might slide into dominant comfortable energy. But more, you would miss the opportunity to build a common ground and align the organization around a shared new perspective that will encourage excitement and engagement.

Let's begin with a closer look at the first task of phasing down the company's negativity. Beyond just identifying that negativity early, as a

FIGURE 3-1

Moving from corrosive to productive energy

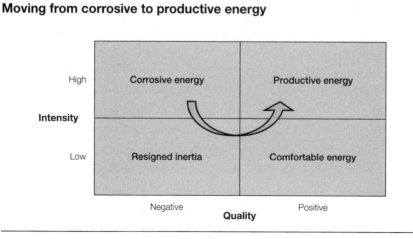

leader you need to bring it into the open, where you can encourage people to actively deal with it. Our research has turned up three important tools that you can use to start this process: creating release valves for letting off steam, instigating emotional shake-ups, and identifying and supporting toxic handlers.

Create Release Valves for Letting Off Steam

Corrosive forces often develop over a long time before they break out. These extensive periods of hidden corrosion are extremely dangerous for your company as well as for the employees and executives involved; this is when corrosive tendencies intensify and at the same time solidify themselves, absorbing increasingly more time and attention. As a leader, you must thus facilitate events where organizational members can express their anger, aggression, or frustration. We call these purposefully provided occasions to let off steam *release valves for negativity*. For the valve to have a calmative effect, the venting should take place in a protected environment or be accompanied by active counseling. Corrosive forces then are not simply discharged indirectly but can purposefully be refocused or abolished.

What might this look like? For example, when it became clear at ABB that its former CEO, Percy Barnevik, had paid himself a $116 million pension during the heart of the company's financial troubles, ABB moved swiftly to put in place procedures to deal with the problem before the corrosive power of this widely criticized revelation began to eat away at employees.[8]

To help the company as a collective whole deal with the shock, sadness, and anger associated with this announcement, ABB employed specific contact people to work with the negative thoughts and emotions of its employees.[9] Human resources established a short-term hotline to field questions regarding Barnevik as a person. An overwhelming number of the ABB employees called in. Some asked informational questions, and others used the hotline as an opportunity to talk openly about their feelings and anger. "How could this man, whom we had so loved, admired, and honored, have done this?" was a common theme. Still others looked for concrete, practical advice for managing their anger and emotional paralysis. Many employees called several times and expressed the same feelings over and over. People reported that having this opportunity to diffuse their discouragement and anger helped them considerably over the short term. For ABB, it was a successful measure to break up the spirals of destructive forces from the very start.

Some companies implement forums where tensions can surface even before a crisis hits. When CEO Gabriel Marcano, head of the Spanish division of a global telecom company, wants to introduce a new idea, he regularly uses a technique that the company calls "pussycat and tiger" to identify opposition and potential aggressive forces in an early stage and to make such forces manageable.[10] It works like this: the management team holds a meeting in which the members are divided into two groups. The "pussycats" are asked to identify the positive aspects of the new idea and to defend them in a debate, while the other group, the "tigers," search for negative arguments against the idea. The debate lasts about forty-five minutes, after which all arguments are structured and documented. All participants receive a list of the arguments discussed and are given the opportunity to rethink the issues after they have taken a step back. Each team then gathers further information and finally presents new arguments in a meeting that takes place a few days after the initial debate. Not until this meeting is there a final decision about the new idea—which is made by Marcano or, if necessary, by the whole team. Marcano has found not only that the decision is usually unanimously accepted after this procedure, but also that the process acts as a release valve and goes a long way toward diffusing any underlying dissent and corrosive forces.

In companies where deep-rooted dissent already exists—for example, where conflicts between office and field staff or between marketing and production are commonplace—everyone involved must have the opportunity to vent any pent-up aggression. But at the same time, people need to have sensitive guidance aimed at overcoming the dissent so that a solution can be based on a mutual agreement.

A large bakery located in Southern Germany, with 250 employees and twenty-seven shops, provides an example of how one company helped neutralize corrosive energy by enabling its employees to let off steam. Customer satisfaction had steadily decreased, and employee turnover drastically increased because of constant conflicts between the sales staff and the bakers. The antagonism had gotten so great that the bakers had started to purposefully delay bread production and to do other things that would make the sales staff's lives difficult, such as mixing in day-old cake with the freshly produced cakes. The sales staff also came up with creative ways to harm the bakers—salespeople would delay returning the cases for the pastries to the bake house or return them dirty; they hid equipment and even removed machine parts.

The overall energy state at the company had been spiraling down for almost three years before Hans Berg, founder and owner of the bakery, started to actively fight the corrosive energy.[11] Berg did not understand many of these processes; he did not have a clear picture of the situation and had to watch the destructive racketeering of his employees helplessly for quite a while. Not until his chief pastry cook quit did he take action. He began by having an initial open conversation with ten key people from the two departments. There he learned that the situation between the departments had reached a deadlock, with mistrust and trauma all around.

In a series of six sessions with the two departments, every bone of contention, every negative emotion, and all the negative experiences of the past were revealed. Berg hired an external moderator to ensure that no more harm was caused during this process. The participants agreed on rules of cooperation, and they used open-feedback methods such as always framing criticism as a personal perception, keeping feedback descriptive rather than accusatory, and not defending or justifying themselves when receiving feedback. The participants formulated joint goals and arranged so-called rotation afternoons, in which the bakers and sales staff exchanged roles to better understand one another's position. They also agreed to hold monthly gripe sessions to let off steam and to keep negative energy at bay.

Over the course of these initial six meetings, the two groups confronted each other with all the things that annoyed them and everything the customers had criticized. During the final meetings, they collectively planned how to make things better. The six sessions ended with a dinner in which they ate their own bread and cake and discussed, in the same structured way, what they liked about working together. There was a great deal of enjoyment and self-mockery—key to the success of such sessions.

Since those six initial sessions, both customer and employee satisfaction have jumped. And although conflicts continued to regularly erupt between the sales staff and the bakers, the monthly gripe sessions provide a valve for these inescapable frictions, ensuring that they do not develop into corrosive energy.

For you as a leader, then, the first step is to overcome negativity by simply allowing your employees a chance to let off steam. The bakery needed the managed workshops as an initial forum. This, combined with release valves such as monthly gripe sessions and biweekly visits by Berg's assistant to conduct informal conversations about employees' feelings or concerns, enabled people at the bakery to release their pent-up frustration, to vent anger, or simply to express what was bothering them.

As a second step, you need to ensure that your organization goes beyond just letting off steam and works on real solutions to solve the problem at hand. To overcome corrosive energy jointly, especially in a workshop situation, employees need to accept their conflict and be willing to understand each other's perspective. This step can be challenging indeed; in a state of corrosive energy, most people have difficulty perceiving their conflicts and fights from anything but their own perspective. Invested in their own negativity, they often have trouble freeing themselves of bad feelings long enough to see things from their opponents' side.[12] You should therefore create models of joint successful activities. Berg did this by establishing rules for cooperation during the workshop, helping participants to develop common goals that they formulated jointly, and holding a dinner where the warring parties were able to express what they appreciated about one another. With such small successes, you create the foundation for future productive energy and safeguard the organization from decline.

Companies can approach these delicate topics in lighthearted, easy ways. One particularly playful way of dealing with corrosive energy comes from the Otto Group, a German leading retail and service company with fifty-three thousand employees. In September 2005, the executive board decided to use a special forum to highlight the need for change between different departments and to offer an opportunity for employee feedback. Guided by professional actors, the managers were divided into ten teams in which they each developed and rehearsed a skit that incorporated the new strategic success factors and cultural values represented by the new plan for 2012. As each team presented its skit before the larger group, the benefits of a theatrical approach became clear: the humor and irony with which each group enacted its perception of other departments and the company took the edge off somewhat delicate topics, without reducing the relevancy for the whole company. As Alexander Birken, member of the Otto Group executive board, Human Resources and Controlling OTTO, put it, "We started to playfully understand our own weaknesses and began to ask ourselves, How customer-orientated are our controllers, our HR members, our colleagues from the services department? In doing so, we were able to mirror the truth and to abolish blinders and shields."

The group found that much of the possible negative tension and concern about the future was eased through the role-playing. For example, one skit made it clear that the reception area was not perceived as customer oriented at all. As a result, the concerned department started a project called Happy Gate to establish the reception area and its staff as the friendliest in Hamburg. Criticism was thereby voiced in a way that became constructive feedback that individual departments could act on. The overall result of this kickoff workshop was that the new vision for the future was communicated and implemented with great dedication and energy.

Use Emotional Shake-ups to Overcome the Denial of Corrosive Energy

Some companies suffer under corrosive energy for a long time. These require something more substantial than simply a release valve for dealing with brewing negativity; they need a dramatic wake-up call. We have found that after months or even years of hostility and animosity, the nature of the destructive behavioral patterns becomes chronic. Organizations develop a culture of distrust, blaming, and aggression. In corrosive cultures, people lose focus on the company's overarching goals and often deny that their behavior is corrosive. Why? They've become accustomed to this behavior. This is when release valves no longer function; since corrosive energy is not perceived as an exceptional state, it has become part of people's work life.

That's when as a leader, you need to do something to emotionally shake up the company, confronting people directly with the consequences of destructive energy. And what is the main effect of such shock-like interventions? A breakdown of the most deeply entrenched internal perspectives—those that tend to neglect company goals, desired results, customers, and strategies. If the intervention is done well, a new, shared external perspective will emerge after such a shake-up. Shake-ups usually work best early in the game; once negativity has started to settle in, people often won't be open to solutions that could overcome corrosive attitudes—even when there is no alternative. We've found that two kinds of shake-ups work well: openly confronting the organization about its corrosive energy and using destructive brainstorming.[13]

Candidly confront the organization about its corrosive energy. As a leader, you should openly talk to people about their destructive behavior and how their internal, destructive conflicts hurt them as individuals and, more importantly, the company. For example, you should bluntly present the facts about lost customers, lost revenues, the cost of internal fights, and the impact of all these problems on employee turnover and missed business opportunities. Share specific quotes from disappointed customers—things that highlight the effects of poor performance on their lives and businesses.

Martin Frerks, a department head at a U.S.-based chemical company, used just such a shake-up at his company after trying fruitlessly for eight months to integrate employees from four sites with similar functions into one logistics unit at a new location.[14] His team of thirty people continued to argue about the same topics—not wanting to travel to the new location, not having as powerful an IT system as they had enjoyed at the old location, and on and on. What's more, Frerks was accused of favoring the employees from his former site. Although the strategy, business processes, and customer needs had changed, the employees refused to accept that their previously independent units were no longer relevant. The atmosphere was tense—a mixture of frustration, conscious undermining of the new colleagues, and open hostility toward one another and toward Frerks. As a consequence, the measured level of quality and reliability were 50 percent—far from the formerly achieved level of 95 percent that the company had set for the department.

It wasn't until Frerks tried a new approach that things began to change. Working closely with his boss, Frerks confronted his department with new rules for the change process: first, the unit had to improve performance radically. Without improvement, he told his people, he himself would be transferred or probably be forced to leave the company altogether. So it was then about Frerks and his future, which came to the department members as a huge surprise no one had considered an issue before. And the department was also at stake—tasks would be outsourced. This shock-like wake-up call for the employees curbed the corrosive forces. To avoid this distressing scenario, management would support the change with additional resources, above all with internal business developers as well as quality and change experts. The message was clear: improve, or else. Frerks announced that he would set up personal meetings with each unit member to discuss his or her opinions and expectations and to collect ideas on how to plan for the change.

In his talks with individuals, Frerks learned that the people had not understood the seriousness of the situation until now. But now, they realized what was truly happening and they saw that Frerks had clearly put his own job on the line for the department. Through Frerks's drastic action, everyone now understood that the company's leaders had run out of patience. The talks had worked as a catalyst for change, and Frerks was now able to develop a strategy to dismantle the previous weaknesses. Using a short-term, well-timed shock had broken the existing destructive tension and allowed the department to overcome its previous differences and create a productive collaboration. Three months later, the department's quality and reliability measures had significantly increased, and one year later, it was the top revenue producer of the whole group.

Use destructive brainstorming. Once negativity has started to settle into an organization, people will seldom easily embrace solutions that could overcome corrosive attitudes—even when there is no alternative. Typical reactions are cynicism and an inability to even think about possible improvement, especially when it comes to interacting with the "other" party. As a leader, you therefore need to create for your people an even more drastic emotional shake-up that will in turn help refocus the organization's forces. In these truly dire cases, you can work with your teams (and it is important that the conflicting parties are present and contribute) to jointly develop worst-case scenarios for the organization, a schema of facts and events that highlight the consequences of continued destructive behavior. This type of *destructive brainstorming* facilitates a deliberate change of perspective.[15] Before corrosive energy can be overcome and a collective search for solutions can take place, the employees are asked to initially work on the exact opposite task: what do we need to do to harm our company? The task has a somewhat ironic, even funny, aspect that helps to dissolve mental blockages and emotional calcification.

Destructive brainstorming usually takes about a day. Here is how it's done: ideally with a small group (eight to fifteen people), all of whom are involved somehow in the negative conflict, the participants jointly develop the goals of the workshop, such as overcoming a crisis, improving customer retention, or explicitly overcoming corrosive energy between departments or hierarchy levels. Next, the participants engage in destructive brainstorming by approaching the defined goals from an opposite direction, for example, by asking, "How can we drive the company into bankruptcy as soon as possible?" or "What can we do to scare away our customers once and for all?" or "How can we handicap ourselves so efficiently at work that we accomplish a maximal failure?" This inversion of the problem, which essentially forces everyone to look at corrosive tendencies freshly, can be especially helpful for removing mental blockages around structural conflicts or crises.

All ideas are collected on flipcharts and assigned a priority, so that the group can deal with the ideas later in the process. The group members examine every idea and *reverse* it to come up with concrete actions—so that they form constructive ideas to deal with certain problems. By the end of such brainstorming workshops, participants are often surprised at how constructively they have worked together and feel inspired to jointly implement their positive ideas for change.

Negative brainstorming has several benefits. The collectively developed worst-case scenario not only helps the participants overcome blockages, but also clearly shows which direction their corrosive behavior is leading them toward. Moreover, the participants experience positive interactions with former "enemies." This is especially helpful when it comes to building common ground for implementing the jointly developed ideas.

What does negative brainstorming look like in practice? An example is what happened when three formerly unconnected companies with three business areas—gas, water, and electricity—were integrated into a European energy company. The new organization demanded intensive internal cooperation. Yet there was intense infighting within the newly integrated boards, with a massive gap between the mind-sets of the "old" CEOs (now division heads) and the new integrated board members.

Because the CEO himself was a member of the fractured executive board, he hired an external consultant, who began with a two-day strategy workshop with the whole management team to refocus all present toward a shared perspective for the integration process. The consultant began by asking all the workshop participants if they personally were willing to contribute to a solution to the conflict, but although they were all willing at a rational level to cooperate, he could not get them to discuss the heart of the issues. Therefore, his next step was to initiate a destructive brainstorming session around the future alignment of the company. He asked all participants to come up with as many ideas as possible on how to *ruin* the company quickly and how to most effectively scare away customers.

At first the participants were irritated because they perceived the task as absurd. But once they were persuaded to participate (after all, what did they really have to lose?), soon they got into the spirit of the session. They had filled two flipcharts with creative ideas that would be used later in the workshop. Even more important, after the brainstorming, the mood of the participants had changed dramatically. They were more relaxed and even able to laugh together. That afternoon and the next day, the board members amicably discussed concrete measures for the future strategic alignment of the company. They talked about visions, strategies, risks in the market, and the concrete change needed to establish an integrated company. They were able to use the ideas from their destructive brainstorming as a starting point for each topic, reversing those ideas and relating them to concrete action in the company. Where one of the destructive ideas was "All board members should pursue their own hidden agendas and initiate conflicts among staff members," the team now reversed the statement: "We all pull together. When we talk to our employees, we speak with one voice. Our joint success is more important than the goals of individual divisions."

A few caveats to remember if your organization decides to use an emotional shake-up to overcome corrosive energy. First, for maximum effectiveness, targets of the shake-up need to feel that ultimately everyone in the team or organization is in the same boat—that is, that only if everyone works together will the company succeed in refocusing its energy.

Second, executives often react at first with reservations when confronted with this very direct and even drastic form of addressing corrosive energy. Their reservations are usually based on wrong assumptions, namely, the fear that they or their unit will be exposed and that people in the organization will learn that they face a serious problem. But, of course, the method or intervention is not the problem; the problem already exists and people are already aware of it.

Third, pulling the organization out of a corrosive state is ultimately a task that rests squarely on your shoulders as an executive. It is up to you to find the right approach to make the consequences of negative energy concrete and vivid in your people's minds and to lead your organization toward a more positive state. This is true even when you yourself are part of the corrosive dynamic; you must find ways out of the corrosion trap, even if that means getting support from external specialists.

Finally, you must recognize that whenever people in an organization come in contact with corrosive energy, the toxicity of that interaction has far-reaching effects. That brings us to a third tool that you should use when dealing with corrosive energy: identifying and supporting toxic handlers in the organization.

Identify and Support Toxic Handlers

There is a final tool you can use to clean up and refocus your organization's corrosive energy. While managing corrosive forces is essentially your task as a leader, other people in the organization can also take on a significant part of this task of refocusing energy, however informally. Peter Frost and Sandra Robinson call these people "toxic handlers."[16] These are the people whom employees and leaders alike trust and thus share their negativity with. Toxic handlers also appear in more formal positions, such as members of the human resources department.

David O'Connell is a senior ad campaign manager and an HR manager at a media agency with more than forty people, and as a nineteen-year veteran at the company, he's that guy whom other employees tend to approach when they are frustrated or angry or have difficulties with their superiors or colleagues.[17] O'Connell has heard stories about everything from perceived unfair treatment and lack of recognition to difficulties in communicating effectively with colleagues and anxiety related to change. His colleagues told us that talking to this toxic handler makes them feel heard, and in many cases, just the conversation itself reduces the magnitude of the problem—all while helping O'Connell's coworkers continue to function at their jobs. O'Connell often helps develop a solution as well, sometimes carefully approaching the other party in a conflict. And because of his role in HR, O'Connell can synthesize the information he gets and feed it to the senior team to initiate systematic changes in the company when needed, for example, in the way the company works with its people.

What's the theory behind this? Toxic handlers absorb negativity from individuals, acting as a human release valve. They help their colleagues avoid or overcome anger, aggression, embitterment, and annoyance by actively listening to them.[18] Through intimate conversations, toxic handlers establish trust and help people in the organization to work out their negativity.

For their part, employees regain their emotional balance by sharing their negative experiences and getting support and ideas for solutions—all while the toxic handler keeps that aggression from spreading destructively throughout the organization. These special people thereby contribute fundamentally to the success of a company; they notice corrosive developments early on and diffuse them so the company can maintain its productive energy.[19]

Then leaders retrieve from the handlers critical information about corrosive energy in the company. Toxic handlers are often trusted not only by employees but also by leaders. Listen to your toxic handlers, and signal your openness to learn from them about the sources and potential outbreaks of corrosive energy. To systematically find and establish this kind of exchange with toxic handlers, you can seek out the company's informal opinion leaders, engage in direct dialog with people at lower levels, and actively foster a dialog with people who have, by the nature of their jobs, a trusted relationship with employees, such as HR managers, social workers, or labor representatives. You're not looking for people to blame or target—just for information to gauge the energy levels of the organization and to symbolize leadership's openness.

Finally, since people frequently turn to toxic handlers during particularly trying periods in organizations, you need to offer the handlers systematic support to cope with the intake of negativity. After all, the positive work of toxic handling can come at great personal cost to the handlers themselves.[20] We have often observed that while toxic handlers are adept at ridding others of negativity, they themselves often lack the ability to digest all the negative or corrosive information they take in. As a result, these people run a high risk of physical, mental, and emotional burnout. You therefore need to develop systems that support and unburden the toxic handler.

Begin by publicly acknowledging toxic handlers' crucial role, especially if that role is more formal (as for an HR employee). Then be sure to provide the resources these handlers need for their important activities—such as counselors or other professionals who can help them deal with their own burnout.[21] Another useful tool is to work with toxic handlers to predefine periods of time and the conditions under which they will deal with a particular issue, so that the process is less emotionally exhausting. This way, toxic handlers get time-outs to recharge their batteries—and to be available again at a certain point to help battle corrosive energy and refocus the energy on the shared goals of the company.

You may also want to consider bringing in toxic handlers from the outside. See, for example, the box "Using Social Workers to Handle Toxicity at Lidl."

Preventing Corrosion by Building a Strong Organizational Identity

Once you have accomplished the first task for escaping the corrosion trap—phasing out the negative energy in your organization—you are ready to move on to the second task: recharging the organization to prevent corrosion from emerging again. The bad feelings that penetrated a company during a period of corrosive energy do not easily or quickly disappear—even when the organization appears to be cohesive and collaborative on the surface. Our research shows that without an explicit investment in positive behavioral norms and attitudes, people are likely to fall back into old patterns and negativity will return.

Using Social Workers to Handle Toxicity at Lidl

As described in chapter 2, Lidl is an international discounter chain with over eight thousand stores worldwide. When the company entered the Swiss market in March 2009 with the goal of opening twenty-nine shops in the first year, it met with considerable resistance. Another discounter had already entered the Swiss market in 2005 and struggled with the local media and labor unions about its working conditions—and there was a concern that Lidl would encounter similar problems. What's more, a scandal in Lidl's own German parent company, regarding hidden surveillance of employees, had become public. With its Swiss labor force growing swiftly (Lidl had hired over six hundred employees before the Swiss stores' opening), Lidl's management agreed that employees would need special training and support to deal with direct confrontations from customers and the Swiss public.

The management team of Lidl decided to establish a contact point for all workers, to serve as a bridge between employees and the executives. Two social workers were recruited to proactively meet with employees to give them support. The workers visit approximately two stores per day to ensure constant availability and to give employees the opportunity to reduce their stress.

The social workers also rigorously trained the teams of all twenty-six stores opened in the initial launch, using Lidl Switzerland's corporate principles and mission statement as guidelines. These guidelines represent a certain security for the employees as they build a framework for a good work environment. Even though the principles are part of each contract of employment and therefore available to every staff member, "a special focus is laid on individual training to make sure all employees know their rights and can internalize them," said Silja Drack, head of HR Lidl Switzerland. In general, every newly hired worker is trained by one of the social workers, to guarantee that every employee is well-informed from the start.

Besides these instructive workshops, the two social workers' main responsibility is now to assist and support all employees in any matter, be it social, professional, or private. If an internal problem develops within a team or with management, the social workers meet with the involved parties to resolve the issue, with the goal of supporting employees and keeping a motivated and positive atmosphere. Through such communication and assistance with problems, the social workers effectively reduce the staff's negative energy. In the case of severe problems, the social workers alert Lidl management to take action.

During the intense start-up phase in Switzerland, between March and May 2009, the social workers were truly put to the test as the toxic handlers for Lidl, since staff and management alike faced significant physical and psychological stress. Besides handling various private issues that employees expressed, the social workers dealt with a serious internal problem regarding negative management behavior during that period. Staff members contacted the social workers to inform them, for example, that some store managers were possibly acting against corporate principles.

To handle this type of issue, the social workers use a standard procedure. As a first step, they talk to the employee who reported the grievance. If the problem turns out to be severe, small, anonymous working groups are then put together to talk to other employees and get the relevant manager or area manager involved. Even though the executive managers are informed about an existing problem, they don't know who and what store is affected. This guarantees anonymity and security for the reporting employees and managers. When the social workers have gathered all the required information from the discussion groups, the problem is evaluated objectively. Whether the problem is with an employee or a manager, the social workers provide support to these people. If the problem is a leadership issue, the leader receives personal coaching. Besides help from the social workers around the specific problem situation, an additional manager is put in charge to support the relevant person over a period and to release some pressure.

Regarding the reported leadership problems during the Swiss start-up phase, the problems were usually resolved and the situations went back to normal. Clearly, with two social workers as an independent contact point for all staff members, Lidl Switzerland is now able to proactively manage negative energy within the corporation. These toxic handlers play an important role in identifying possible threats and negative influences as early as possible and therefore make it easier for management to respond.

How, then, do you prevent corrosive energy from reemerging? You do so by building a strong organizational identity—essentially, a healthy team spirit in the organization.[22] People who share a robust organizational identity have strong bonds, shared values, and a sense of "we" deriving from past achievements. What's more, they aspire to the same future goals—which makes it very likely that they will collaborate well. Finally, conflicts, mistrust, and other destructive activities must be actively prevented.

As a leader, you can leverage two elements that combine to create a strong organizational identity: organizational pride and a shared future perspective about the company.[23]

- **Organizational pride:** This means the extent to which people share a sense of achievement in the company's past successes. If organizational pride is high, employees feel closely linked to their company or organizational unit. They are proud to be a part of it and to make a contribution. If organizational pride is weak or not present at all, then the company lacks one of the most important elements for cohesion, and people will be more likely to maximize personal benefit over the good of the whole. Under these circumstances, corrosive energy thrives and employees increasingly see themselves as simply individuals and less as a part of a larger whole, namely, the company. Our research has shown, for example, that when employees possess high levels of company pride, the organization has lower corrosive energy (17 percent) and higher productive energy (10 percent) than companies where people experience low levels of pride.[24] Our data that looked at how well people identified with their organizations clearly supported this picture. Companies where employees showed high levels of company identification had lower corrosive energy (16 percent) and higher productive energy (11 percent) than companies where people felt little organizational identification.

- **Shared perspective:** This element describes the extent to which people share a strong vision, ambitious goals, or a common focus regarding company strategy. When employees have a shared perspective, they are engaged in a joint overarching purpose and the company enjoys a clear direction for aligned action. On the other hand, if shared perspectives about the organization's strategy are weak or absent, there is confusion regarding which activities are most relevant to pursue. The company does not pursue a uniform, future-oriented path, but rather goes after many different, often contradictory initiatives—and the likelihood of corrosive energy increases. Indeed, we found that companies that had high levels of shared perspective, that is, a strong shared vision throughout the organization, had higher productive energy (14 percent) and lower corrosive energy (19 percent) than companies where people experience low levels of shared perspective.[25]

If you look closely at these two dimensions—organizational pride and a shared future perspective—you can determine which of the four types of organizational identity dominates your company: complacent identity, drained identity, rootless identity, or sustainable identity (figure 3-2).[26] These identity types are not meant to match up to the four energy states of the company—rather, we are emphasizing that a strong, sustainable identity helps to prevent and counteract corrosive energy.

Companies with a *drained identity* are weak on both pride and perspective. Organizational identity has been exhausted and broken up, and

FIGURE 3-2

Organizational identity matrix

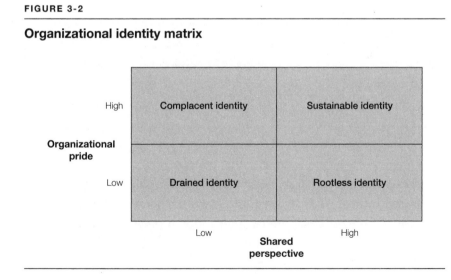

employees do not feel strongly tied to the company. A strong, shared, future perspective can be destroyed through uncontrolled growth, over-diversification, or over-decentralization, which goes hand in hand with silo thinking and prioritizing unit goals above company goals. Pride is either missing or related to the unit rather than to the entire company, so that people are more likely to fight for the success of their unit against others within the same company—and corrosive energy emerges.

Companies can develop a *rootless identity* when they have low or no organizational pride combined with strong, joint future perspective. They often successfully pursue a strong, shared strategy, but employees no longer take any pride in it. These companies soon lose a sense of cohesion, and employees do not feel strongly tied to the company or to their team. More critical, low feelings of pride only allow for a very limited look back on past achievements, because employees don't trust their colleagues. The situation becomes a breeding ground for corrosive energy. Employees know which goals they have to follow, but they lack the decisive, shared sense of success that could change a rootless identity into a sustainable identity. Although employees with a rootless identity share a common goal, corrosive dynamics can quickly emerge because a strong, shared feeling of pride is missing.

A *complacent identity* arises in companies with high organizational pride but low or absent joint perspectives about the future. The complacent identity is often based on a very positive organizational past. We frequently see a complacent identity in older companies that have been doing business for decades and that are generally very successful in their markets. Employees are proud of what they have achieved and of the company's image, and management tends to be fairly self-satisfied. These companies do not foster very ambitious or strong goals. Rather, there's a complacent identity that is often initially accompanied by a very low state of negativity and aggression. People in the organization have a strong feeling of pride concerning past achievements and feel comfortable with the living-in-the-past attitude. In such a setting, corrosive energy typically emerges when parts of the organization start to question past achievements and future plans to launch innovative initiatives, and people generally feel impaired in their forward-looking process.

Finally, companies with a *sustainable identity* are characterized by strong organizational pride and strong future perspectives. These companies are the least likely to reengage in corrosive activity. For example, the company has a focused, ambitious strategy or the company's strategic initiatives are highly prioritized and considered a shared challenge. Employees put their whole energy toward the shared company goals and see themselves as an important part of the whole. This combination of a high shared pride in the company and its achievements and the pursuit of a joint ambitious perspective helps companies prevent negative energy in the long term. The trust that comes from a shared successful past and from knowing that people jointly strive for future goals creates a strong bond in the company as well as a high sense of readiness to cooperate and avoid destructive engagement.

When your company lacks a strong identity or possesses strong identities in some units that compete with its central identity, you need to foster the organizational pride and shared future perspectives of the whole.[27] You should therefore first concentrate on *establishing or improving a shared perspective* about the future since you can address that comparatively quickly. Second, you should *nurture organizational pride*. Compared with the steps needed to improve a shared future perspective, attempts to build or rebuild pride take more time.[28] Executives regularly disregard organizational pride either because they don't understand its importance or because they don't know how to systematically influence it. But make no mistake: there is no real alternative to nurturing pride continuously over a long period. Answer the questions in "How Strong Is Your Organization's Identity?" to see what areas need improvement in your company's overall identity. Once you have an idea of how strong your organization's identity is, you can then work on specific levers to boost both your company's perspective and pride. These levers are discussed in the remaining sections.

Develop Shared Perspectives About the Company's Future

Creating a shared future focus or perspective for the company—around which every unit and every member of the organization can rally—requires two basic actions. First, you need to refocus the company's joint goals, and second, you need to create collective commitment.

How Strong Is Your Organization's Identity?

This checklist summarizes the typical indicators of a sustainable identity. Answer each question and add up the score. (More than 11 "yes" responses: your company most likely has a strong identity; 6–10 "yes" responses: beware—some early warning signals of a weak identity; 5 or fewer "yes" responses: danger zone—the company is likely to struggle with a weak identity.)

Pride

- Are your employees proud of your company?

- Are people in your company aware of its past achievements?

- Do people in the organization share a view of the successful past of the company?

- Are the employees of your organization aware of the strengths and competencies of your company?

- When someone praises your company, do employees perceive it as a personal compliment?

- Do people tell others that they are proud to work for your organization?

- Do employees recommend your company to their friends as an employer?

- Do you explicitly emphasize and celebrate exceptional successes or achievements in the whole company soon after they occur?

Perspective

- Does your company have a focused, ambitious strategy that people collectively pursue?

- Is there a shared understanding of the vision of your company regarding the whole organization?

- Are people in the organization fully committed to a joint, ambitious perspective?

- Do employees have a shared view on challenges and opportunities in your company?

- Is there a shared emotional tie to common goals in your company?

- Do people in the organization prioritize the company future over the success of their individual subunits?

- Are the company's strategic initiatives highly prioritized and considered a shared challenge?

- Is there a high level of identification with the company goals in your organization?

Refocusing joint goals. Most often, strengthening a common perspective through refocusing goals means overhauling the entire strategy of the company, reshaping the big picture, and communicating the new direction clearly to everyone in the company.

As we recounted earlier in the book, when Juergen Dormann took the helm as ABB's new CEO in 2002, the company was on the brink of bankruptcy, and organizational pride and identity were at an all-time low.[29] He started by simplifying the business model, with a focus on the traditional strengths of the company and a reduction to only two business areas, power technologies and automation technologies. All other areas were put up for sale, and the remaining divisions were dissolved. Dormann also brought in a new leadership team and reduced the executive committee from eleven to five people—ensuring that his own strategic focus was shared and accepted by the other top managers. Moreover, Dormann introduced a more comprehensive, open, and clear communication style throughout the company (including his famous Friday letters, mentioned earlier) to explain the new strategic focus and the shared perspectives, get employees behind the new company direction, and thus generate shared commitment for future tasks. As a result, both customers and employees slowly began to understand again what ABB stood for, and organizational pride has been restored.

Creating collective commitment. After periods of corrosive energy, it is paramount that you as a company leader foster collective commitment, a collectively felt, deep obligation to the new unifying direction—a commitment that is ideally shared and accepted by every member of the organization. That is how you ensure a shared willingness to invest people's energy and develop and maintain loyalty for shared initiatives. Commitment among all people creates high levels of effort and enduring concentration on important objectives.[30] This is key for overcoming corrosive energy in an organization or preventing the return of destructive behavior.[31] But how can you build this sense of collective commitment to company goals?

The German automotive systems and tire manufacturer Continental AG reveals how previously conflicting units developed shared goals and a strong collective commitment. When Hubertus von Gruenberg took the helm in 1991, he led Continental AG from a growth-by-all-means strategy, in which conflicts and indifference were the norm, to a combined focus on profitable growth and innovation.[32] All units and processes needed to contribute to profitability. This demand also included over one thousand engineers and technicians in R&D.

Von Gruenberg introduced a quarterly research-development-engineering (RDE) meeting, gathering the board of the tire division, marketing directors, and project leaders from R&D. At RDE meetings, engineers presented their projects at an early stage and received feedback directly from marketing and top management. Innovations were balanced with existing products and market trends. For the respective projects, the participants defined shared goals and project steps. The direct participation of both R&D and marketing and sales employees in goal setting, the involvement of the top management, and the clear importance of individuals' contributions to the group strategy led to a strong emotional attachment and shared commitment for implementing the projects. The meeting achieved a shared commitment in two areas: R&D employees committed themselves to innovations that would enable market success, and the marketing people committed to the need for extraordinary technology.

The following leadership strategies can go a long way toward creating such shared commitment regarding the future within companies and individual units:

- Make sure that the shared direction is not only clear and focused but also perceived as challenging and meaningful.[33]

- Ensure that the new focus of your company becomes a shared view among all employees, including those who have fought each other bitterly.

- Whenever possible, involve all your employees and managers in defining the company goals. Self-set goals produce higher goal commitment.[34] After times of corrosive energy, this is one of the most challenging tasks for leaders. But you can do this through personal meetings with selected representatives of different work units, agenda-setting team dialogues, or the involvement of the whole company, for example, in a large survey on joint vision or values.

These instruments enable you to prevent or overcome the dividing forces in your company and to protect or reestablish a shared determination and commitment to pursue the new strategic focus over longer periods.[35] We have observed, in fact, that once units of the company rally around common goals, they become actively reluctant to deviate from the new, unifying purpose.

Build and Rebuild Pride

To build a sustainable identity that prevents companies from spiraling toward corrosive energy, you as a leader must focus on a shared sense of organizational pride. In companies with strong pride, people are aware of their joint achievements and share an intense feeling of belonging.[36] Employees and managers support and step in for each other, focusing on solutions for shared tasks or problems.

But how, exactly, can you build or strengthen that sense of pride in the organization? A core instrument is to *explicitly recognize accomplishments, successes, and strengths of the company*. In our experience, executives seldom systematically and credibly analyze the successes of the past. More commonly, they focus on the future, on deficits, and on goals that have to be accomplished. Although the future is undeniably important, pride about reached goals and past successes highlights the organization's shared history and the important connections between different departments or teams.

Juergen Dormann used the Friday letters not only to explain a new strategic focus but also to help restore employee pride in the company by openly describing how he felt about ABB's past success. "I have already told you," he wrote early in his tenure in October 2002, "and that impression is reconfirmed daily—how strongly I have been struck by the determination, pride and fighting spirit of people in our company."[37]

You can further strengthen pride by *stressing the special characteristics of the company* and by underscoring aspects that differentiate the company from other companies. What makes your company so special? What differentiates it from rivaling companies? Why is it special to be part of the company? How difficult is it to become part of the organization? In answering these questions, you should stress the commonalities among the organization's divisions and individual members, strengthening pride in being part of *this* company.

Another way you can support a strong organizational identity and the feeling that everyone is pulling together is by making *visible and credible investments in the company* or by making *visible personal sacrifices*.[38] We often see that when the top team reduces its own salaries in times of crisis, as the Phoenix Contact executive board did in 2009—even though the action was largely symbolic—this does help to ease anger and frustration and demonstrates to employees how important the company is to the executives.

Consider, for example, the ways that Dormann helped ABB rebuild a sense of pride:

- By concentrating on the core competencies and traditional business areas of the company, Dormann reflected back to employees their previous successes and competencies.

- In addition, he explicitly emphasized the strengths and past successes of ABB in his Friday letters, awakening a sense of the shared history and future potential in the company's employees.

- Dormann gave many managers great freedom to act and strengthened accountability in the whole ABB Group. Thus, he increased managers' long-term identification with company goals, helping everyone to feel responsible for ABB's further development.

- Dormann performed numerous symbolic acts (such as getting rid of status symbols and the privileges of the executive committee), which emphasized the commonalities in the company and helped employees to feel pride for *their* company, *their* management, and *their* turnaround. The employees thus regained trust in the integrity and goals of the company management.

- Finally, Dormann explicitly emphasized the company's shared identity—the importance of "one ABB" versus a company that was a collection of different units or companies with their own identities. "We
need to further align our people around the common interests of
ABB," he wrote in one of his Friday letters. "We need to strengthen
your identity as employees of ABB—and not of company X Y or Z
in ABB, still clinging to its identity from 10 or 15 years ago . . . ABB,
the company that communities and nations welcome. ABB, the company whose shares investors want to keep. ABB, the company where
the best talent wants to work and where skilled, experienced people
remain and feel at home. And all of this will happen for one reason:
because we are the preferred choice of our customers, suppliers and
other business partners. Working as One ABB."[39]

Through his confident communications, Dormann moved ABB bit by
bit from a rootless identity to a sustainable identity. He understood that
strategic focus alone is not enough. Rather, custom-tailored leadership
was necessary for reinstating a strong, sustainable identity—and thus overcoming corrosion and mobilizing productive energy.

Dealing with the corrosion trap is a leadership challenge that executives
sometimes overlook or even purposefully ignore because the task isn't
very straightforward; corrosive forces are difficult to handle. Nevertheless,
it is critical that you direct your attention toward the highly negative
forces in your company as soon as you begin to detect problems. As we
have illustrated, even short incidents of corrosion can place a long-lasting
burden on the organization's performance. The longer corrosion permeates a company, the deeper its damage.

As we've seen, corrosive energy occurs in companies that are highly
active (yet this activity and motivation are directed toward destructive
purposes or the benefit of individuals or subunits rather than the company
as a whole). There is one additional trap we often find in companies that
are highly active. Although people usually consider high positive energy a
good thing, we will describe yet another way that it can put a strain on
organizations. The next chapter, then, deals with this acceleration trap.

CHAPTER 4

Focusing Your Organization's Energy

Escaping the Acceleration Trap

In the last chapter, we looked at how to free organizations that have been caught in the corrosion trap. Now we will explore a second energy trap, a very tricky one, because it ensnares companies that seem to be doing quite well and that have reached the ideal of high productive energy. Their fatal mistake? They become overly energetic. Faced with intense market pressures, corporations often take on too much: they increase the number and speed of activities, raise performance goals, shorten innovation cycles, and introduce new management technologies or organizational systems. For a while, they succeed brilliantly, but too often, the CEO tries to make this furious pace the new normal. What began as an exceptional burst of achievement becomes chronic overloading. Although energy levels are high, exhaustion and resignation begin to blanket the company soon enough. We call this problematic situation the *acceleration trap*.[1]

The acceleration trap, then, is a phenomenon that starts out as something positive. Your company is productive and energetic, and there's a sense that it can begin reaping high returns for both employees and shareholders. The trouble is that constantly driving the organization along the edge of its capacities simply isn't sustainable. And although many companies today are naturally geared toward growth, innovation, speed, and performance, highly energetic companies sometimes become victims of their own excess energy. They become caught in a dynamic spiral, blindly forging ahead without examining how they're using their energy. When executives don't regulate their companies carefully, positive high-energy phases can easily move toward negative positive energy and overacceleration.

That is exactly what has happened in surprisingly many companies. In today's rapidly changing conditions, the acceleration trap has become practically an epidemic, especially at large corporations. And while these companies have developed clever ways to adapt, becoming ever more flexible and using powerful new technological tools, many firms fail to see the negative result: exhausted employees and organizations at risk for serious resigned inertia and burnout.

The problem is pervasive, especially in the current environment of speeding up and cost-cutting: half of the 92 companies we investigated in 2009 were affected by the trap. The acceleration trap harms the company on many levels; companies caught in the trap fare far worse than their peers in every area, from employee morale to company performance and efficiency. Specifically, resignation increases by 50 percent, emotional exhaustion increases by 70 percent, corrosive energy and aggression doubles (increase by 100 percent), and turnover intention even triples (increase by 200 percent) (figure 4-1). Performance is also significantly impaired at companies caught in this trap: there are drops in overall performance (–17 percent), employee productivity (–12 percent), efficiency (–24 percent), return on investment (ROI) (–24 percent), growth (–10 percent), retention (–15 percent), and the companies' financial situation (–25 percent) (figure 4-2).[2]

Our research reveals several specific organizational symptoms of the acceleration trap. Companies that have been trapped tend to start many activities simultaneously but don't devote enough time or resources to each, thus overwhelming their people by relentlessly pushing them

FIGURE 4-1

Consequences of the acceleration trap, employees' point of view

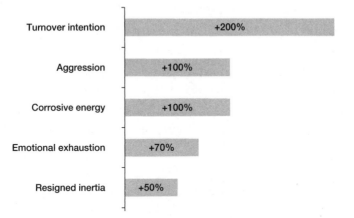

Turnover intention	+200%
Aggression	+100%
Corrosive energy	+100%
Emotional exhaustion	+70%
Resigned inertia	+50%

Note: Data based on a subsample from 2009 in 104 German companies with 3,783 respondents for energy states, 3,777 respondents for acceleration trap, 3,673 respondents for turnover intention and 3,555 respondents for emotional exhaustion.

FIGURE 4-2

Consequences of the acceleration trap, top management's point of view

Financial performance	-25%
Employee retention	-15%
ROI	-24%
Growth	-10%
Efficiency	-24%
Employee productivity	-12%

Note: We asked members of the top management teams to rate their company's performance in relation to the performance of their major competitors at the time of measurement. Data based on a subsample from 2009 in 104 German companies with 3,777 respondents for acceleration trap and 225 top management team members for performance measures.

beyond their limits. Particularly when CEOs have seen what their companies can achieve during a stretch phase of intensive energy, the leaders assume that the exceptional can become the routine. Like the Olympians that we referred to in the introduction, these leaders push their companies constantly beyond the edge of people's capabilities. Although growth and innovation are obviously crucial for business success, they can break your company if they are not managed wisely.

What begins as a positive, exciting journey for the organization can end in an ongoing acceleration, an uncontrolled flood of activities, unfocused and inconsistent managerial action, confused customers, and exhausted employees. People who work in companies caught in an acceleration trap often report a feeling of permanently increasing speed and time pressure, as well as personal disempowerment. Despite the massive effort they put into their work, their load never seems to decrease, and they're left feeling fatigued and vaguely dissatisfied.

Our data provide a sobering look at conditions inside a company that is accelerating too much. At companies that we define as fully trapped (we'll describe the various types of ensnarement momentarily), 60 percent of surveyed employees agreed or strongly agreed that they lacked sufficient resources to get their work done; compare that with 2 percent at companies that weren't caught in this trap. The findings were similar for agreement with the statements "People in this company work under constantly elevated time pressure" (80 percent versus 4 percent), "People in this company often reach their limit because of too much work" (55 percent versus 6 percent), and "My company's priorities frequently change" (75 percent versus 1 percent). Most respondents at fully trapped companies disagreed or strongly disagreed that they saw "a light at the end of the tunnel" of intense working periods (83 percent versus 3 percent) and that they regularly got a chance to regenerate (86 percent versus 6 percent) (figure 4-3).[3]

The acceleration trap leaves both employees and their entire organizations feeling stuck on an increasingly faster hamster wheel of activity and pressure, with too little time to complete tasks and too little recreation and rejuvenation. Rather than continuously investing to build resources and nurturing and regenerating human capacities, these organizations deplete everyone's potential and reserves.

FIGURE 4-3

Consequences of the acceleration trap, employees' point of view at companies both with and without an acceleration trap

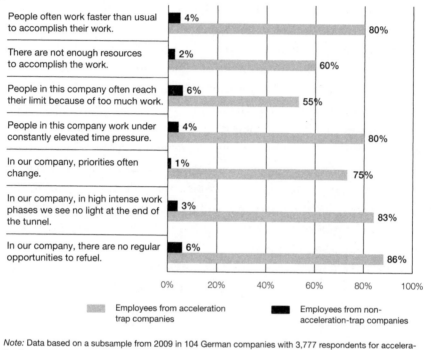

Note: Data based on a subsample from 2009 in 104 German companies with 3,777 respondents for acceleration trap.

Similar to the corrosion trap, the main problem with the acceleration trap is how insidious it can be: most companies don't even realize they've been caught. But beyond detection, even when companies *do* recognize the trap, most take the wrong cure for it. Instead of fighting the cause, they try to fight the symptoms—and aggravate the problem. Executives typically interpret their employees' tendency to withdraw or not work at their best as laziness or lack of motivation—and so the leaders increase the pressure, which only digs the company faster and deeper into the trap.

But it's possible to escape. Companies can sustain high performance over the long term without overtaxing their employees or confusing their customers. To do so as a leader, you must deliberately decrease energy in your organization as a method of bringing it back to productive energy. As a first step, you must identify and analyze the problem in detail—and then take action to consciously scale back the organization's activities. Once your organization is free from the trap, however, your work doesn't end there. Since the acceleration trap can disguise itself as positive growth and activity, you must continually monitor for overacceleration, even when the organization shows no apparent symptoms and when things seem to be running smoothly, such as when your company is enjoying high activity levels and high employee commitment. The challenge then becomes to differentiate between appropriate activity levels, that is, ones that allow for sustainable commitment, and relentless activity coupled with exhaustion, low employee morale, and increasing resignation or detachment from tasks—all typically the harbingers of ensnarement in the acceleration trap.

In this chapter, we'll show you how to recognize the acceleration problem, how to start to move your company in a different direction, and how to make cultural changes that will prevent future entrapment. We'll look at three forms of acceleration traps—overloading, multiloading, and perpetual loading—and offer some tools for avoiding them if you can, and escaping them if you have to. But first, as we did with the corrosion trap, let's look at specific signs and symptoms that can tell you when you've been caught.

Detecting Acceleration

When determining whether your company is overaccelerating, keep in mind that the acceleration trap actually comes in three forms: what we call *overloading* (too much to do), *multiloading* (too many activities), and *perpetual loading* (monotonous, continuous work). Overaccelerated companies exhibit at least one of these three patterns, and most companies exhibit several at once.

Overloading

Some 35 percent of the firms in our sample fell into this type of acceleration trap.[4] These companies become overloaded when they find themselves increasingly involved in too many activities of the same kind—without sufficient resources to handle the work. The result is often too-rapid company growth, exploding demands, and overly ambitious business expansions, such as breaking into new markets and establishing new offices. You know that such activities have veered into overacceleration when your employees voice concern that they can't handle the multitude of activities or when they can't foresee increases in activity level and can't anticipate future developments. Also, if the resources to handle the increased demands are either unavailable or late in coming, the company has probably been caught in an overload situation. When these kinds of developments persist, overload becomes a problem, leaving employees with the sense that the exceptional conditions of a high workload have now become the norm—with no end in sight.

Sulzer, an industrial company based in Winterthur, Switzerland, with 120 locations worldwide and employing 12,000 people, found itself overloaded in 2008. It had increased sales by 94 percent (from $1.7 billion in 2003 to $3.2 billion in 2007) and, over the same period, had increased its operating income by more than 580 percent (from $39 million to $261 million). By the end of 2008, Sulzer's workforce was working at the limits of the company's capacities, a situation that restricted the company's future growth prospects. In the same period, when Sulzer's net sales had increased by 94 percent (between 2003 and 2007), the company's workforce had grown by only 29 percent. Remarkably, Sulzer was doing nearly twice the sales with only about one-third more employees. What's more, the company had gone through a turnaround that required a tremendous amount of energy from Sulzer's employees. Although operational efficiency improvements had increased productivity per employee, by 2008 the company's workforce capacity was reaching its saturation level.

CEO Ton Buechner was aware of this challenge and told us that the problem was finding new, highly qualified employees to help ease the work burden. As a result, Buechner put enhancing its brand as an employer on top of Sulzer's strategic agenda in order to ensure hiring enough good talent to do the company's work. Buechner charged the company with enhancing its brand as an employer, and he put this challenge at the top of Sulzer's strategic agenda. Subsequently, Beat Sigrist, the head of corporate HR, set up a project designed both to retain and motivate the current workforce and to position Sulzer as an attractive employer. The project focused first on the core values of the company and, second, on the employer brand, which was built on these core values to ensure consistency of brand messages both within and outside the company. This approach led to a highly credible and effective long-term solution that worked even during the extreme market downturn in 2009. Today, Sulzer's attrition rates are low, and the company has substantially increased its attractiveness in the labor market.

Multiloading

Some 35 percent of firms in our sample suffered from multiloading.[5] When a company loads its systems with *too many different things* to do (as opposed to too much of the same thing, as we just described with overloading), it can lose focus, misalign its various activities, or flipflop the company's priorities one too many times. You know you have entered multiloading territory when the organization initiates too many change processes simultaneously without a clear strategy. When a company asks employees to do too many kinds of activities, both the company and its employees become unfocused, and activities are misaligned.

That's what happened at ABB.[6] As we've recounted in previous chapters, when the company was founded in 1987 after a merger between two European groups, it was one of the world's largest industrial groups, with 170,000 employees. At first, the company responded extraordinarily well to CEO Percy Barnevik's radical restructuring; costs were reduced, new acquisitions were effectively integrated, and the company rapidly built its position in a number of new markets. Over this period, the company's revenue grew from $17.8 billion to $36.2 billion, while its operating income leaped from $854 million to $3.2 billion.

But after eight years of permanent growth, the first signs of overacceleration became visible in the company, and it became clear that all of this growth had put the company into severe multiloading. Individual sectors suffered from constant internal conflicts, and the entire company soon degenerated into confusion and redundant activities.

It was on this already exhausted organization that the new CEO Göran Lindahl imposed his drastic reorganization of September 1998. Yet the expected success of the reorganization never came, and by the end of 2000, sales had fallen by $1.7 billion (to $23.0 billion), net profit fell to $1.4 billion, and the company's stock price lost almost a third of its value.

And when Jörgen Centerman replaced Lindahl in January 2001, Centerman's reorganization of the company into seven customer groups led to yet more disastrous results, with ABB's debt level growing to a record-breaking $5.2 billion by mid-2002. Worst of all, the reorganization meant that ABB's people again lost many of their well-established working relationships and had to begin working under new, younger, and typically more ambitious and aggressive business-area executives.

ABB demonstrated classic symptoms of organizational exhaustion: poor prioritization, unrealistically high expectations, and diffuse attention management. In undertaking too many restructuring plans and a variety of acquisitions, ABB had pressured its people to achieve radical improvements in a too-broad range of areas. As a result, most of ABB's field managers were in a state of frenzy, spinning their wheels without focus and achieving little effective change. Sensing this exhaustion but applying the wrong cure, first Lindahl and then his successor Centerman put even more pressure on the company. As performance continued to decline with rising criticism from shareholders and the business media, the acceleration trap finally took complete hold of the company by 2002, leaving it with little reserve of energy left to revitalize itself.

Perpetual Loading

A third kind of acceleration trap emerges when leaders *constantly push their companies to the edge of their abilities,* perpetually loading them with too much activity. In this case, the problem is not so much the amount of work, but rather the monotony and uniformity of the workload. Some 30 percent of the firms in our sample were affected by perpetual loading.[7] These companies, which persistently operate close to capacity limits, tend to be the hardest on employees. Just about anyone can tolerate overloading or multiloading for a while, especially if there's an end in sight, but when leaders neglect to call a halt to periods of furious activity, employees feel imprisoned by the debilitating frenzy. You know your firm is perpetual loading when the workload never seems to let up and there are no possibilities for regeneration or retreat. When companies fail to alternate intense work cycles with cycles of exertion and recreation, then employees will either individually take time-outs or hold back energy, even if this obstructs the company's goals.

As described earlier, Lufthansa began a long-term change process in 1991, when the company first faced bankruptcy.[8] By 2003, Lufthansa had a decade of constant energetic exertion behind it, a relentless process that led the airline to organizational burnout and its workers into a deep malaise and fatigue. As Holger Hätty, then a member of the executive board of Lufthansa Passenger Transportation, put it, "We are in a business in which the only thing we are ever able to say to our employees is, 'Economize, economize, economize!' And our people respond by asking, 'When is the economizing going to come to an end?' They are exhausted . . . The pilots' strike and excessive demands were no coincidence. This problem will return to haunt us. Maintaining the change momentum is becoming increasingly difficult." Added Silke Lehnhardt, then head of the Lufthansa School of Business: "Burnout is a challenge. Everywhere, people are feeling the need for peace and quiet and hoping that once we've stood this through, everything will return to normal and we'll be able to rest. People still have not grasped that that moment will probably never come." Finally, with the hiring of CEO Wolfgang Mayrhuber in 2004, Lufthansa successfully extricated itself from the trap by easing its formerly relentless—and exhausting—focus on cost control. Although cost sensitivity remains important, Mayrhuber allowed the firm to recover from the seemingly never-ending process of savings by shifting the focus more toward innovation, a service culture, and diversification. He also further decentralized the company and gave employees more freedom to work at their own pace.

When it comes to the acceleration trap, the three forms we've just examined—overloading, multiloading, and perpetual loading—are often interrelated and occur simultaneously. But even though the symptoms, perceptions, and consequences of the forms of overacceleration can be the same, you should try to form a clear, early picture of your particular situation so that you can apply the best coping strategy—as early as possible. Work through the box "Early Warning Signs of the Acceleration Trap" frequently, so that early on, you will recognize the signs that your company is falling into an acceleration trap.

Now that we have defined the different ways that a company can have too much energy and how these ways can lead a company into the acceleration trap, let's look at some coping strategies companies can use to climb out of this trap—and avoid falling into it in the future.

Early Warning Signs of the Acceleration Trap

Overloading

- Speed and time pressure are permanently increasing within your company.

- Employees have to work faster and faster to keep up with the increasing workload.

- Employees are unable to take breaks or vacations because of the increasing workload.

Multiloading

- Top management lacks clear priorities.

- It is hard for your employees to prioritize their tasks, because of the multitude of activities they are involved in.

- Priorities in your company change constantly.

Perpetual Loading

- A constant feeling of overload and tiredness pervades your organization.

- Employees feel they don't see the light at the end of the tunnel, because of constantly elevated work demands.

- Good employees are leaving your company.

Stopping the Action

The acceleration trap stems in part from a number of trends in today's business environment, including the demand for speed, the diffusion of new technology, globalization, shortened innovation cycles, and intensified competition. These trends are not new, yet their interplay is relatively new and creates a particular dynamic that implies an ever-greater acceleration for individuals and the organization as a whole. This dynamic becomes escalated in extreme situations—in exceptionally prosperous times as well as tense economic situations.

Because the acceleration trap is still a relatively new phenomenon in organizations and has rarely been explicitly addressed by managers, few best practices have been developed to help organizations to escape it. Nevertheless, a few courageous executives have initiated highly innovative, often counterintuitive approaches. Almost all of these solutions carry one overarching message to leaders: take a break from initiating new activities, that is, *stop the action*.

You can use stop-the-action initiatives in situations where the symptoms of overacceleration and excessive energy are already noticeable. Essentially, you as the leader stop for a moment to regroup, deliberately reducing the organization's activities and looking at how to refocus. This is not about figuring out what to do next. Rather, it's about deciding what the company needs to *stop* doing immediately. In stop-the-action initiatives, companies or work units reevaluate their projects, goals, and commitments; rank them in order of importance; identify the essential ones; and then rechannel their energy toward those. For stop-the-action initiatives to work, you need to already have a clear strategy in place for the organization and a reasonable understanding of the future. When organizations stop the action, they can get their energy back and refocus on the core business.

Why would you choose to stop the action? Basically, this approach helps companies get off the treadmill of continually starting new projects and adding new goals and tasks to the agenda—which often results in uncontrolled growth and, more importantly, the activities fueling this growth. Stopping the action helps you identify less-important activities and systematically reduce them or get rid of the dead weight entirely. (Dead weight might include activities that aren't really productive, are a waste of energy, and ultimately cause individuals, work units, or even the entire organization to get caught up in busyness or projects lacking direction.)

In the companies we've studied, leaders have stopped the action through a two-step process. First, they ask, "What should we stop doing?" (rather than "What new idea can we pursue?"), and second, they do some serious spring cleaning throughout the organization.

Ask Employees, "What Can We Stop Doing?"

Most companies have a suggestion process in place, through which ideas get generated. The people behind these processes are always asking,

"What should we start doing?" But with the stop-the-action initiative, the idea is to *reverse* that idea-generating process.

In one Swiss pharmaceutical company, for example, about 150 employees routinely submitted between 150 and 180 ideas throughout the year. These ideas all implied new projects, additional activities, and potential innovations, which meant new activities for the company. As a rule, a full 10 percent of those ideas—some of them quite large, new projects—were implemented. But in 2005, CEO Peter Moser realized that the company had started an unusually large number of new projects—and he began to doubt the company's idea-management system.[9] "We do not know how to implement all those ideas with the resources we have," he told us. "Does it really help us to keep generating even more ideas?"

His conclusion: even though people in the company were still excited about coming up with and implementing new ideas, it simply wouldn't be possible to begin additional innovative project ideas. There was no way that all these projects could be completed. And in fact, there were signs in the company that many projects were being completed ineffectually or slowly. That's when Moser had a eureka moment: "Why don't we take an inverse approach?" he thought. Instead of asking, "What new project can we begin?" he challenged the company to ask, "What should we stop doing?"

The response was almost instantaneous. Employee ideas about what to *stop doing* began to pour in—540 ideas in all—for what needless tasks, projects, and goals could be eliminated even though they were already in progress throughout the company. Eventually, the company carried out 145 of those ideas for what to *stop doing*. These stop-the-action initiatives amounted to a full 40 percent of the firm's projects, resulting in a significant increase in efficiency. In the end, without making a single cut in the workforce, Moser trimmed the company's dead weight and liberated it from needless overactivity.

Institute Spring Cleaning

Another method for breaking free from the acceleration trap and ultimately shifting the organizational culture involves what Fredmund Malik calls "systematic waste disposal."[10] Since some companies do this every year in the springtime, we call it *spring cleaning,* but companies caught in the acceleration trap will want to do this immediately, regardless of the season.

Typically, company leaders, particular departments, or sometimes the entire company will meet or conduct a workshop to analyze all existing activities to differentiate between what is of central strategic importance and what isn't. As a leader, you should divide all company activities into three categories: those considered very important and that need the most focus and energy, those that are central but not urgent and that can easily be put on hold, and those that are truly unimportant and that the company can and should stop doing immediately. At the end of this process, leaders report feeling refocused, reenergized, and refreshed, knowing that the company can now pursue its most important tasks with much more attention and energy.

For example, when the Otto Group went through a restructuring, managers found themselves burdened with 20 to 30 percent more work. So in 2007, the company initiated a spring cleaning. Each executive was asked to select a single project that he or she wanted to complete by all means. But that still left too many in play, according to Thomas Grünes, then head of central services. The list was then halved, according to each project's required investment, its value-to-cost ratio, and, in certain cases, its symbolic value for employees. For example, the final list included a redesign of reception areas and staff restaurants, which increased pride and performance "and thus was a very important initiative, although the economic value was not obvious," Grünes told us. At the end of the process, the managers had reduced their activities and projects by 50 percent. The other half of the projects were filed away, to be reconsidered during future spring cleanings. To guard against bloat, the company has made this winnowing process an annual activity. Grünes stressed that in the end, the decision about which projects are initiated isn't a question of whether there's a particularly powerful executive behind them—rather, the group selects only those that it can argue are reasonable to do and that are key for meeting company goals.

Of course, a spring cleaning isn't always a positive experience. You might have trouble letting go of pet projects. And sometimes, your company's culture can get in the way of the workshop. For example, in a culture where commitment and reliability are guiding values, you might find it particularly hard not to complete activities you've already started.

Keep in mind, too, that apart from escaping acceleration or using spring cleaning as an annual process, you can also use the method quite effectively when the company is engaged in a change involving rationalization, cost-cutting, or streamlining. Often, the beginning of such change processes spawns new executive responsibilities on top of your old ones, as well as added acceleration of company activities, leading to employee stress and exhaustion. By introducing a spring cleaning in the midst of such change, you reduce ineffective activities that only hinder forward movement. (See "Spring Cleaning at Phoenix Contact.")

Finally, you can also use spring cleaning when evaluating the results of an employee opinion survey or when measuring organizational energy. Typically after such a survey, companies conduct workshops to generate ways to improve the problems that employees identified. Our research has shown that, far from being helpful, these workshops often just add more stress to the workforce since they usually generate new tasks and responsibilities. In companies already operating under the pressure of increasing acceleration, employees see such new responsibilities as just more dead weight, additional work, and needless bureaucracy. In extreme cases, especially in companies already caught in an acceleration trap, employees purposefully list only positive responses in company surveys, simply to keep their workload from increasing—making the whole process a farce. See the box "Doing Spring Cleaning" for a summary of ways to make your organization's spring cleaning successful.

Changing a Culture of Acceleration

Just as important as escaping the trap is the prevention of future entrapment by changing the culture of acceleration in the organization. Sometimes, this means refocusing the company's management systems step by step, gradually reducing activities by outsourcing, for example. We will also describe other methods, such as taking time-outs, slowing down to speed up, and using feedback systems. (See "Summary of Steps to Prevent a Culture of Acceleration" for a quick list of the recommendations we put forth in more detail on the following pages.)

Spring Cleaning at Phoenix Contact

Sometimes, executives use change management or crisis in the organization as excuses to send their companies into an overaccelerated mode. Although this is an understandable response, in such tense times leaders should actually do the reverse. Not only can they stop the action during crisis management, but they must. Only by pausing and regrouping can leaders give their employees a clear understanding of the most important activities. That way, employees can participate in the necessary change activities on top of their normal jobs. Companies should always do some spring cleaning at the beginning of change processes, as this leads to openness for new actions. Moreover, it has a psychological benefit for employees. Stopping the action helps people overcome change fatigue and the feeling of overload, emotions that often appear at the beginning of change processes and that can lead to procrastination and a sense of paralysis.

As described in chapter 2, the German electronics developer and manufacturer Phoenix Contact responded to the fiscal crisis of 2008–2009 by requiring employees to work short time (not working one or two days per week) starting in April 2009. Although the company consequently did not dismiss a single employee, its capacities were significantly reduced by about 20 percent even while the overall workload stayed at the same levels.

Sensing the beginning of overload in the company, Gunther Olesch, executive vice president and member of the board, initiated a systematic process to reduce the workload across all units and hierarchical levels. In April 2009, Phoenix Contact started a worldwide ABC program, with all forty-six affiliates participating. The aim of the program was to reduce the workload by 20 percent and to prioritize tasks and projects. Projects of each business unit were ranked A, B, or C in order of priority, with A representing a necessary project, B an important task that would be postponed for a time, and C a project that could be delayed for two years or canceled. Managers were required to meet with their teams and classify all current and future projects of their divisions. Though the participants met within their own divisions, the decisions were made according to the relevance of each project for the entire company.

"At first, people said, 'We have only A tasks,'" Olesch told us. "I answered, 'Then classify your tasks as A1, A2, and A3. We have to move and cancel activities; otherwise, we burn out and we do not manage to come out of the crisis in good shape. We want to stand in a good position after the crisis. This means that we have to stand there ready to shoot when the race starts again, and this is only possible if we invest in innovation . . . during the crisis . . . and save our energy.'"

Even though it meant a reduced salary and intensified work, employees understood the necessity of the work-hour reductions. Through the ABC program, they identified between 20 and 40 percent of their activities that they could stop or freeze, which allowed them to manage the crisis while investing in innovation at the same time.

Doing Spring Cleaning

- Challenge your company by asking, "What should we stop doing?"

- Use the spring-cleaning method regularly, ideally every year and especially during change processes or after employee opinion surveys.

- When you do decide on a spring cleaning, follow a specific, standardized protocol that is well understood by all participants.

- Continually check the strategic importance of goals, tasks, and projects, and eliminate less-important activities.

- Use three categories to differentiate activities: *top priority, on hold,* and *stop doing.*

- Ask yourself, "What activities today would we not start again if we had not already begun them?"

- Use spring cleaning at both the company level and the division or work-group level.

- Involve all managers in the process.

Refocus the Company's Management Systems

As an executive who wants to protect your company from overaccelerating in the long run, you must learn to periodically refocus your company's management system. This method can be used in addition to

Summary of Steps to Prevent a Culture of Acceleration

Refocus the Company's Management Systems

- Use a management-by-objective (MBO) system that demands focus.

- Allow only three top-priority goals.

- Help your managers to understand the purpose of a new MBO system and its applications.

- Introduce stop-the-action initiatives and goals.

- Critically evaluate new projects before you start them.

- Use project-burying systems.

- Encourage your managers and employees to monitor projects constantly.

- Stop a project deliberately but compassionately if it seems unpromising.

Take Time-outs

- Help your employees to understand time-outs as an opportunity for regeneration that facilitates high performance on the next project.

- Act as a role model for time-outs.

- Design time-outs that serve both your company and your employees.

- Use organization-wide time-outs (e.g., a year without change), especially after periods of massive change or high performance.

Slow Down to Speed Up

- Systematically alternate high-energy phases with periods of calm or regeneration.

- Don't lower your expectations—instead, focus your company's engagement, attention, and effort on things that matter.

- Clearly define key activities and change phases.

- Establish beginning points and endpoints for key tasks.

- Create a pit-stop culture by establishing norms of focusing, refocusing, and slowing down to speed up.

Use Feedback Systems

- Watch for symptoms of excessive labor and overacceleration.

- Offer periodic employee self-assessments, 360-degree feedback, employee surveys, or a combination of these.

---

stop-the-action initiatives, since both ambitious and less dynamic organizations will always need a certain level of refocusing. You can choose between three methods of refocusing the company's strategy.

Pare down your goal-agreement system. Most companies have an internal system by which goals are set and agreed upon. But too often, this system can move a company toward an acceleration trap; rarely does it function as an instrument for disciplined focusing. Why? Usually, there's no limit on the number of objectives defined. A multitude of projects and tasks get listed in the yearly goal-agreement plan, making it difficult for individual employees and the company as a whole to escape the activity load. If the company's top levels start this overreaching process, then these decisions will cascade down, and overacceleration will spread throughout all company levels.

You should therefore limit the number of objectives you set each year. Some companies, finding themselves becoming caught in the acceleration trap, are purposefully changing their management-by-objectives system into a system that demands focusing.

For example Hans Schulz, when he was CEO of Balzers, a big international industrial enterprise headquartered in Liechtenstein, declared, "In our company, managers are no longer allowed to set or agree upon ten top-priority goals. The point of goal agreement is to give people an orientation, and to focus their action, attention, and energy. That's why we now expect them to focus on no more than three priority goals. These goals become our 'must-win battle'—goals that must be reached at any price and are not negotiable." This focused targeting resulted not only in a much more coordinated mode of operation, but also in the actual attainment of significantly more goals. Whereas before the new process, goal pursuit was diffuse, with employees all pursuing their individual ten priorities with little coordination, now everybody knows what is important. In the long run, the company was able to reduce an excess of energy and kept clear of the acceleration trap. "Our employees still work very hard," said Schulz. "But now it's a more satisfying job without the constant need to hurry. For our managers, the process meant a huge change—they have to show more courage now in their choices and they need to carefully manage their people toward each goal."

To be sure, old habits die hard; managers sometimes have great difficulty adjusting their behavior to a new, "decelerated" goal agreement system and often find many reasons why the system can't work in their particular case—and try to circumvent the obligation to focus. But focusing on just a few pared-down goals is important if your company hopes to stay out of the danger zone of acceleration. You might have to work extra hard to help your managers understand the purpose of the new system and to refocus on just a few key goals. You'll also have to offer managers help in applying the new rules (e.g., by coaching your people or through specialized workshops). In the end, this kind of visible involvement and unmistakable commitment by the top management should help the new system eventually take hold in your company—and help you then take the company one step further in paring down and focusing goals. For example, some companies focus on three top priorities and then allow three subgoals for each priority, making things a bit easier for managers who come from a long tradition of an accelerated management-by-objective (MBO) system.

Other companies handle their MBO system in an even more restricted fashion by requesting their managers to set or agree on stop-doing goals—a distinct number of activities or projects the employee stops during the next period—*with* their subordinates. Why? People tend to stick to their old and beloved activities and do not easily distance themselves from these projects. Therefore, it is important that initiatives that the company decides to stop doing are treated as seriously as the goals that employees set to achieve—and that they're given full top-management support.

At Hilti, for example, managers are sensitized through the company's cultural training program around the importance of energy and focus.[11] This also involves questioning existing activities and assigning them to stop-doing lists alongside management's usual to-do lists. These focusing and prioritizing activities are regularly discussed, and even at the top management level, both lists take top priority in discussions between the executive board and the executive committee.

Ultimately, by developing the discipline to concentrate on just a few key activities, and with the courage to disengage and abandon excess goals and tasks, you as a leader can transform your goal agreement into a system that helps your company focus and change a culture of acceleration.

Modify your project management system. A second way that you can refocus the company's systems strategy is to make sure that your project management system keeps the organization out of the acceleration trap. A project management system can be a great opportunity to help bundle, focus, and prioritize the firm's activities. But the systems often become overly bureaucratic rather than allowing the organization to purposefully assign resources to the most important, strategically crucial projects. As a result of many such systems, companies find themselves confronted with a flood of projects. In other words, the project management system is another process that you need to closely monitor and manage to keep it from becoming yet another source of overacceleration.

What can you do? We've seen companies modify their project management system by introducing two mechanisms. One mechanism is used at the beginning of a project cycle to ensure that the company separates the most important projects from the flood of other, less important projects. This mechanism comes in different shapes and forms. It can involve certain rules such as, "We start only a new project when another one has been finished." This mechanism can also be a version of playing devil's advocate and imply an early meeting in which everyone is invited to be skeptical and ask critical questions about the project. Or it can mean that people who want to initiate a project must show where the resources will come from and what they are ready to stop doing in order to start a new initiative. As a rule, then, it becomes much more difficult to actually start a project, which will help companies in the long run. Rather than allowing people to get caught up in the euphoria and excitement (and little reflection) that often accompanies the beginning of a new project, this mechanism ensures that critical questions get asked, such as, "Do we have the resources for this project?" "Who will lead and own the project?" and, the most difficult of all, "What other project or projects do we leave behind in order to have the capacity needed for this new project?" Experience shows that this mechanism leads companies to start far fewer projects—and focus on only those that are key to the organization's ultimate success.

A second mechanism that you can use, *project burying,* applies to later stages of the project cycle. It allows for projects to be stopped consciously and with dignity, rather than what often happens in companies—where even obsolete projects continue on with minimal effort. And even if these lame-duck activities are finally stopped, the people working on them try to hide that fact, because the company culture doesn't support a formal burying process and instead attaches a sense of guilt or shame to noncompletion. The whole process becomes totally absurd if a project is carried out pro forma long after everyone has realized that it isn't really promising.

Through project burying, employees and managers are explicitly encouraged to monitor projects and to stop a project if it turns out to have an unpromising future or no longer makes sense, given new priorities. At that point, the project is ended publicly, and employees go through a process of letting go of, and grieving over, what may have been a favorite (but doomed) project.

Such a culture of burying allows for employees and managers to take time to reflect on questions such as "What are the odds that this project will really be successful?" and "Are our resources and commitment well invested?" In many cases, answers to these questions will result in an even greater commitment for the project. But often, people already have a gut feeling that their answers will mean the end of a project. So the question then becomes "Do we have the courage to bury the project now, with dignity? Or do we wait until the project has to be taken off the company's agenda—without dignity?"

Project burying is particularly useful in very innovative areas; at the project's beginning, it's hard to estimate the chances that it will succeed. Only further into the project, after more information gathering, can the project's prospects be known—and then can be buried if necessary.

Focus on one thing only for a limited time. Preventing the growth of new activities is only one aspect of avoiding the acceleration trap. There's another crucial component: changing the company's hurry-up culture. Specifically, a special problem of an acceleration culture is that large projects do not get appropriate attention, space, and focus. Other activities stay unaffected, and centralized activities are continued alongside normal business. At the same time, expectations of extraordinary workloads and particularly demanding projects are often managed insufficiently. In acceleration cultures, it is often not the task itself that overexerts a company, but the time and effort it takes to plan and organize how the task will be accomplished. Ad hoc activities come on top of an already tense task situation, so that employees have no idea how long the stages of the exceptional efforts will last, when they'll see a light at the end of the tunnel, and how they should manage their energy.

That's why it is important for you to help your company to put on blinders for a specified period to pursue strategically important projects without distractions. When Lidl focused on opening twenty-nine supermarkets in Switzerland, the company underwent a massive growth. Lidl Switzerland grew from 70 people in November 2008 to 631 people in January 2009. To protect the employees at that time from overacceleration, Lidl called for a company-wide project ban between May and September 2009. All employees knew that they could exclusively focus on the opening of the twenty-nine supermarkets in Switzerland and would not have to expect any additional project work or unexpected extra activities. "We would never have been able to manage this enormous show of strength without this project ban," Andreas Pohl, CEO of Lidl Switzerland, told us. All ideas for potential future projects were collected on a list. But people knew that this list would not be discussed before September 2009. Once the stores had opened and were running well, Lidl declared an end to the strict focus period and Lidl executives discussed collected project ideas and prioritized them.

Take Time-outs

In the race for success, wise leaders create opportunities for the company to regenerate, to take a time-out. On the one hand, these time-outs provide employees with breaks from their day-to-day work. On the other hand, time-outs constitute an essential business task: a relaxing opportunity for creativity, reflection, or exploration.

Our research shows that, unfortunately, within a sample of service companies, an astonishing 78 percent of the employees complained that after stressful phases in their organizations, there wasn't enough time for regeneration. But as a leader, you need to have the courage to counteract this norm and allow for, or even actively establish, time-outs from project activity. And while you might fear that employees will lose momentum or become too relaxed, you still need to insist on these times of regeneration while communicating that a time-out does not mean a work break. Rather, it creates a period of regeneration to help employees prepare for high performance on the next project. It's not unlike the pit stops that race-car drivers take during races. These aren't meant to allow drivers to relax, but rather to prepare for the next stage, when they'll need to drive even faster. Time-outs in organizations, then, should serve a well-defined function: to purposefully support the productive efficiency of the company. Ideally, you will act as a role model and demonstrate how to use time-outs in a disciplined way to escape the acceleration trap and to limber up for even higher performance afterward.

A great example of modeling a time-out is Microsoft's Bill Gates. Every spring and fall, Gates retreats to his cottage for a so-called think week, taking with him all the ideas submitted by employees around the world. During the entire week, he is officially off e-mail and instead exclusively ponders the new ideas, thinking them through and evaluating them carefully. The think week is remarkable for at least four reasons. First, it allows Gates, arguably one of the world's busiest men, to retreat. Second, it allows him to focus entirely on a crucial business task—the selection of new directions in Microsoft's product development. Third, it saves Gates from being constantly bombarded with new ideas, which perhaps would have gotten lost or fizzled out during the year in the rush of his daily workload. Fourth, when Gates returns to day-to-day business, he feels refreshed, even though he has worked intensely during the think week. Today, forty-three of Microsoft's top executives follow Gates's pattern, and the think week has become a Microsoft institution. Think-week cochairs were chosen according to their influence and reputation inside the company as experts on particular subjects, along with their openness to new ideas and their ability to get the right ideas to the right people.

Time-outs obviously need to serve the company's goals. But usually, they turn out to be something good for employees, too. For example, Swiss International Air Lines has a policy for its flying staff. Under its "fit to fly" policy, pilots and flight attendants are allowed up to seven days off (in addition to their vacation) if they feel they're not in good condition to fly. At any time, even on short notice, these employees can call in and take up to seven days off without reporting the reason. "We believe our staff knows best when they are too stressed or overworked to fly. We do not ask further questions," explained Captain Thomas Bolli, former CEO of Swiss Aviation Training, the training company for the pilots of Swiss International Air Lines and still an active pilot for Swiss. Most important, Bolli told us, the policy benefits both employees and the company: "Customer satisfaction has clearly increased, because flight attendants who aren't authentically happy take days off. And our flight safety significantly increased. It is much higher than the flight safety at airlines that do not have such a policy."

Not just employees but sometimes entire organizations need time-outs. In the competitive race for IT leadership, Microsoft took a time-out for an entire year. In 2004, after a period of deep organizational change, Microsoft announced it wouldn't introduce any more changes for a full year. The break "helped employees recover from the immense efforts of our restructuring," said Ulrich Holtz, general manager for HR at Microsoft International. It's a tactic we see too rarely. In our study of ninety-two German companies, we found that in the forty-six caught in the acceleration trap, 86 percent of employees complained that their firms didn't provide adequate time for reflection and regeneration after stressful phases. Perhaps that's because leaders tend to view time-outs—of any length—as disruptions. We disagree. Time-outs are periods that allow for creativity and exploration. They prepare workers mentally and emotionally for the next phase of high performance, thereby increasing the company's productivity.

It is also important that you take time out to celebrate successes. Most companies do not celebrate ends. They think the completion of a project is a reward in itself. It isn't. Achievements and outstanding effort deserve acknowledgment. In particular, people need the feeling that a special challenge, a project, or a milestone is achieved and finished, before they are able to be open for something new. Often we are asked how long regeneration phases need to be. From a purely practical standpoint in most organizations, these phases can't last long, and they don't need to. It often is enough for you to clearly and unmistakably show acknowledgement of efforts, to look back on what has been achieved, and to thank the people involved.

As a leader, therefore, you need to make sure your organization stops and takes a moment to reflect and feel proud of accomplishments. These moments are rare, and too often leaders fail to savor them but rather rush full speed ahead into the next tunnel. Even though the tasks and efforts might be identical, the feeling is fundamentally different if you allow for a break in between tasks. The crucial difference lies between an employee's thinking, "One thing comes after the other" or "After this demanding task, there now comes another demanding task," versus "No matter how much we work, things just get more and more intense, and we never have time to finish one thing before they put another one on top." The last sort of statement leaves employees feeling that they can never work hard enough and that they never really achieve a goal, since new tasks can be directed from above, no matter how much effort employees put into the current race. They will always be the losers of this race; the finish line can be moved at any time. So, how fast will people want to sprint? Not very fast.

Executives often fear that if they appreciate or celebrate people's work, employees will reduce their engagement with the projects at hand. Surprisingly, the reverse is the case. True appreciation and celebration of accomplished goals help employees develop the self-confidence and pride they need to create new energy to achieve even more goals.

Juergen Dormann's Friday letters at ABB are a terrific example. In one letter, he set the tone of hopeful appreciation: "So, let's agree to put some champagne on ice. And let's continue our efforts to make our ABB great again, while we wait for the right moment to pop the corks." In a Friday letter a few weeks later, he officially declared the ABB crisis over, and he encouraged celebrations: "What we see today is more than just light at the end of the tunnel. This is the end of the tunnel."[12] Employees felt proud and relieved, though they knew that after the celebrations, the company would turn its attention to the next opportunity—and that everyone would be ready to meet the challenge.

Slow Down to Speed Up

Another strategy that you can use deliberately to protect your company from the acceleration trap is to systematically alternate high-energy phases, in which a great deal of energy is spent, with periods of calm or regeneration.[13] This strategy is especially important for companies going through a major change process. Typically, these companies are working at a very high pace, are exceptionally innovative, and are successful because of their strain and overacceleration, so it's key that they incorporate phases in which they can recharge their batteries.

To be sure, an overacceleration phase because of change initiatives or new strategies can be critical for a company's success. Top managers set strategic goals and formulate initiatives, but these often take the company beyond its limits, and in the long term, it loses focus by trying to do too many things simultaneously—without leaving enough time to complete any of them well or on schedule.

This doesn't mean that you should lower your expectations. Rather, to get out of this kind of acceleration trap, you can carefully define which activities and phases of a change process are key and give those the most attention and effort before you slow the organization down again to recharge and regenerate.

How can you finesse such a careful rhythm within a change process? Start by defining change episodes with a clear beginning and a clear endpoint, deliberately alternating between high-energy and lower-energy periods, thus differentiating between fundamental and incremental change.[14] This differentiation will help you manage employee expectations, among other things. People are much more willing to be stretched to their limits if they know that a phase of lower pace and less pressure awaits them at the end. If this light at the end of the tunnel is missing, they hold back their energy and take regeneration phases anytime and in any way they can get them. That means leaving everyone to find regeneration individually, rather than in a coordinated way across the company.

This strategy can be effective for more than just companies trying to manage fundamental change. In our research, we have seen how high-performance companies can use a rhythm of slowing down and speeding up within the standard business cycle, thereby working against the acceleration trap.

As recounted earlier in the book, the Swiss-based Sonova Group, the world market leader in hearing aids with $1.1 billion in sales, has enjoyed a constant growth rate of about 16 percent. Remarkably, the products the company launched over a recent two-year period generate a full 64 percent of the company's total sales. This is no flash in the pan; it has been part of the company's expected results for years. What's more, the company has shown that it can be exceptionally energetic and innovative over long periods. How? Sonova deliberately orchestrates the rhythm of its high-energy and regeneration phases.

With the appointment of CEO Valentin Chapero in 2002, the company committed itself to launching two completely new product generations per year.[15] Before these product launches—one each in mid-April and early November—the entire company goes into overdrive. R&D and marketing, the technicians, and the sales force work almost around the clock to ensure that another new product makes a precision landing. It is only through the workforce's readiness to regularly test the company's limits and, when required, to go beyond them that Sonova can maintain its extraordinary results in innovation. By regularly and systematically unleashing the organization's enormous power, Chapero consistently achieves peak performance—all while continually monitoring each phase in the company's ebb and flow. He makes sure he keeps a close eye on energy levels throughout the organization for signs of wear and tear from excessive energy use or from over-acceleration, which could lead to busy work.

The result? Sonova is significantly more innovative and growing faster than all its competitors. The company's two latest product generations are a case in point. In November 2006, Sonova joined with Steinway & Sons to bring to market an impressive, high-end hearing instrument, the Verve Steinway Edition. Its elegance and discreet design (high gloss, in piano black or piano white and bearing the Steinway logo) are targeted at the most demanding clientele. It sets new technological standards in the hearing care industry: Verve is the world's first hearing system to deliver information about its functions by "speaking" to the wearer in a clear, natural voice.

Five months later, in April 2007, Sonova launched Audéo, a "personal communication assistant" (PCA). Combining an innovative blend of cutting-edge engineering with award-winning design, Audéo is a tiny, light, and trendy hearing aid, and the first product designed to counteract the prejudice and resentment traditionally associated with hearing aids. Aimed at a younger—or at least younger-thinking—breed of consumers accustomed to wearing trendy Bluetooth earpieces and Apple iPod earbuds, Audéo comes with all the appeal of a must-have accessory.

Audéo is the most decisive step that Sonova has taken to realizing its vision that people in the future will all wear "hearings aids" as innovative gadgets for listening to music, catching the latest news when the devices are connected to the Internet, and telephoning (when the aids are combined with cell phones). And yes, sometimes the devices will be used as hearing aids. But Sonova's main vision is to produce hearing devices that are part of a chic, progressive lifestyle that combines the latest technology with modern design and brand value. The company is pursuing this vision while nurturing its high innovation momentum and taking care to sustain its energy by not overaccelerating. Indeed, the company's most recent returns show that the organization is achieving record results: in 2006–2007, revenues rose 23.8 percent to $1.1 billion, while its full-year net profit rose 40 percent to $226 million.

Create a pit-stop culture. Perhaps the most sustainable strategy of all for mastering the acceleration trap is for you to engage the organization in fundamental culture change. That process begins with a close examination of your culture for the signs and symptoms of overacceleration. Only when you have a clear picture about the type and severity of the acceleration culture within your company can you actively intervene to begin changing deeply rooted basic beliefs and the values (see the box "Building a Pit-Stop Culture at Hilti").

Use Feedback Systems

As a leader, you can use feedback systems to help change a culture of acceleration. In chapter 5, we will point to more specific ways that you

Building a Pit-Stop Culture at Hilti

Hilti, the Liechtenstein-based market leader in the construction and building maintenance industries, has achieved a culture change that centers around confidence, energy, and focus.[16] By regularly taking time out to examine priorities, company leaders ensure that Hilti concentrates on only its most important tasks while avoiding overactivity and overload. "Employees and the company culture are not soft-strategy elements, but key drivers of the company's success—one of the biggest secrets of our success," Michael Hilti, son of the founder and former chairman of the board of directors, told us. At Hilti, therefore, it has become possible to say "I am overloaded" or "This is too much." Employees know they can say no when they sense they are becoming overworked.

One important time-out occurs in the form of regularly scheduled workshops called Our Culture Journey. Every twenty-four months, all Hilti teams meet off-site for two days of reflection on their culture and their contribution as teams and individuals to Hilti's purpose and strategy. Christoph Loos, an executive board member responsible for human resources, finance, and IT, described the process: "We expose people to the envisioned culture and do exercises around it. We take them out of their comfort zone so that everyone can reflect on their own contributions." For example, each team and each individual is asked to define their main work focus. Eivind Slaaen, senior vice president of HR, told us, "When you ask people to list the things they should stop doing, this leads to defensive reactions. Therefore, we ask the question 'If we weren't already doing this activity, would we start it today?' This allows people to concentrate on the question of whether an activity is the right thing for our future."

One team training camp in Our Culture Journey, called Pit Stop, is designed to pay special attention to the idea of slowing down to speed up. Like formula car races, which are often not won on the course but in how well the race team carries out its pit stops, the main idea at this camp is to take a break, to step back, reflect, and align and realign ideas about what Hilti teams do and how they do it. After these pit stops, participants (executives, middle managers, and employees together) emerged refreshed, refocused, and ready to work with even higher energy on their most important tasks. The team camp also includes a so-called personal pit stop, which encourages individual team members to find ways to balance their personal energy reservoirs.

Hilti's pit-stop culture has resulted in many changes, including how leaders schedule meetings. "Business meetings are no longer scheduled past seven p.m., and business trips, whenever possible, start on Monday rather the weekend before," says Egbert Appel, a former Hilti executive board member who is now head of the Hilti foundation. Moreover, Hilti executives systematically try to reduce unnecessary work. For example, the company introduced an executive board workshop, where ideas can be presented briefly and still generate intense discussion—rather than requiring executives to prepare long, polished presentations with hundreds of backup slides. Such new rules, generated from the regular time-outs that Hilti takes to examine its culture, signal the organization as a whole about the expectations, preferred behaviors, and values that the company's top management supports.

---

can introduce and implement feedback systems, but for now we'll say that one special aspect of an acceleration culture is that the tendency to get caught up in too much work, at too fast a pace, is deeply rooted in the organization's behavior patterns. For example, you might notice that your employees routinely talk about how much they work, and they try to outdo one another with their stories. You can take this as a clear sign that some of the rules and norms of the organizational culture need to change if you hope to avoid the acceleration trap.

A feedback system can help you turn this culture around. Rather than watch employees complaining to each other about their workloads, for example, you can create a way for employees to give feedback on signs of possible overload and you can encourage them to do something about the problem. This can mean anything from periodic employee self-assessments, 360-degree feedback, or employee surveys.

Serview GmbH, a thirty-person IT consultancy headquartered in Bad Homburg, Germany, effectively uses feedback to address the challenges of its high-energy environment. The company regularly operates in the high-productive-energy zone, showing an above-average growth of 25 percent during the last four years.[17] The company's services demand a high amount of customer contact, travel, and commitment to high-quality-standards in the training programs Serview carries out. How does it maintain its energy without overaccelerating? It fosters a strong feedback system that the company specifically developed for this purpose. Called SMART, the system provides all employees with a monthly external assessment and self-assessment concerning fourteen aspects of the business that were jointly developed by the Serview employees. Among the fourteen aspects are factors like work quality, innovativeness, and personal appearance, but other aspects concern how the employees deal with regeneration and energy.

Since Serview established the SMART feedback system, a pronounced change in behavior has emerged. Employees not only take care of their own energy, but also look out for their colleagues' energy levels. They have learned to watch for symptoms of excessive labor and overacceleration and jointly work to develop solutions to overcome such problems as they arise. Moreover, SMART supports the company's high level of innovation. The system asks every employee to submit at least one innovative idea every month. Those ideas are not evaluated by the executive board, but rather by an internal employee group that assesses which ideas can realistically be implemented and which might lead to overacceleration.

Ideally, a company is fueled by what we call *sustaining energy*—a joyful urgency that is shared among employees and that can be constantly renewed and never burns out. Many CEOs get glimpses of this ideal, especially in energy-intense phases such as during high-speed growth or innovation, or in crisis situations, when the entire workforce is highly motivated to achieve critical goals. But if you as a leader get greedy, demanding the same level of urgency every day, the energy eventually fizzles and performance sinks, despite your employees' heroics. So the best advice we can give you is this: don't drive your company constantly to its limits. That often ends in an ongoing acceleration, a loss of focus, an uncontrolled flood of activities, organizational fatigue, and burnout. Be cognizant of the exertion that underlies every burst of effort, and work toward making sure the firm's energy is sustainable. This means continually monitoring, even when things are going smoothly, for signs that your company is slipping into the acceleration trap.

Now that we've looked at the acceleration trap, let's examine one final trap in which companies can find themselves: the complacency trap. This trap becomes a problem when companies have trouble sustaining productive energy. In the following chapter, we show you how to use a vitalizing management system that keeps the company operating with a proactive sense of urgency and a high level of productive energy.

Does an Acceleration Culture Permeate Your Company?

This checklist summarizes the typical symptoms found in companies with an acceleration culture. Answer each question and add up the score. (Up to 5 "yes" responses: virtually no acceleration culture exists; 6-10 "yes" responses: beware—some acceleration culture is present; more than 11 "yes" responses: danger zone—the company culture is already caught in the acceleration trap.)

Input Versus Output Orientation

- Do you value attendance more that goal achievement?
- Do you value hard effort over tangible achievements?
- Are your employees made to feel guilty if they leave work early?
- Do you hear your employees talk a lot about how big their workload is?
- Is busyness something that is valued within your company?
- Do you implicitly expect your managers to act as role models by being involved in multiple projects?
- Is *no* a taboo word to use in your company, even by someone who has already taken on too many projects?

Lack of Focus and Discipline

- Are activities started too quickly in your company?
- Is it hard in your company to get the really important things done because there are too many activities?

Lack of Courage to Stop Activities

- Is ending activities considered a sign of weakness within your company?

(continued)

- Are projects carried out pro forma, just because people fear ending them publicly?

- Do the employees in your company like to stick to routines and familiar tasks?

Lack of Regeneration Phases

- Does your organization have a tendency to constantly drive itself to the edge of its capacity?

- Are your employees chronically overworked?

- Is it impossible for your employees to see the light at the end of the tunnel because there is always too much to do?

Excessive Use of E-mail and Other Communications Technologies

- Is there a subtle or even an explicit expectation in your organization that people must respond to e-mails within minutes?

- Do countless people routinely get copied on e-mails, simply because employees are trying to protect themselves?

- In their free time, do employees keep their cell phones or messaging devices on because they feel that they always need to be reachable by someone in the company?

CHAPTER 5

Sustaining Energy to Rise Above Number One

Getting Beyond the Traps

While the last three chapters have shown how you can boost your company's energy and avoid getting caught in the complacency, corrosion, and acceleration traps, this chapter explores how to move beyond these traps altogether, toward *sustaining* your company's energy over the long haul. How can successful companies, organizations that are already top in their industries, stay agile and keep growing or changing? How can they rise above number one?

In some ways, this chapter particularly builds on what we learned in chapter 2 about escaping the complacency trap and energizing the company. Certainly, it's about avoiding complacency—but because it's about sustaining that energy for the long haul, it goes beyond the immediate solutions we have recommended for all three traps.

Even highly energetic and successful companies frequently become complacent and lose their ability to change and reenergize. Why? Our research shows that although leaders may know how to unleash energy, few know how to systematically sustain it. This brings us full circle, back to Lufthansa chairman Juergen Weber's critical question in the introduction: "What I really need to know now," he asked us, "is, how can I keep the energy at Lufthansa high in *good* times?" All highly successful companies, all market leaders, all companies that are number one in their industry, struggle with this challenge.

The Problem of Sustaining Energy

Leadership activities designed to increase your company's productive energy and to make your company *become* number one differ fundamentally from those needed to have your company *stay* number one. Specifically, executives find it hard to facilitate, on their own, what Hilti CEO Bo Risberg has called "a proactive sense of urgency." And this is a Herculean task. Sustaining the vital forces of enthusiasm, alertness, and high effort over the long term, while keeping energy loss at bay, is much more demanding than igniting the vital forces in the first place. No single leader, or single process, can possibly foster exceptional engagement, innovative thinking, emotional involvement, and passion for company challenges over the long term.

Think back to how much Lufthansa's success when fighting its crisis originally relied on Weber's influence, or how much ABB's turnaround early on depended on Juergen Dormann. Certainly, they were great leaders, "batteries" who gave their companies the charge to succeed—but they didn't *sustain* the changes in their companies all by themselves. Indeed, if the top management team is an organization's main and often only source of battery power, then the company is likely to be operating far below its potential. That's why both Weber and Dormann acted decisively to develop strong leaders everywhere in the company, to build organizational structures that empower people throughout the organization, and to develop a culture of action that would sustain momentum with the help of many sources of energy.

As a leader you need to establish and build a strong, *vitalizing management system* for sustaining productive energy and building a network of "batteries" throughout your company. Our research has shown that rather than relying on a few individuals who identify challenges (dragons) or opportunities (princesses) and energize the rest of the organization from the top to pursue them, the best organizations build systems with many batteries. That is, you should create a working environment where people are constantly stimulated, encouraged, and asked to challenge the status quo, to identify opportunities as well as possible challenges, and to take initiative to achieve at the highest levels. And an environment that constantly channels these activities toward a joint, ambitious goal of the organization.

What does such a management system look like? It's a highly vitalized version of the three basic organizational components: strategy, leadership structures, and culture. Essentially, you have to establish a unified system that converts *all* your people into batteries—triggering a proactive, widespread sense of urgency without losing your organization's focus.[1] Such a system comprises the following:

- Vitalizing *strategy processes* through which the strategy itself and its development and implementation are handled in an energizing way.

- Vitalizing *leadership structures* in which strong leadership is spread throughout the company, not concentrated just at the top.

- A vitalizing *culture* that promotes a proactive sense of urgency at every level of the organization.

These three components of a vitalizing management system literally keep the organization's energy running at full power. They create batteries in every area of the company. For several reasons, they work much better than just one source of energy (i.e., the company's top leaders). As we observed in many organizations that rely on a single top leader, when the CEO leaves (for whatever reason), energy plummets and the company begins showing signs of resignation or even paralysis.

The opposite could be observed at Hilti, a company whose executives have long invested in a vitalizing management and whose energy and performance is less dependent on the "big battery" at the top. In 2007, however, Hilti faced a test of its management system when three of its four executive board members were retired within a two-year period—including

CEO Pius Baschera. How truly independent was Hilti from their sources of energy at the top? "Yes, it is a change of people, but it is continuity in the culture and values and it is continuity in the direction and strategy of the company," Baschera, today chairman of the board of directors, told us. January 1, 2007, marked the official start date of the new company leadership, and the transition went very smoothly—almost silently. We describe later in the book how Hilti developed the vitalizing management system and managed the transition.

Companies that, like Hilti, use many sources of potential ideas and inspiration and people who perceive challenges or opportunities, are much more energetic, swift, and adaptive than others. That's why CEOs should enrich their own worldview through systematically tapping into their staffs, the people closest to the market. Your challenge as a leader, then, is not to energize individuals but to create an environment where people are continuously encouraged to be alert and agile and to take initiative around the company's joint focus of energy. In June 2008 when the global financial crisis showed its first signals, Swiss CEOs participated in a debate about whether, and to what extent, CEOs could manage the risk to their business.[2] Participant Valentin Chapero of Sonova argued for precisely this kind of energized management system: "I cannot control the full risk on my own. But it is my task to create an environment where people are sensitized and actively alerted and take action when there is smoke or fire."

When innovation, customer relationships, and flexibility are important for an organization's success, companies have to rely on many sources of inspiration, ideas, and instant reaction to market changes. This is true for all organizations, but particularly relevant for those led by CEOs whose jobs separate them from daily market developments. George Day and Paul Schoemaker studied the importance of open-ended foresight among CEOs.[3] Only 23 percent of the companies in their study were headed by CEOs who regularly looked for weak signals outside the company and applied strategic foresight. The other 77 percent relied only on their CEO to carry out innovation or strategic change, and therefore, such forward thinking was limited.

To sustain energy and move beyond the energy traps, then, you should develop and foster a vitalizing management system that allows and encourages your managers and employees to be sources of high productive energy.

Organizations should actively use all three components of their management system simultaneously—strategy processes, leadership structures, and culture—and align them closely with their work to vitalize the organization.

Let's look now at how the first component, the strategy process, can work to help sustain high productive energy.

Vitalizing Strategy Processes

To develop strategies that systematically instill a proactive sense of urgency in the entire organization while sustaining its productive energy, you must invest not just in the *what* of a strategy, but also in the *how* of the strategy process. This process involves four steps (figure 5-1):

- **Craft a shared strategy:** Include unambiguous, ambitious goals, milestones, and interim successes.

- **Home a radar for weak signals:** Involve people in identifying relevant trends, opportunities, and the need for change.

- **Overcome blinders:** Include different perspectives in strategy development.

- **Regularly review strategy:** Seriously question the status quo.

FIGURE 5-1

Components of a vitalizing management system: strategy processes

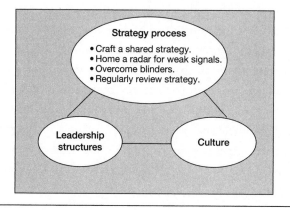

Craft a Shared Strategy

A strong strategy that is shared and internalized by everyone in the company will help your company sustain energy and instill the enthusiasm, mental alertness, and effort that will last over time. *Involve as many people as possible* in creating the strategy process, either in developing the goals and in communicating them, so that people make the goals their own. Not only must you lay out convincing reasons for the goals, but you also need to engage employees' emotions around those goals to make the connection to their own work tangible.

For example, in the summer of 2009, top executives of Germany's BMW, one of the leading corporations in the automotive industry, discovered that their employees were not sufficiently internalizing their company's Number ONE (named for "new opportunities" and "new efficiency") strategy. A survey had shown that although the strategy was well known throughout the company, not all managers and employees could equally relate to it in their actual day-to-day work. In the fall of 2009, the executive board therefore launched an initiative called Number ONE on Tour—a large-scale series of strategy workshops for BMW managers.

Between the fall of 2009 and the summer of 2010, more than 8,000 middle and lower managers attended the ten-hour workshops, which were facilitated by 180 executives and an additional 250 internal specialists in cross-divisional teams—a further demonstration of the shared, organization-wide commitment to the company strategy. Participants not only learned more about the strategy content, but also viewed new product developments and discussed the Number ONE strategy in groups. They also engaged in activities designed to cement their commitment and motivation, such as viewing motivational videos about BMW's past and future. "The personal commitment and open communication from top management was persuasive," one participant reported. "I feel highly motivated now to bring these messages back to my own team." "The high level of discussion quality and enthusiasm was impressive," added Harald Krüger, BMW board member and mentor of Number ONE on Tour. "We achieved our main target to gain a common understanding of our strategy, and we surpassed our own expectations, creating and encouraging optimism and a shift towards a high-performance organization."

The return on investment of such an activity far outweighs the investment—under one important condition: continuity. The strategy must stay in place over a reasonable length of time. In companies that lack continuity and change their strategies too quickly, the building of a shared understanding of the strategy will be too costly and time- and work-intensive. The project head of Number ONE on Tour explained this: "Number ONE on Tour was an enormous amount of work and coordination for top management, the human resources management, and the whole organization. But it was fully worth it. The engagement at all levels is now apparent, with everyone focused on shared priorities."

It's those priorities that can make all the difference; to make a shared strategy effective, you must concentrate on a selected *set of clearly defined goals* that will create a distinct focus for the company. That doesn't mean reducing expectations or engagement around other aspects of the company's performance. Rather, choose very carefully which objectives are paramount, so that people's enthusiasm, attention, and effort can flow toward those objectives rather than toward their daily routine. For example, one of Lufthansa's successful company-wide strategic initiatives, Program 15, was designed around reducing just one metric, the cost of transporting one aircraft seat one kilometer, from 17 to 15 German pfennigs.

These goals for your top activities should be *ambitious*. As with Lufthansa's Program 15, the goals need to be challenging, creating a realistic stretch for employees, and be meaningful enough to continuously energize them.[5] At Phoenix Contact, the company goal is simple and clear: to be "best in class." And these goals must be shared; what makes Phoenix Contact unique is how it combines this ambition with an impressively broad scope of commitment—all units, from information technology to human resources and marketing, are included in the company's goal setting.

However, you also need to go beyond shared commitment to ensure that your managers and employees engage in *joint activities* to act on the organization's strategic goals. At Continental AG, former CEO and chairman Hubertus von Gruenberg noticed a deep division between the strong research-driven R&D group and the marketing and sales group (the two groups basically were not working together on some important products). As described in chapter 3, he started holding so-called

research-development-engineering meetings (RDE meetings). By join-
ing these differing groups regularly and giving them a significant role in
setting strategy and by allowing individuals to express their views freely,
von Gruenberg actively involved various groups of people in important
decisions. The RDE panel was immediately able to set its strategic priorities, provide resources, and develop joint commitment and activities
around each project—thus instantaneously bringing together differing
company factions to take action.

Milestones that you set for your strategies can punctuate the long-term
journey with defined energy peaks and phases of normal engagement, as
discussed in chapter 4. Milestones are also perfect tools to systematically
mark and celebrate an interim success. They work both to positively
stimulate the organization, creating more energy, and to remind everyone
that the final goal still looms on the horizon. These milestones are particularly important to sustain the human forces in your company over the
long term.

Lufthansa used a sequence of strategic programs (Program 93, Program 15, Operational Excellence, D-Check, and Upgrade) to maintain
energy for more than a decade. The company developed and launched
these strategic programs step by step, with each program pursuing a time
horizon of three years and a particular focus.

Phoenix Contact launched its Strategy 2020 in a different way. It defined and communicated in advance the main milestones (e.g., communication & leadership, quality, innovation, culture, service, investment,
and personnel) that the company intended to pursue to achieve its overall
strategy. Integrating these milestones with best-class performance in all
parts of the company and integrating them with the leadership system are
what made Phoenix Contact's overall vitalizing management system so
robust and effective. (We'll discuss Phoenix Contact's strategy in more detail later in the chapter.)

Whichever method you choose, a progress dashboard is the perfect way
to keep these milestones front-of-mind. For its D-Check program,
Lufthansa published a monthly "D-Check barometer" describing the
company's interim results. It showed in exact numbers what D-Check had
achieved in terms of cash flow generation and what remained to be done
to meet the program's final objective. Because the report was published

both on the company's intranet and on the wider Internet, employees and outside stakeholders alike could monitor progress and celebrate successes along the way.

Home a Radar for Weak Signals

Once you have generated a strong, shared strategy with clear, ambitious goals and with milestones, you need to turn to monitoring the world around you to understand the threats to, and opportunities for, that strategy. Your strategy should be flexible and tied closely to the market so that it can react at a moment's notice—this will help combat tendencies of complacency, inertia, and overconfidence.[6] For a *highly efficient early warning system* you typically need to include many people in the organization who are sensitized for spotting subtle trends and other weak signals.[7] Employees charged with such a mission feel energized by the mere sense that their perception counts. They are constantly more alert and mentally involved. Although early warning systems have a long and widespread tradition, they often fail to produce real pressure for immediate change, because they emphasize financial data or are poorly connected to the strategy process and therefore do not produce a sustained boost for the strategy.[8] When a company's radar is focused on financial metrics, threats such as losing touch with customer demands or low innovation levels show up too late. Rather than acting with urgency, these companies operate under a false sense of security. The result? Executives realize the need to change so late that only a crisis-oriented mobilization strategy—with high strain on everyone's energy reserves—can keep the company afloat. Furthermore, because early warning systems are often completely detached from the strategy process itself, managers and employees are often unwilling to work with the system and share their knowledge through this system.

Companies with vitalized management systems avoid these pitfalls. The way the Hilti Group handles strategy shows a very careful consideration of energy-related aspects.[9] As a longtime global leader of construction and building-maintenance products, Hilti faced the challenge of generating an ongoing sense of proactive urgency throughout the company. To address this challenge, Hilti instituted the Competition Radar tool in 1994. The company observes its competitors, relying especially on

Hilti employees who have regular, direct contact with customers.[10] All of the company's salespeople—60 percent of its employees—are integrated into the process. Each person with customer contact is called upon to analyze the market, actively talk with customers not only about Hilti but also about competitors' activities, and record the relevant or new developments that customers mention about a competitor. The salesperson enters this information into the Competition Radar. Thus, Hilti maintains a systematic market orientation, and company leaders are constantly able to observe weak signals in the environment. What's more, executives do not keep the competitor information to themselves, but instead circulate it regularly throughout Hilti. In this way, people in different parts of the organization can become aware of market developments, stay alert, and realize the possible needs for change. The general managers of Hilti's marketing groups meet every six weeks to discuss with their teams the implications of the Competition Radar tool, particularly the strategic activities of competitors Bosch, Black & Decker, Würth Group, Fischer, and Makita.

Hilti uses two more sources of information to complete the picture and identify new directions. First, employees are regularly asked about their experiences and impressions; second, Hilti periodically conducts comprehensive customer satisfaction surveys. "The various sources of information we receive are like the tiny tiles in a mosaic depicting the market situation," Baschera told us. "We are constantly measuring ourselves against them." Hilti acts very early on the first indication of irritation before a crisis emerges, rather than only after external pressure arises. Despite its market leadership and therefore increased risk of complacency, Hilti systematically stays on top of market developments, and the company's alert employees significantly contribute to this awareness.

The best strategic early warning systems use four key operating principles that enable organizations to react early to initial weak signs of an opportunity or crisis:

- Adopt a radar process, so that employees are not just stumbling on threats by chance.

- Include quantitative and qualitative as well as externally and internally oriented indicators.

- Engage employees across the organization to watch for weak signals.

- Regularly share radar information throughout the organization.

How do you incorporate these broad findings into the strategy itself? That's the next step in the strategy process.

Overcome Blinders

Often, a company is operationally blind and misses market developments because it relies on only a small senior management circle—the board of directors and a few selected senior managers—to develop its strategy. With the early warning system in place, you as an executive should include in any strategy review the valuable feedback that comes from units close to the market, as well as external expert opinions. This not only keeps the strategy focused and realistic, but also keeps complacency at bay. It means that strategic decisions are backed up by the most current information, and thus it is easier to unlearn basic misguided assumptions and frameworks. Furthermore, when remote units visibly participate in strategy, alertness for new developments and necessary changes increases both in the units and at the top of your company. Finally, this connected strategy process connects the decentralized strategies with one another and with the overall company strategy.

Companies that merely pay lip service to such a process do so at their peril. In one organization we studied, information was collected from decentralized units, but the company leaders ignored the information when making their final strategic decisions. As one manager recalled, "We were asked to regularly report on trends on the market. 'What are the customers saying? Can you identify moves from competitors when you talk to your clients?' I got curious and tried to find out internally what portion of all this information ever got used by our executives. No one could tell me, not even whether it was condensed and processed for presentation in strategy meetings. After we discovered that reality, you can imagine how quickly the flow of information ebbed, at least from me and the people in my unit." This kind of mistake quickly destroys employee engagement and ensures a loss of energy in the long term.

To sustain energy by ensuring that the company direction isn't driven solely from the top, IBM created a format, called jam events, to involve all its 399,409 employees worldwide in contributing to strategy and cultural development. Beginning with its first WorldJam in 2001—a three-day online discussion between employees from all divisions, geographic locations, and levels in the hierarchy during which people posted six thousand comments in seventy-two hours, with over 6 million hits on the intranet page—IBM has used its global intranet to enable employees to participate in discussions, express their opinions, and offer ideas. Sam Palmisano, IBM's CEO, president, and chairman, said that the jam events helped IBM "create a management system that empowers people and provides a basis for decision making that is consistent with who we are at IBM."

Since the first jam event, IBM has conducted a series of annual jam sessions, each focused around a different issue, such as culture or innovation. They have proven to be a powerful tool, illustrating the importance of employee involvement in strategic decisions and trend monitoring. Strong feedback from employees has indicated that they appreciate being taken seriously and have become more interested in the company's strategy as a result. What's more, IBM can now be sure that its strategies are based on the most current information, perception, and experience of people at all levels and areas of the company. The events have proven lucrative as well: ideas generated during two Innovation Jams, in 2006 and 2008, resulted in a total estimated $700 million-plus in revenue. The company has served as a role model for other organizations: Nokia and Swiss Re have adopted similar kinds of company-wide innovation sessions.

Regularly Review Strategy

With all this information in hand, you need to regularly review your company's strategy and openly call it into question. By regularly reviewing and questioning your company's strategy, you are enhancing your company's ability to gain "second-order learning."[11] Additionally, by reevaluating your company's actions, basic philosophy, and norms—its entire framework—you are keeping it viable and responsive to change. Doing so will maintain enthusiasm, alertness, and a high level of activity for the organization's overall goals.

This doesn't mean that you automatically change the strategy drastically each year. That would only promote executive burnout and potentially drive your company into the acceleration trap. It is much healthier when you continuously develop the company's strategy using several perspectives and then defining the necessity and scope of any change in strategy.

Take, for example, the Hilti Group's strict process for reviewing its strategy.[12] The executive management group (EMG) monitors the overall strategy in a so-called strategy control process. In the ten largest countries and then in all business units, the EMG scrutinizes each respective strategy annually to ensure that Hilti continually evolves as a company. Since 2001, the four members of the executive board and fifteen managers from the next level convene an annual three-day workshop. There, they scrutinize the progress made in the last year regarding strategic goals and projects; put themselves in the shoes of their main competitors for identifying opportunities and threats; and, finally, draw conclusions about Hilti's existing strategy. Their analysis draws on information from sources as varied as customer surveys, Competition Radar, employee surveys, and employee breakfasts.

"The EMG meetings provide a means for facing facts in the most brutally direct way," said Baschera. "And the effect has been phenomenal— you can see the changes throughout the entire company, even just one day after the meeting. A sense of urgency around key topics emerges in the company once again, along with the commitment to really take them on."

This strategy process—from creating a shared strategy to keeping that strategy humming through regular checking—is a key element in keeping your organization engaged and energetic over the long term. But to execute the strategy, you must have the right leadership structures in place, and they too must be energized.

Vitalizing Leadership Structures

The responsibility for mobilizing and maintaining an organization's energy falls uniquely to leadership. But especially when it comes to maintaining energy, as one of the company's top leaders, you cannot go it alone. Rather, you must develop a leadership system that prepares, enables, and fully involves all people throughout the organization, turning each of your managers into strong leaders. This helps leaders at all levels be the source for enthusiasm, alertness, and effort of their team and thus sustains productive energy in the company. Leadership must become a core capability of your organization. Today's environment of flattened and networked organizational structures makes sharing leadership necessary—and yet too often, it is still not the reality.

Leaders are often reluctant to make their organization less dependent on them, for a number of reasons. First, executives may fear that sharing leadership will make them redundant. But we argue that instead, it will energize the company at all levels—including their own. Second, some leaders do not believe that line managers want or need to be involved in understanding the company's strategy. One company asked us to measure its organization's energy, but only wanted us to survey the first four of its six managerial levels. One leader made his reasoning quite clear: "These supervisors are not knowledgeable enough. They do not need to know the details. I also suspect that a typical team manager is not interested in the logic and potential conclusion for her or his units. They only want to focus on their daily business." Not only did this firm openly doubt the abilities of many of its managers (and those managers' potential for initiative, innovation, and role modeling), but it also was engaging in what we consider systematic and sustained energy destruction. After all, this was a company whose business success relied almost 100 percent on how well employees at the lowest hierarchical level interacted with customers. There is no reason that the energy level of these employees should not be measured—or developed—just as any other employee at any level.

Energy measurements such as the Organizational Energy Questionnaire (OEQ) can clearly reveal to what extent you as a leader are succeeding at this goal. Run the assessment twice, the first time evaluating the energy in the team of your direct reports and, the second time, evaluating the energy in the whole company (or in the area for which you are responsible, in larger companies). The first energy profile often shows significantly better results than the second one; this shows that while you might be able to lead the members of your team, you might be less able to turn that team into leaders themselves. In other words, executives are often able to transfer the energy spark to their team, but many neglect to transfer it to others as well.

Managers often aren't even aware that they're expected to lead, and if they are, their daily responsibilities preclude their ability to look for opportunities, challenge the status quo, and instill enthusiasm in their people. These leaders are not properly prepared to sustain energy in their own people. But that's exactly where the first patches of complacency or inertia begin to emerge.

A first step toward developing strong leadership in the entire organization is to simply tell managers that it is their job to inspire and energize their teams. A second decisive step is a systematic approach to leadership for the entire organization—one that keeps productive energy flowing freely from the top down to the lowest levels of the company and back in order to instill a sense of proactive urgency throughout. To do this, you need to work on several facets of leadership structures (figure 5-2):

- Develop energizing leaders across all hierarchical levels.

- Develop flexible structures that encourage informal relationships.

- Create and leverage energizing customer touch points.

FIGURE 5-2

Components of a vitalizing management system: leadership structures

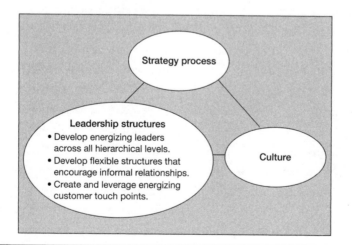

Strategy process

Leadership structures
- Develop energizing leaders across all hierarchical levels.
- Develop flexible structures that encourage informal relationships.
- Create and leverage energizing customer touch points.

Culture

Develop Energizing Leaders Across All Hierarchical Levels

The first step in developing leaders who are energizing is simply to encourage strong leadership behavior among all managers and employees, across all hierarchical levels. As a top leader, you must ensure that people at all levels feel a true sense of accountability for continually questioning the status quo and sustaining the productive energy of the company. You also need to enable managers throughout the hierarchy not only to lead actively themselves but also to foster a strong leadership climate down through their own units. Middle managers and front-line line managers must be perceived as strong leaders who lead with one voice—demonstrating leadership behavior that sustains organizational energy rather than drains it.

ABB learned this lesson the hard way. As recounted in chapter 3, during the era of Percy Barnevik, ABB relied on this CEO's charisma and strengths. The firm prospered, but Barnevik's presence made it difficult for new talent to grow. As HR director Gary Steel told us, "Like a large tree with strong roots and solid foliage, he overshadowed everything that grew beneath him so that it could not flourish." As a result, ABB leadership talent dwindled not only near the top but also throughout the entire organization.

The response was a new ABB people strategy, created by CEO Juergen Dormann and his executive board members, especially Steel, who articulated one of the strategy's three basic principles: "Leadership within ABB is not restricted only to managers and positions with people responsibility. Leadership is self-leadership and leading others. Leadership means finding the right composition of delegation and accountability to enable an individual contribution for achieving the objectives of ABB." People throughout ABB, therefore, now were expected to live the new ABB community spirit—one that embodied elements such as openness, transparency, willingness to engage in dialogue, respect, clear responsibility and accountability, and goal implementation.

Of course, while you must encourage energizing leadership everywhere in the organization, for this approach to be taken seriously, you need to back up this encouragement with formal leadership development and continuous feedback. Sound leadership development creates better leaders and a foundation for healthy, high levels of excitement, alertness, and effort throughout the company. For example, to make this idea an integral part of ABB's activities, the company started the so-called Leadership Challenge Program in 2003. The program worked on the capability of each employee to show leadership behavior that would contribute to ABB's sustainable success. By 2010, more than forty thousand people had taken part in the program—ABB employees as well as contractors and customers—over the course of 1,100 seminars in fifteen languages and in forty-three countries. As an executive or board member, you must embrace leadership development as a key responsibility with exactly this kind of programmatic drive to oversee, steer, and engage in nurturing leadership talent in every corner of the organization.

But what, specifically, should the content of this development of energizing leadership be? Top management needs to clearly communicate what good leadership means in the organization and to ensure that these principles apply to every employee with leadership responsibilities. Keep away from facile clichés such as "be cooperative," "be a team player," or "communicate openly," and instead make your goals for good leadership company-specific. However, there are some leadership behaviors that have proven to sustainably energize employees and foster performance across all organizations, and two we find particularly effective are inspirational leadership and prevention-oriented leadership.

Foster organization-wide inspirational leadership. Inspirational leadership is the leadership style associated with the winning-the-princess strategy in that it calls on leaders to place a positive and emotionally compelling goal or vision in front of their people and to then act on the vision. As with the winning-the-princess strategy itself, this leadership behavior can be extremely effective for activating positive energy in units or entire organizations. It can be used by leaders at all levels, from senior executives to middle and lower managers.[13] A long research tradition has supported the positive impact of inspirational leadership.[14] Our own empirical research shows that companies with high inspirational leadership, compared with those with low to average inspirational leadership, possess better energy profiles (figure 5-3). These companies have significantly higher productive energy (14 percent) and comfortable energy (17 percent) and significantly lower corrosive energy (−19 percent) and resigned inertia (−14 percent). Furthermore, the companies with strong inspirational leadership

FIGURE 5-3

An inspirational leadership climate

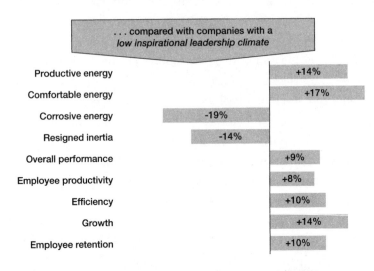

... compared with companies with a
low inspirational leadership climate

Productive energy	+14%
Comfortable energy	+17%
Corrosive energy	-19%
Resigned inertia	-14%
Overall performance	+9%
Employee productivity	+8%
Efficiency	+10%
Growth	+14%
Employee retention	+10%

Note: Data based on a sample of 14,300 employees from 104 German companies in 2009.

scored higher on overall performance (9 percent), employee productivity (8 percent), efficiency (10 percent), growth (14 percent), and employee retention (10 percent).[15]

Four behaviors have been established as the major levers of inspirational leadership: (1) acting as a role model, (2) inspiring people for a joint vision, (3) intellectual stimulation, and (4) individualized support.[16] CEO Martin Strobel of the Baloise Group, for example, relied on these four behaviors to help his employees follow the company's new customer-promotion strategy while they honed their own individual leadership abilities.[17]

When inspirational leaders *act as role models,* employees identify with these leaders and are inspired to do similar things. For example, Strobel mobilized his organization by personifying the necessary learning that needed to happen if the unit were to succeed, and he modeled that learning to his people through his visit to U.S.-based Progressive Insurance and his subsequent working sessions to share his findings—knowing that any new understanding of the insurance business would have to begin with himself.

Strobel also demonstrated *inspirational motivation*—which charges leaders to articulate and communicate a vivid, attractive, and compelling vision and thereby energize leadership capabilities throughout their teams. As we discussed with the princess strategy, because employees feel motivated when they know they are contributing to something larger than themselves, managers who can articulate a tangible and inspiring vision for the future can inspire their people to invest their full energy toward that vision.[18] Strobel provided a clear picture of the rather bold company vision to improve the customer-promotion focus of his employees, by offering many examples and descriptions of his findings to his employees of what the immediate and future work environment of the company would look like—thus helping his people develop a personal connection to the end goal. For example, Strobel used a series of three training seminars to present eighty of his employees with many examples from Progressive Insurance and other companies such as UBS and Hilti. These examples illustrated what Baloise Switzerland's new strategy would look like and what it would mean for each manager and employee. The employees thus experienced concretely what it meant, for instance, to identify the right customer needs—that is, those that also made the business profitable—and it applied to every individual insurance offering that Baloise made.

Strobel *intellectually stimulated* his followers as well, encouraging them to take risks and to challenge the established ways of doing things and charging his people with trying out new ideas and solutions to old problems. For example, by drawing on the mission statement of Wells Fargo, a U.S. bank that focuses on how employees can help customers feel enthusiastic and deeply emotional about the company, Strobel helped his people to grasp the excitement that the new strategy meant for the organization. By crafting a similar statement for his own employees, he was able to unleash their passion to get their customers excited about the company's insurance offerings—something that few people even inside the company thought would be possible. In addition, Strobel drew on his knowledge of Progressive Insurance to develop a new vision for innovative insurance offerings at Baloise. The American company charged different rates for its auto insurance depending on the city and related volume of traffic, and Baloise decided to follow a similar model. At the same time, Strobel chose a different way to challenge the thinking of his sales force. He started by looking internally at the sales representatives' best practices and concluded that the top 5 percent of the force were already working with the new concept. Strobel then used these examples to open up and stimulate the thinking of others in the sales force.

Finally, Strobel offered his people *individualized support,* acting as a coach and taking into account the leadership-development needs and potential of each employee. Strobel and his team also worked with outside career coaches, who trained the sales force individually on the job to develop their strengths and to implement the new strategy in customer interactions.

Ultimately, Strobel's inspirational leadership approach greatly improved the situation at Baloise Switzerland by mobilizing his people for the new vision and strategy. When the press reported the positive developments at Baloise, Strobel used these reports to further reinforce the change, and by 2006, Baloise was able to report a before-tax profit of $272 million.

Foster organization-wide prevention-oriented leadership. While leading with inspiration focuses on potential gains and opportunities (winning the princess), *prevention-oriented leadership* focuses on possible losses or harm, as in the slaying-the-dragon strategy. This method can sustain even more energy, because leaders can mobilize their teams' potential by inciting them to prevent possible damage from an identifiable dragon.

Leaders at all levels of the organization can draw on three specific behaviors of prevention-oriented leadership: (1) emphasizing existing and potential threats, (2) strengthening people's confidence that they can cope with the challenges, and (3) nurturing employees' sense of progress and impact.[19] As with the slaying-the-dragon strategy, prevention-oriented leadership is based on leaders' readiness and courage to deal with problems directly, openly, and uncompromisingly by involving team members in a shared problem-solving process. Our own empirical research shows that companies with high prevention-oriented leadership have better energy profiles than companies with low prevention-oriented leadership (figure 5-4). The companies with high prevention-oriented leadership have higher productive energy (3 percent) and comfortable energy (1 percent), but lower corrosive energy (–4 percent) and resigned inertia

FIGURE 5-4

A prevention-oriented leadership climate

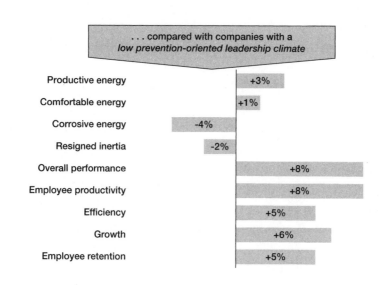

... compared with companies with a
low prevention-oriented leadership climate

Productive energy	+3%
Comfortable energy	+1%
Corrosive energy	-4%
Resigned inertia	-2%
Overall performance	+8%
Employee productivity	+8%
Efficiency	+5%
Growth	+6%
Employee retention	+5%

Note: Data based on a sample of 14,300 employees from 104 German companies in 2009.

(–2 percent). What's more, companies with strong prevention-oriented leadership scored higher on overall performance (8 percent), employee productivity (8 percent), efficiency (5 percent), growth (6 percent), and employee retention (5 percent).[20]

Because prevention-oriented leadership complements inspirational leadership in a meaningful way, you should balance each within your company's leadership principles with these two concepts. In this way, you convey a compelling picture of the future while at the same drawing attention to short-term challenges and possible threats.

Foster a general leadership climate in the organization. A leadership climate doesn't describe single leaders and their behaviors, but describes the collective, shared pattern of behaviors in the leadership of your organization. For example, an inspirational leadership climate would be defined as the shared degree of inspiring behaviors that the leaders within an organization collectively direct toward their subordinates.[21] Our studies show that in the eye of the employees on average, only 16 percent of the companies actually have a strong inspirational leadership climate, whereas the majority had a medium (69 percent) or weak (15 percent) inspirational leadership climate.[22]

Build management structures to align with leadership principles. Only when the top team ensures that all managers align their behavior with the company's leadership principles will such principles become credible (see the box "Leadership Principles at Phoenix Contact").

You need to make sure that the company's leadership principles are reflected in the management system—its structure and incentives. When leadership principles clash with incentives—if a principle calls for team orientation but the company awards individual performance—the principles will never be considered relevant in daily business. But by creating this alignment, you can make the company's leadership principles explicitly an important factor in any decisions—for instance, for all personnel decisions such as selection, evaluation, feedback, or promotion as well as sanctions or even dismissals.

In fact, all business-related issues should be decided within the rubric of the company's leadership principles—for example, change-management issues, the implementation of a new strategy, or relationships with partner firms. This approach is followed at Fujitsu Microelectronics Europe (FME), a supplier of semiconductor products for a range of markets.[23] Leadership quality is a core mission for FME's strategically oriented human resources department. In 2003, the culture and values of the company were discussed and explicitly defined, including FME's leadership principles. Since that time, leaders have been selected and trained according to the principles, and the principles are part of the 360-degree feedback process. Moreover, all managers are regularly assessed on their leadership style and goal achievement—an assessment explicitly based on the company values and leadership principles.

How you deal with those who deviate from the norm is also important. Many companies hesitate to penalize employees when behavioral principles or leadership guidelines are ignored or violated. But rather than considering good leadership a "nice to have," you as a member of top management need to communicate the vital importance of company values and leadership principles and the penalties for not taking them seriously.

Be on your guard when managers deviate from the established leadership norm. Our research has clearly shown that it takes only a few outliers

Leadership Principles at Phoenix Contact

In 2003, Phoenix Contact set a goal to not only maintain the company's number one status in its core business but also to become best-in-class in all other areas such as IT, marketing, human resources management, and logistics. The top management team was aware that this ambitious vision could never be realized without strong leadership at all levels. Accordingly, Phoenix Contact developed a long-term and company-wide program to develop leaders at all levels. This program trained managers to prepare for challenges that the company envisioned up through 2010, and taught them how to inspire their teams for the new vision and involve them in identifying problems.

Phoenix also listed its corporate principles in a document known simply as "The Principles." The document provides a basis for any actions that Phoenix employees take, and the executive management team reviews and discusses these principles every two years in a strategy workshop focused on the future position of the company.

These corporate principles are the guidelines for everyone at Phoenix and provide a strong basis for maintaining high energy and strong leadership throughout the ranks. Phoenix executives put a great deal of effort into communicating these principles after they were developed. In forty workshops with small groups of eighteen people each, the management team sat together with about seven hundred so-called multipliers—team members of various business units who were then charged with communicating the principles throughout their business units and handling possible questions from their coworkers. In this way, all employees could learn about the new strategic ambition. How the multipliers spread the new strategic ambition to their team was left to them; they could choose the most suitable way to teach their team. Today, the corporate principles are omnipresent at Phoenix; a copy of them has been hung in every office and meeting room, reminding all employees of the company's global mission and their own leadership roles at Phoenix. By weaving the company's leadership principles into everything your organization does, you ensure the greatest amount of adherence to—and excitement about—those principles.

to destroy the positive effects of a strong leadership climate.[24] Even when most company managers are leading in exemplary manner and are motivating and inspiring their teams and fostering success, organizational performance will still lag behind if some managers employ a laissez-faire or nonactive leadership style. Therefore, you should demand active leadership from all your managers to facilitate productive energy and ignite high performance throughout your organization.

Develop Flexible Structures That Encourage Informal Relationships

It's one thing to understand the need for strong leaders at every level of the organization. It's another to put in place specific leadership structures and processes that increase employees' ability to take action and that enable strong, decentralized leadership in every company unit.[25] To create these leadership structures that maintain healthy and high levels of excitement, alertness, and effort in the company, you need to follow two guidelines: create decentralized leadership structures and facilitate company-wide networks.

Create decentralized leadership structures. Although some hierarchical, centralized organizations do manage to create and sustain high, productive energy, in our experience they are not the norm. Most often, these kinds of leadership structures and processes promote inertia rather than ongoing momentum. When combined with lengthy decision-making process and high levels of formality, this inertia seals off the company from the outside world. Productive energy is decreased, and companies often fall into complacency or widespread resignation. Our research shows that over the long term, however they develop their leadership, executives need to make their companies adaptive from within, with low levels of centralization, high flexibility, and widespread, shared responsibility and accountability way down the hierarchy.[26] Only then can individual employees or teams show increasing and sustained engagement. In one large-scale quantitative study, we conducted a survey with 125 companies and 16,144 employees. We found that decentralized structures contribute significantly to strengthening an inspirational leadership climate and thereby indirectly benefit productive energy in organizations.[27]

Hilti shapes leadership structures in just such a sustainably energizing way.[28] Perhaps the most crucial aspect is how it uses direct sales to keep the company decentralized and close to the market. Hilti works successfully with structures that empower its people in direct sales to engage in comprehensive, direct contact with the end customer. This enables the company to identify new tendencies, needs, and changes in customer behavior early on. As a result, Hilti employees often end up developing new solutions with customers themselves. This way of sustaining energy could not occur in a hierarchical structure, where every decision must be checked with the boss or the boss's boss before the employee can take action.

But at Hilti, flexibility works at the very top. Hilti promotes equality and a decentralized structure with its Rule 56: members of the executive board must step down when they reach the age of fifty-six. By ensuring that the next level and generation of managers below have a chance to step into a board position, Hilti keeps its leadership pipeline charged, generating a proactive sense of urgency.

In 2007, however, Hilti faced a test of its ideals when three out of its four executive board members—including CEO Pius Baschera—would turn fifty-six within a two-year period. The time had come to examine just how independent Hilti truly was from the big batteries at the top.

In most companies, this exceptional situation of the departure of three-quarters of the board would have certainly warranted a counterruling that would allow at least some members to stay on past age fifty-six. Early on, however, Hilti instead worked on a succession plan. Back in 2002, the board had decided that the best way to ensure a smooth transition was to empower the management level below to do the work of the executive board. Egbert Appel, former executive board member and today the trustee of the Martin Hilti Family Trust, explained it: "We could reduce the risk of the transition by exchanging not three out of four executive board members—seventy-five percent—but by instead exchanging three out of twenty—fifteen percent. So I suggested what we always said we wanted to do anyway: to empower the next level."

Until 2004, the next level, the executive management group (EMG), consisting of sixteen managers, gathered once a year to discuss the current strategy with the executive board. The EMG members were responsible for their regional goals, but had no profit responsibility for the corporate results. Like any other team within Hilti, the EMG went through regular team camps in February 2004 and June 2005, when the group learned about the company's culture-development process. A salient topic within this group was how the members could work together as a real team, rather than acting as individuals in their respective fields and, subsequently, defining their role as the EMG. They wanted to gain the confidence of the executive board to provide them with more responsibility, but did not take it as a matter of course. As a result of the team camp in June 2005, the group was renamed the executive management team (EMT) and was made responsible for 50 percent of the company's overall financial results. Only three areas exclusively remained with the authority of the executive board: corporate strategy, the recruitment and succession planning for the thirty key positions of the company, and the corporate culture. Everything else involving Hilti's governance was placed into the hands of the new EMT.

By the end of September 2005, three members of the EMT had been named as successors for the three departing executive board members. Each departing member was assigned a new position, including Baschera, who took over the position of Michael Hilti as chairman of the board of directors (Hilti remained a board member). To ensure a smooth transition, the executive board worked closely with the incoming members from June to December 2006. For instance, the old and new executive boards revised the strategy together. Yet the final decision on the new strategy was made by the new executive board alone, even before it officially took office. January 1, 2007, marked the official starting date of the new company leadership.

Creating a decentralized leadership structure, however, isn't only about creating autonomy and freedom to act. As an executive or a manager, you also need to communicate and show other managers and your employees how much influence they have in the organization and how important they are to it. You must tell your people exactly how much room they have in which to act and have an impact—often more than people know or see.

We monitored the organizational energy and its drivers at one industrial service company for a few years with an annual employee opinion survey. We were struck by the fact that people repeatedly indicated low values of autonomy for their units. They didn't feel empowered to make decisions on their own; nor did they feel they could follow through on any decisions without continually checking with upper levels. But when we talked to senior management and looked at the responsibilities allocated in the organization charts, we got a different picture. This company in fact allowed considerable freedom among its unit and teams. So where was it stuck?

After conversations with lower ranks and a session that brought senior executives and front-line managers together, everyone saw the disconnection. While top executives thought they were allowing a great deal of autonomy, they had not managed to communicate this sense to lower managers and employees. Part of the problem was that a number of years before, the company had been deeply embedded in a hierarchical structure. When executives decided to create a flatter organization, they neglected to retrain their lower-level managers to act more freely within this new, wider freedom. Top management, then, launched an initiative to communicate the change to employees across all hierarchical levels and ensure that they began to act on the freedom they actually possessed.

Facilitate company-wide networks. Developing energy-sustaining structures in an organization requires consciously working with informal structures such as internal networks. Companies like Lufthansa, the automotive systems supplier Continental AG, Baloise, Hilti, IBM, and Swisscom all facilitate and encourage managers and employees to create their own informal networks across departmental boundaries.[29] At Hilti, for example, leaders leverage intense work in small working groups to foster close personal relationships in a stable working environment; additionally, leaders systematically rotate among teams to sustain flexibility, to help people develop personal networks, and, most important, to help employees understand different needs, perspectives, and goals in the organization.

Since 1998, Lufthansa's School of Business has made working in networks an essential element of management development. Explorers 21 is a development program in which junior managers improve their competencies by initiating real changes in the company.[30] During the year-long program, 210 junior managers from all Lufthansa divisions and nine partner companies divide up into thirty crews each of seven people. Each crew is assigned to one of the company's divisions, say, passenger airline, cargo, or technical maintenance. These crews regularly identify and initiate actual changes in the division, for instance, creating a manual to train project leaders in cultural awareness or designing a Web site to integrate the online activities of Team Lufthansa, a group of regional airlines within the airline. The participants learn to act collectively in informal interactions, creating relationships with managers from other units and nourishing them over time, sometimes ten years or longer. The program has been so successful that in 2010, Lufthansa had already run Explorers 21 for the seventh time. The company has worked with other large-scale change and learning networks such as ProTeam for young talents, STEP for high performers, or C-Experience to optimize informal leadership structures and networks throughout the entire group.

Programs like Explorers 21 help reduce the strain on the formal hierarchies that otherwise need to digest every initiative. Through these programs, employees develop high-quality connections and personal ties in structures parallel to the hierarchy. What's more, these kinds of programs empower employees to take action and individual units to develop a proactive sense of urgency while reducing internal political conflicts and destructive energy.[31]

What can you do to help craft these informal networks as a backbone for company-wide, sustained energy? Begin by applying a set of systematic levers to relationship building:

1. **Remove the obstacles and bridge the gaps:** As a leader, you need to eliminate or reduce formal borders and communication barriers between units and departments, making it easier for managers to talk to each other without always involving upper management.

2. **Increase the likelihood of building high-quality relationships:** Rather than leave networking to chance, create intentional opportunities for your managers and employees to directly engage in cross-border relationships. These exchanges aren't just about pure

networking, but rather about creating opportunities for employees and managers to establish high-quality relationships that can inspire and energize them.[32] This is especially true (and especially easy to facilitate technically) in today's social-network-friendly world. This is what Explorers 21 did for people at Lufthansa, and most companies can develop something similar, where people work on a practical challenge or project together and get to know each other in an intense process of joint experiences and interaction.

3. Establish communication and information flow throughout the value chain: Although companies often use division-related meetings and other formal efforts to encourage teamwork, communication and collaboration can also be fostered informally among the ranks and between divisions to create added value and provide services to customers. In our work with companies, we encourage leaders to overcome silo thinking and to measure, and then boost, the energy up and down the value chain. You can play a very active role in this process as a role model who fosters collaboration, communication, and team-building events between divisions and units that have to work together.

Create and Leverage Energizing Customer Touch Points

Finally, a vital foundation of productive energy is customer experiences. Intense customer experiences have the power to serve as so-called affective events, that is, incidents that naturally generate strong emotions and energy.[33] Usually, organizational units closer to the market have markedly higher energy than units that are more removed from the customers or to the end product. You should use the existing customer touch points—intense customer interactions that raise employee emotion—much more as sources of positive energy and create more customer touch points for desk-bound employees. Often, these units that are unrelated to the customers or product have trouble being in touch with the market and what it demands, and therefore, they often don't appreciate the need for innovation and change. They find it hard to be passionate, because they are only loosely connected to the customers and customer responses and they are emotionally detached, unlike units that are regularly and sustainably energized through the adrenaline they receive from close contact with the market and the customer experiences. Creating more of these customer touch points is a leadership responsibility, and therefore, you must design tasks and organizational structures that allow most units to have these touch points.

To take advantage of the natural market sources for the kind of adrenaline that energizes employees, make sure to give each employee the chance to develop a sense for the market. Foster instant customer feedback, and recognize employees for outstanding customer reviews. Finally, leverage the passion of your fans to give your employees a tangible, vivid picture of why these enthusiasts do what they do.

Give every employee the chance to develop a sense for the market. Employees who have had lively exchanges with a customer about how the person uses and appreciates the company's products and services never forget that up-close experience. They will always associate aspects of their work with the customer feedback they got about certain benefits of products and services. To ensure that all employees have the opportunity to engage with real customers, you can invite customers to share their experiences with the company's offering.

For example, Sonova Group regularly invites customers to its headquarters for product information events.[34] Occasionally, children who need a hearing device attend these events and interact with employees. One executive who had worked ten years for Sonova told us how meaningful it is especially to meet Sonova's youngest customers: "We get to see what we are working for every day. These children can hear."

Similarly, a Swedish insurance company regularly has managers from different parts of the company cook meals for customers, as a metaphor for (and an effective practice of) direct customer service. One of the rooms in its headquarters is transformed into a kitchen and a nouvelle-cuisine restaurant. Every six months, twenty people from the company are selected a "chefs," and each is allowed to invite one customer. One of the participants told us, "I participated twice already. We were all so excited when preparing the menu, we all gave our best because the feedback was so immediate. The relationship to my customers is much more intense now. But what is more important for me personally is that I remember this emotional experience vividly. I often draw on this excitement and passion for my customers to motivate me."

But there are other ways to build emotional attachment between employees and the company products and customers. For example, Stryker GmbH & Co. KG, headquartered in Duisburg, Germany, is a leader in the medical engineering industry and a maker of prostheses. Not only does Stryker invite customers to the company to share how its products improve their lives (such as enabling them to walk again with a Stryker prosthesis), but employees from all units also regularly go into the field (such as to hospitals) to see how Stryker products are applied. Another example is the German company Securetec, which develops leading-edge technology for rapid test kits for the detection of drugs and hazardous substances globally. The R&D division of Securetec employs a wide range of assistants and scientists, including chemists, biologists, and engineers. But although these employees are usually ideally educated for doing research and developing novel detection systems and innovative in vitro diagnostics, they work far away from where their substances are applied as end products: namely, the police and customs officials. To give these employees a sense for the market, customer needs, and the products, CEO Rudolf Zimmermann sends every new employee—and this includes people from R&D, quality control, and marketing—to observe customers at work. So for one week, the employee might be on a traffic-control beat with police and another week working the night shift with highway patrol officers. One Securetec employee spoke of how this practice affected him: "This extensive experience with the police—our principle customer—is with me all the time and motivates me in my work, especially when difficulties appear or when I'm challenged to develop new ideas and innovative, practical solutions."

The goal of creating as many customer touch points as possible enables the majority of employees to feel the adrenaline from the market. Hilti creates touch points by instituting a guideline that at least 60 percent of employees need to do some direct-sales work, which effectively puts them in contact with the market. Direct sales—which Hilti conducts exclusively—enables employees not only to explain their product, but also to sense the market and bring new initiatives into the company while having as many customer touch points as possible.

Foster instant customer feedback and employee recognition. To sustain organizational energy, you need to foster contagion processes as part of a system that absorbs and channels impulses from the market and distributes them throughout the organization. Organizations throughout the retail and hospitality industries use mystery shoppers. For example, at Vapiano, a fast-growing restaurant chain, shoppers regularly visit and then meet with all personnel for a feedback session in which they discuss specific problems and together decide on direct improvements and innovations. The mystery-shopper experiences is used as well for internal benchmarking and new shop openings.

Likewise, Serview, which specializes in consulting and training for business IT alignment, posts customer feedback on the company intranet directly after every customer event or seminar, including new-product launches, trade fairs, or key customer acquisitions.[35] Behind-the-scenes employees benefit especially from such feedback and encouragement, which offer them a glimpse of why (and for whom) they are working. Because it includes lively and direct comments from testimonials, this instant customer feedback also allows employees to perceive the effects of their own services on the market, almost as if they had attended the workshop themselves. This instant feedback therefore critically supplements the more structured customer-satisfaction surveys that are conducted less often.

Beyond putting your people in close touch with customer feedback, you should give every employee a chance to be applauded, literally or figuratively. At Itemis, a medium-sized German software company, all employees work on customer projects to develop and implement software solutions.[36] To keep the energy high even when customer projects are finished, Itemis gives all its employees the opportunity to research topics of special interest within the software area. They are then invited to present these special topics to other employees and to customers at conferences, to share their new insights, and to publish them under their own name. Not only is it rewarding and motivating to receive time for this kind of research and knowledge development, but it also can potentially recharge employee energy. Moreover, the attention and accolades employees receive as a result of this extra effort create the chance for them to become "famous" within the community. Through this system, Itemis has become a well-known and attractive employer. While most companies in the soft-ware industry have trouble finding skilled personnel, Itemis has no prob-lem and receives many applications from talented people.

Another example is ABB subsidiary Busch-Jaeger, the electrical installa-tion technology leader of some one thousand people in Lüdenscheid and Aue (Germany). CEO Hans-Georg Krabbe deliberately creates an ongoing stream of external enthusiasm and emotional public resonance, which infects employees from the outside and nurtures their sense of pride and meaning. Krabbe introduced a system with various origins of external feedback. For instance, without exception, all executive managers at Busch-Jaeger have to visit customers to get their personal feedback directly from the market. In addition, the company regularly participates in competitions. In past years, Busch-Jaeger has won several awards, such as the Ludwig-Ehrhard Award for top performance in 2006, the iF Product Design award in 2007, and the red dot "best of the best" design award in 2008, which inspired his employees, stimulated their engagement, and filled them with pride.

Further channels that are increasing the external reputation of the company are local TV commercials; Busch-Jaeger employees get ap-proached by people who ask them about the company and its products for their own private use. Their pride in the company increases with this ex-ternal excitement. Local politicians and other prominent people are in-vited to exhibitions, and the feedback of these people and customers is shared with employees via an intranet or in person. This, too, helps trans-fer the outsiders' excitement to the employees, and the excitement thus spreads from the outside in.

Krabbe described how he purposely uses the external communication channels to successfully sustain the high energy in the company: "Similar to soccer, the company is on the field, and energy and enthusiasm is cre-ated when the fans are cheering. And this effect can't be achieved with internal praises only—it is necessary that it comes from the outside. Financial success is good and important for a company, but it doesn't cre-ate enthusiasm or identification or pride—this is coming from the external positive resonance." The emotional infection that Krabbe systematically and purposefully generates for Busch-Jaeger is, interestingly, taken for granted in sports. The energy that top athletes and teams get through the fans' cheering is even physically visible. In fact, athletes often actively encourage their fans with gestures and other expressions to cheer and show their enthusiasm—with an obvious energizing effect.

Leverage the passion of your customer fans. You can spread energy around your organization by using the enthusiasm of your most passionate customers—your fans. When you have big fans of the company, you know that you've achieved the kind of service excellence that turns a shopper into a lifetime customer.[37] Especially since the advent of social media, fans are not only infinitely loyal customers, but also potential ambassadors and advocates for your products or services in the marketplace, because they tend to rave about your company's offerings and feel emotionally attached to the organization. But they can also be a central source of energy for people in organizations.

Hilti constantly checks the proportion of fans among its customers and asks every department to find ways to increase this proportion as far as possible. The passion and deep loyalty fans show for the organization and its products and services has a contagious effect for employees.

Georg Schneider VI is another leader who leverages the enthusiasm of his company's fans. He does this through special employee and customer events to promote his brewery's beer. For instance, the Schneider Weisse brewery teamed up with Brooklyn Brewery to brew and present the Schneider & Brooklyner Hopfen-Weisse to the public with a big event launched simultaneously in Bavaria and New York. The brewing process itself was made into a public event and received much customer attention and enthusiasm. After the event, the German brewer traveled to New York to present the beer along with his American counterpart. The fifty-plus Schneider Weisse fan clubs all over the world now conduct more and more events, which Schneider personally attends with a rotating delegation of employees such as the brewers themselves. These events both honor the brewery's fans and allow Schneider to bring back photos and other impressions to the organization as inspiration for employees.

The potential to create fans or use the energy of the fans of the company is not limited by industry or restricted to certain kinds of products. Stryker, for example, provides a comprehensive range of products and services in the orthopedic industry, including prosthetics—not an obviously "sexy" market segment. Yet even such a manufacturer can build passion and fascination for its products that then translates to employee excitement. At Stryker head-quarters, an exhibition displays all the products as if they were art, with special layouts and a fascinating light installation. Moreover, the company owns pieces of art that integrate Stryker products in a very aesthetically pleasing manner—abstract depictions of prostheses and so on. In addition, the company promotes the product of the month, which is introduced to, and celebrated by, all employees. All of these elements together contribute to developing fans outside and inside the organization; these practices encourage and spread passion for, and pride in, the company's products.

Vitalizing Culture

We've just seen how, for the long-term management of an organization's energy, you need to engage in a systematic approach to leadership behavior and structures—essentially, creating a strong leadership climate. Such a vitalizing leadership, combined with the strategy processes that we explored earlier in this chapter, go a long way toward maintaining an organization's productive energy. But companies need to strengthen yet one more component of the management system if they hope to sustain productive energy over the long haul: the culture.

Again and again in our research, we've observed how the organization's culture can be the make-or-break factor in keeping companies energized over a long time. *Culture* describes the basic assumptions, values, and beliefs that are shared by members of an organization and shape how people unconsciously operate and view themselves and their organization.[38] Whereas a strong leadership system aims at fostering an energizing leadership climate and thus primarily the way leaders act in the organization, culture represents the unique character of an organization. An organization's culture provides the context for action, determines how organizations conduct their business, and can be a key source of energy if properly nurtured and orchestrated.[39] It can also significantly block or sap energy if not properly developed.

Companies such as Novo Nordisk, buw, and Phoenix Contact provide a positive example. In addition, Hilti has for more than twenty-five years engaged in deliberate culture development through its INNO training

FIGURE 5-5

Components of a vitalizing management system: culture

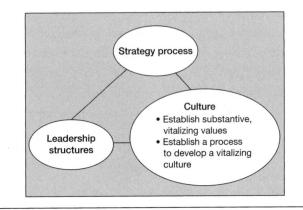

and Our Culture Journey, which we will explore later in this chapter. The company has invested massively in these phases of cultural development. Over the last three years alone, Hilti employed sixty-seven team "camp" facilitators, called Sherpas, and spent over $10 million per year on cultural training. All told, the workshops represent more than thirty thousand annual workdays spent on cultural development alone.

Our research has shown us that, like Hilti, organizations that manage to stay in the productive energy zone work consciously to develop their company cultures toward active engagement and initiative in the whole organization. Specifically, as a leader, you need to create company-specific solutions that makes sense for your culture. These can include the establishment of substantive vitalizing values and a process that develops a vitalizing culture (figure 5-5).

Establish Substantive, Vitalizing Values

Which values should make up the foundation for sustainable behavior and expectations in the company? From an energy point of view, you should promote a set of energy-sustaining values that encourage a proactive sense of urgency—values that signal, for instance, how the company deals with personal initiative, action, or feedback. There are no one-size-fits-all sets of values, however. Rather, you must find a value set that's right for your organization. For example, Zeiss, the German optical and opto-electronic high-tech company, articulated the values of serve, empower, act, and win.

As a side benefit of this process, you can use the task of finding a specific value set for your company as an opportunity to role model value-driven behavior. Employees are very quick to observe and evaluate senior management vis-à-vis any newly introduced values, so as a leader, be sure that you set values and standards by which you and your team can live. Executives sometimes get confused about what it means to have a strong culture. Just because a company has an established set of values that are deeply shared throughout the organization does not automatically sustain organizational energy. The key to sustaining energy over the long term is to have a set of *substantive* values, that is, values that are still relevant and essential to the organization. Although many organizations have historically established some core company values early on, these values may or may not still be relevant to the organization today. You should therefore periodically review your company's values and make sure they still apply. And if they don't apply, then it's time to craft modified values that are sustainable but that apply specifically to current circumstances.

In our work with companies, we have identified a set of values and cultural norms that help to sustain energy. The values include innovation, open feedback, and personal initiative (we'll explore these values and more later on in this chapter). But these can only serve as a guideline. As a leader, you must first find the values, belief systems, norms, and behavioral patterns that fit your organization's unique situation and ambition and, second, reconsider them regularly. At Lufthansa, for example, until the early 1990s employees strongly believed that they worked for *the* German airline, a company without peers, far and above all other airlines. As we saw in chapter 1, such rigid and non-proactive beliefs nearly sent the company into bankruptcy. Lufthansa's strong organizational culture directly supported its complacency, hindering personal initiative and change and crippling the entire organization. So although Lufthansa adhered to a set of very strong values, in their content these values were misguided; they had to be substantially overhauled to save the company. Therefore, the first step you must take is to consider whether your company's values, norms, and behavioral patterns sustain or endanger high positive energy in the first place.

Let's return again to Hilti. Not only does the company have a history of developing actionable values that it communicates throughout the organization, but it also is willing to adjust its value system periodically when needed to sustain energy and success. The company's culture training program is a good model. In the first phase, INNO training, all the teams were introduced to five basic behavioral principles and their application at a three-day seminar.[40]

The company's five principles themselves are a good model for energizing values:

1. **Rules:** Because Hilti employees are sensitized to the importance of rules for collaboration and coordination, this first principle emphasizes that rules should not be seen as constraints to people's actions but as a defined freedom to take action and that this freedom promotes internal entrepreneurship.

2. **Circle of habit:** Everyone can fall into routines that hinder new experiences; the key is to be aware of them and to resist the dangers of mechanical routine. Employees therefore are called upon to leave their "circle of habits" and try new moves, rather than just talk or think about doing so.

3. **Freedom of choice:** "Love it, change it, or leave it": it is up to each individual to decide whether he or she can identify with the work—and if necessary, whether to change things, or leave them as they are, which can mean accepting what you cannot change and concentrating on things you can influence. But "leave it" can also mean that you refuse certain assignments or should even consider leaving the company if, after a longer time, you cannot identify with your work. Most important, at Hilti people are well aware that they have chosen their work and conditions and that they can influence these. Therefore, if there's a problem, they can take an active stance and change their environment— rather than complaining and spreading negative energy.

4. **Swing of life:** The *swing of life* refers to setbacks and failure. Hilti employees understand that things can go wrong when people take a new path or initiative. Every new idea can draw positive

experiences, but could also potentially fail. As Michael Hilti emphasizes, "The biggest mistake you can make is to make no mistakes at all." This principle encourages risk-taking.

5. COTOYO: This acronym comes from the phrase "commitment to yourself." Hilti employees are expected to commit fully to everything they do. This principle reminds people that only those who feel committed to a personal path will be able to overcome stumbling blocks and setbacks while pursuing their goals, whether those goals are personal or organizational.

For years all Hilti teams explored these five principles during the three-day INNO training. This was the foundation to an innovation-oriented culture at Hilti. This culture purposefully sustains the company's emotional, mental, and behavioral energy. As a result, internal entrepreneurship and individual initiative have become key drivers for innovation and ongoing improvement from inside the company.

Even when your company develops a strong value system like Hilti's, sometimes you need to step back and put the company's values to the test. This ability to reconsider its culture and value system allowed Hilti to respond effectively when, in 2003, the worldwide construction industry hit a crisis of unprecedented depth and breadth. Hilti's executive board immediately began scrutinizing the larger business challenges, but particularly its culture. Specifically, Hilti reexamined whether its system of decentralized responsibility and high employee autonomy that the company had intentionally introduced was still appropriate, given the industry's weakened state. Could Hilti pursue a fundamental transformation, the board wondered, while still respecting the personal responsibility and autonomy of each employee?

Hilti's management responded with a clear yes. Whereas most organizations might have opted for a top-down apporach for fundamental change, Hilti kept to its course. Values must not remain simple lip service or fair-weather principles. The importance of culture and values is demonstrated not in good times, but rather in bad. That's when you face a dilemma—often between economic musts and values. If you decide against values, you will gain in the short term, but will lose in the long term.

Hilti's board decided not only to adhere to its established culture, but also to even reinforce it. As a follow-on to INNO raining, the company introduced Our Culture Journey in 2005 as an improved way of instilling cultural development in individuals and teams.[41] In Our Cultural Journey, the company culture and codes of conduct are effectively linked with business processes. This was a leap forward in defining what is culturally essential to facilitate innovation and sustained energy. Hilti condensed its value framework to four core values: integrity, courage, teamwork, and commitment. Each team at Hilti participates in three consecutive training camps—named Foundation, Rubicon and Pit Stop (which was described in chapter 4)—to learn more about the company values, translate them in their working routines, and connect them with their business processes. Later in this chapter, we will look at these training camps.

To sustain high productive energy, organizations need to build cultures that keep comfortable energy at bay and that counteract corrosive energy or resigned inertia and typical energy traps—such as the acceleration trap that leads to fatigue and burnout. From our experience at companies with innovation-oriented cultures such as Hilti, IBM, Phoenix Contact, Novo Nordisk, and Lufthansa, we recommend that you consider seven key value areas for an energy-sustaining culture.

Innovation versus routine. For an energy-sustaining culture, you need to develop a culture for innovation in which people regularly contribute new ideas and question what the company thinks, expects, does, and plans. Such a proactive stance toward innovation fosters organizations that purposefully counteract inflexible traditions, narrowly defined norms, and yes-saying.[42] Novo Nordisk, for example, strongly emphasizes innovation in its deliberate culture development.[43] The Novo Nordisk way of management states that every individual is encouraged to innovate: "Everyone must continuously improve the quality of their work." And people are encouraged to share their knowledge and foster innovation across units and teams: "Each unit must share and use better practices."

Our research shows that organizations with high *contextual ambidexterity,* that is, a working context that fosters efficiency-oriented behavior while at the same time encouraging innovative engagement, have significantly better energy profiles and performance.[44] The results of our study show that in companies where employees perceive their working context as ambidextrous—that is, their working context supports adaptability (innovation) and alignment (efficiency)—performance is improved. Productive energy (5 percent) and comfortable energy (6 percent) are increased, while corrosive energy (–9 percent) and resigned inertia (–5 percent) are significantly reduced.[45] Furthermore, the companies with high contextual ambidexterity scored higher on overall performance (7 percent), employee productivity (16 percent), efficiency (16 percent), growth (6 percent), and employee retention (9 percent).

Entrepreneurial initiative versus obedience. Another key value area involves developing an entrepreneurial culture in which employees see themselves as internal entrepreneurs who feel responsible for the company while taking initiative, being proactive, and making choices. At Audi, this form of self-driven behavior for the good of the company is called "creative disobedience." Aware that some of the most significant innovations and successes of the company are the result of lateral thinkers who take creative, new ways to realize their projects, Audi deliberately promotes the entrepreneurial spirit by encouraging a healthy degree of creative disobedience.

The lesson, then, is to avoid pressure toward conformity and consensus, since overly conforming cultures reduce individuals' engagement and initiative.[46] The effect of entrepreneurship on energy in organizations is impressive: our research shows that in companies where employees feel that management is open to new suggestions, and their working context encourages them to take responsibility for new ideas, productive energy (12 percent) and comfortable energy (15 percent) are substantially increased, while corrosive energy (–20 percent) and resigned inertia (–13 percent) are significantly reduced.[47]

Integrity versus opportunism. Since we define productive energy as the degree to which a company has mobilized its potential in pursuit of *shared* goals, it follows that such collective engagement gets destroyed through any kind of egoistic, opportunistic, or uncooperative behavior. A culture that contributes to sustaining the productive forces in the organization is based on deeply rooted integrity throughout the organization. In cultures that take integrity seriously, dishonesty, maximizing personal benefits, diva-like behavior, and silo thinking are not tolerated. At Hilti, integrity is one of the company's core cultural values; it is relevant for everything that people do at Hilti, even if it may imply personal cost or economic disadvantage.

Focus versus busyness One of the greatest threats to sustaining productive energy and full engagement in the organization is a culture of busyness, where people are energetic and chronically active, involved in multiple activities, and constantly under pressure, but lack focus.[48] Productive energy requires that people consciously focus their efforts and engagement on the right things. To help your company overcome a culture of busyness in favor of a sharply focused one, you should actively support values and behavioral patterns that make people throughout the organization select, prioritize, and concentrate their effort and emotional involvement. This doesn't mean that people reduce their efforts. Rather, people should just be sure they pursue the right things and "dare" to pay less attention to insignificant activities.

In its earlier culture development program (INNO), Hilti encouraged people to make conscious choices about their work by instilling behavioral norms around the principle of freedom of choice. Today, in the Our Culture Journey program, Hilti focuses more explicitly on the importance of energy and focus, encouraging its people to concentrate on key activities. By making focus a crucial element of the culture, individuals as well as whole organizations counteract busyness, burnout, and the acceleration trap.

Open feedback versus overtolerance. To sustain high energy, you need to work against one common cultural characteristic that prevents top performance: overtolerance. Overtolerance occurs when you and other leaders throughout the organization shy away from open feedback, criticism, and actively dealing with underperformance or stopping deviant behavior. People start out being overtolerant for a positive reason, that they like and accept each other. But it works against top performance and sustainably high energy when people stop voicing their opinions because they do not want to criticize other people's performance. Particularly as an executive, you need to fight *organizational silence,* a behavioral pattern we often see in firms with strong norms of holding back information.[49] Critical issues and differences remain under the surface, burgeoning eventually into destructive forces.[50] Executives with repellent, destructive, or dishonest communication and feedback—or who are averse to new ideas—create these norms. The typical result: employees disengage from the innovation process.

In a Friday letter titled "Clear, concise, and direct communications," Juergen Dormann addressed this superficial communication culture: "Now, nearly every time I have asked for information in the past month, I have received a sizeable PowerPoint file. Is this the corporate language? I thought it was English . . . I don't want to be sold to when we are discussing real-life business issues within the company—I want facts, views, arguments, context. I don't want self-promotion, I want someone to lay out the issues at hand so we can examine them and find solutions. I'm not saying we should ban PowerPoint slides and stop presenting to each other. I'm saying, let's minimize it. Let's build a culture of analysis, dialogue, decision-making and disciplined action . . . Otherwise, where's the Power? And what's the Point?"[51]

As we've discussed previously, to move beyond number one, companies must facilitate open feedback so that critical information—beyond just praise for the status quo—actually reaches leaders. And you need to develop a culture that encourages people from all parts of your organization to be as critical as possible to help the organization learn. At Hilti, people are empowered to discuss and analyze critical issues—to "confront the brutal facts," as Hilti phrases it. They do this even when the facts are not always easy to accept or when they sometimes create discomfort, but open feedback helps people grow and helps the company continuously challenge the status quo and exploit its full potential.

The need for excellence versus the need for mandatory performance levels. To move your company beyond number one, you need to nurture in your people the inner desire to strive for maximal performance—for going beyond what is required of them. In a vitalizing culture, it is this shared mind-set, rather than top management's trying to impose high performance standards on people, that drives high engagement. Pius Baschera described the inner need for excellence in the Hilti culture when he was

CEO: "People in our organization tend to set themselves overly ambitious goals which are often not realistic. But I'd rather hold people back at Hilti at times than moving them along with the whip."

An organization that has internalized this need for excellence like almost no other is the German soccer club FC Bayern Munich. This record-beating winner of national soccer titles stands for sustainable top performance as few other organizations do. Like any exceptional company that delivers ongoing, extraordinary performance, the club has committed to a philosophy of being number one. For this club, not being on top is simply not an option. Such an uncompromising commitment to peak performance has attracted the best players. "The club has a long standing tradition of success," said Oliver Kahn, longtime goalie of FC Bayern Munich and the German National Team and winner of more than fifteen national and international titles.[52] "The people responsible for the club only talk about the maximum that is achievable. Everything is about being at the top. Anything else is not even discussed." Similarly, you need to ensure that this need for excellence is internalized in the whole organization if you hope to become number one and even more so if you want to move your organization beyond number one.

Courage versus uncertainty. Innovation, entrepreneurial initiative, focus, open feedback, excellence, and integrity all require one key ingredient of a vitalizing culture: courage. Don't confuse courage with arrogance or haughtiness, which are the worst enemies of productive energy. Uncertainty, anxiety, and risk aversion only produce reactive behavior, hesitation, or inertia.

Hilti fosters courage as one of its values and links it to leaving the "circle of habits." To move beyond number one, companies need a similar culture of courage: the courage to lead; the courage to be passionate; the courage to find, define, and take new roads; and the courage to commit.

Although the seven value areas can guide you to develop an energy-sustaining culture, in the end you need to ask, "What is the right culture for us? What do these values mean to our particular organization and people? And how can we make the values a regular part of the activities of all organizational members?" The specific culture of an organization can be developed, but it can never be altered quickly and easily. When nurturing a certain culture, you should consider the roots of the specific organizational culture and try to build as much as possible on the particular vitalizing values, attitudes, and basic beliefs that already exist in your organization or were vivid in the past. That is how the process of culture development and implementation becomes vital.

Establish a Process to Develop a Vitalizing Culture

Developing a culture toward truly sustaining organizational energy can be a long and sometimes bumpy road. Before starting down that road, you need to consider the following questions—and be able to respond with a clear yes:

- Is the leadership task of culture management more to us than a fad that has grabbed our attention for a few months? Or is it rather a process that we have the stamina to see through, over the long haul?

- Are we willing to invest our time as top executives and a considerable amount of time from all our managers and employees?

- Are we willing to invest the financial resources for a culture development that reaches all organizational members?

- Are we willing to treat culture with the necessary seriousness and forcefulness to ensure that our cultural values will be honored and adhered to?

We have seen too many companies that halfheartedly tried to build a culture but did not persevere, which resulted in a loss of integrity for top executives and a sense of failure throughout the organization. There is no magic formula for how to build a culture that frees employees to engage in high levels of energy, emotional involvement, or creative thinking and behavior to further the company's goals and sustain organizational energy. Since culture is largely a subconscious element in companies, you can directly change and influence the company culture only over the long term and in limited ways. But every employee can help to shape the culture in some way. Therefore, you and other executives should facilitate a guided cultural change and make continuity and consistency central. This process must be very systematic to help people both endure the discomfort of implementation and have the discipline to live the culture in everyday routines.

Leaders who succeed in promoting energy-sustaining cultures pursue a process that features six distinct steps (figure 5-6).[53] Again, Hilti provides a good example of some of these steps, as we'll illustrate below.

Analyzing the current culture. In many companies, the current culture is not explicit or well understood; even senior managers only have a gut feeling about it. So as a first step, you need to understand and define the current culture and make it transparent. You need to share a clear idea about the present values, norms, traditions, and practices. As a leader, you should therefore facilitate in-depth interviews with stakeholders such as customers, employees, suppliers, and collaborators, or alternatively, use surveys or take a close look at the kinds of early warning systems we've already discussed.

Defining the preferred culture. Often, a company's values and behavioral norms simply grow and develop unchecked. But it's critical for you to be firmly in the driver's seat when it comes to examining and defining the de-

FIGURE 5-6

Six steps for systematic cultural development

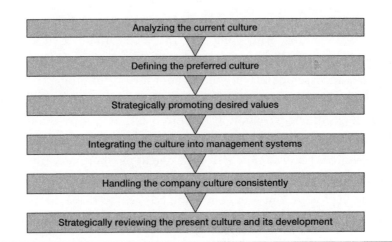

sirable values, behavioral patterns, and traditions. Earlier in this chapter, we described some possible value areas for sustaining energy, including innovation, internal entrepreneurship, and developing excellence. Core values like honesty, openness, dedication, cooperation, strength, perseverance are so focused and easy to understand that people can internalize them deeply and can constantly refer to these values.

Strategically promoting desired values. Some executives feel their job is done once they've announced the desired culture. However, the process must introduce the desired values and behavioral patterns to *all employees* and systematically connect these values to employees' work. To ensure that these values are implemented successfully, you need to develop *and participate in* a coherent stream of promotional measures, including workshops, training sessions, or interactive feedback.

Integrating the culture into the management system. A company's top executives are responsible for seeing that cultural processes are connected to the strategy and leadership system. Otherwise, the cultural process will fall flat and won't take hold over the long term. For instance, incentive systems that focus purely on individual gains often contradict values for cooperation or promote behavioral patterns that are counterproductive. In contrast, as a leader you should make cultural elements a permanent component of management tools and practices, through instruments such as employee surveys, competency models, appraisal systems, recognition, promotion, and leadership guidelines. You can do this by monitoring behaviors that are consistent with or divergent from stated values, by considering values when giving feedback or rewards, and by connecting values with management goals and making them part of other management systems.

At Hilti, culture is considered part of the company's strategy. Additionally, culture is the golden thread for personnel decisions; for the selection, performance appraisal, and staffing of key positions especially within upper management, cultural factors are always crucial. When, in 2007, three of four positions within the executive board were restaffed, cultural factors played an important role—especially factors such as teamwork, integrity, and courage.

Handling the company culture consistently. When you opt for cultural development, you need to find ways to make the company values compulsory for everyone in your organization. It should be clear to everyone that culture development is taken seriously, and you should demonstrate in your actions that you do.

Hilti executives openly promote individuals who live the desired culture. We favor linking values with feedback or reward systems, for example, management objectives. Yet organizations should not refrain from taking tough action, either, when people do not stick to the norms and values. Hilti's top management agrees that despite the great challenges necessarily attached to the culture, the company cannot afford to make compromises; it must consistently live the culture in a credible, disciplined manner.[54] The members of the executive board, therefore, not only give each other extremely candid feedback on a regular basis and challenge one another's actions as they relate to Hilti's values, but also are consistent and uncompromising regarding violations against the Hilti culture. "This is not about intolerance," said board member Michael Hilti. "Quite the contrary, it's about fairness. Our rules of play are clearly defined and give people a lot of freedom. But certain things are just not up for debate. It's just as if someone showed up to a soccer match with a tennis racket. You'd either have to ask him to start using his feet and the soccer ball or to find somewhere else to play tennis. It would be cowardly to let the tennis player play, because he would be blocking the other twenty-two players and notice only later that he'd never get anywhere in our game. If an individual is not committed to what we do, it is our responsibility to change that quickly: 'Change it, love it, or leave it' applies here, too."

This issue of job promotions has put to the test just how serious Hilti is about cultural work. "Our performance appraisal is made along two dimensions: business performance and cultural fit," said Egbert Appel. About 70 percent of the dismissals at Hilti are due to insufficient compatibility with company values and the required competencies. The company even dismisses managers whose performance is outstanding if these individuals do not live the Hilti values, for example by promoting their own agendas at others' expense.

Carl Zeiss was pushed even more to stand firm to its values during crises. In 2008, the German optical and opto-electronic high-tech company was one year into a program called Corporate Agenda 2013 when the company was hit by the recession. President and CEO Dieter Kurz explained, "Carl Zeiss was doing well, but had to reenergize and to improve if it wanted to continue its course, which is set on growth on a global level."

As part of Corporate Agenda 2013 Zeiss introduced the Cultural Journey to refine and strengthen its culture. It was running full gear when the recession hit—the executive board members met the top hundred-and-fifty senior managers in an Executive Summit and were conducting a Passion-to-Win Tour, in which they spoke to almost all employees. In numerous two-day team summits—some twelve hundred in all—Zeiss introduced with the help of internal facilitators a new set of values (serve, empower, act, and win). Yet, with the crisis at hand, Zeiss had to work immediately on its cost basis and efficiency to stop the strong cash drain. Despite discussions to put the Cultural Journey on hold for efficiency gains, top management was convinced that the cultural change would benefit Carl Zeiss in tough times as well as good. And top management needed to stand firm and have the courage to continue with what it felt was right. Living the values was deemed critical to the company's future. "The Cultural Journey is for Carl Zeiss a bit like the Red Cross in the Geneva Conventions. The Cultural Journey is safe, and no one is allowed to attack it," said Florian Mauerer, vice president of Strategic Corporate Development.

Moreover, the value of empowerment in particular shifted leadership deep down into the hierarchy—decisive for the success of Zeiss's cost-cutting program. Top management defined the overall target of cutting a two-digit million-dollar amount of operational costs. However, instead of asking all business units top-down to achieve the same level of cost-cutting, top management empowered its people and asked the heads of business units two things: What amount could they contribute to cost savings in view of their specific situation? And how would they facilitate this? The process cascaded down through the hierarchy. "This type of leadership was new at Carl Zeiss," reported Kurz. And managers used the team summits to define cash targets and respective measures. It was a remarkable success for the company. As of March 2010, the program was 20 percent above the initially planned overall cost savings. More important, managers across the hierarchy had experienced increased empowerment and autonomy during the crisis: leadership had grown at all levels.

Strategically reviewing the present culture and its development. To make sure that you stay on track in developing a vitalizing culture, you should regularly review the culture for guided adjustments. Again, this doesn't mean constantly redefining values. But you do need transparency about the effectiveness of values and norms: do they facilitate a proactive sense of urgency and sustain enthusiasm, alertness, and effort? As a member of top management, you should communicate progress, but also address less positive results in the organization and the units concerned. That is how you make intangible cultural change concrete, understandable, and binding. To this end, you should systematically monitor the status of the culture with regular employee surveys, conduct annual top management team internal review sessions as part of your regular review activities, and monitor the performance of the culture on behavior, energy, and financials.

At Hilti, the executive management group coordinates the company's cultural development. Yet, in light of Hilti's specific values, the decentralized units are responsible for improving potential weaknesses. Hilti identifies drawbacks to a large extent with regular culture monitoring, such as the yearly global employee opinion survey. The surveys connect the state of the culture with the performance of the company. The formal process asks every management team of a unit or work group to take these results into its meetings and decide on activities that improve strengths and address specific weaknesses.

Throughout this chapter, we've looked at how you can sustain your organization's energy over the long term. To sustain energy, you must move your company from being energized from the top to an organization with an inner drive, multiple energy sources, and a shared desire to thrive.

You need to prepare the ground and develop a strong *vitalizing management system* for sustaining productive energy throughout the company with three components: vitalizing strategy processes, leadership structures, and culture. To orchestrate the collective energy in the organization, you need to align these components to form a single, integrated management system: strong leadership and a consistent organizational culture will support the company's strategy, and vice versa. In short, if you build them correctly, the components must work together to inspire your people, foster mental agility, and promote joint, concerted action to pursue shared, organization-wide goals throughout the organization. This sustained, full energy is what you need to raise your company above number one.

CHAPTER 6

Energizing Leaders

Personal Perspectives on Boosting Energy

What does boosting and sustaining your organization's energy imply for you personally as a leader? What are the personal requirements and commitments that you must develop? In this concluding chapter, we add a new perspective on the key concepts introduced throughout the book by focusing on the challenges and opportunities you as a leader personally face when energizing your company.

The leadership strategies and activities we recommend—from monitoring your organization's energy to slaying the dragon or winning the princess—work only when *you and other leaders across the organization* are willing and able to manage your own energy effectively. You might ask yourself, for example, Am I energetic, or do I project low energy or too much energy? And how do I affect others? Do I enthuse them, and do they in turn become energizers? Or are they unable to transport the sparkle in their eyes to others, or do they even sap other people's energy and overwhelm or frustrate them?[1] To help you begin to answer those questions, this chapter reviews the personal perspective of a leader who is charged with directing organizational energy along four pathways described in this book:

- Proactively managing energy

- Mobilizing energy around a dragon or a princess

- Forcefully cutting corrosion

- Decelerating

Proactively Managing Energy

Boosting your organization's energy requires that you first understand, assess, and diagnose the state of that energy to get a precise picture of the *human potential* in your organization or unit. The twelve-question Organizational Energy Questionnaire (OEQ) provided in the appendix of this book will help you to do this and to begin to develop focused leadership strategies.

Because people usually understand organizational energy only as diffuse and vague gut feelings, a tool like the OEQ shines a light of clarity on the true state of the company or unit. As we've seen, the resulting organizational energy profile fully reflects to what extent companies have mobilized their emotional, cognitive, and behavioral potential in pursuit of shared goals. Such an energy measurement surfaces the strengths and deficiencies in the organization. For example, the profile might bring to light an otherwise undetected lack of productive energy, a level of complacency, or some misdirected energy such as corrosive energy or resigned inertia. Only when you have a bead on your company's state of energy will you be able to identify the appropriate leadership activities for the respective areas in your organization. But this is only the knowing side of things—you should initiate and implement the necessary activities to both improve the energy state *and* monitor improvements over time. You can do this in two ways: through the choices you make and the behaviors you exhibit.

At Phoenix Contact, executive board member Gunther Olesch's strategic agenda includes professionalizing trust, leadership, and energy in his company. He regularly measures the state of his organization's energy.

"Monitoring the state of Phoenix's human potential must happen regularly, every year, just as balance sheets are calculated and measured," Olesch told us. "And then we must ask, 'How can we purposefully steer and control our soft factors, the human resources?'" By comparing the energy of your company or unit against benchmarks, you can ultimately set ambitious goals for leveraging your organization's energy.

To forcefully manage the company's energy, you must also be ready to lead by example. Mobilizing positive energy toward a shared purpose and overcoming negative energy is ultimately a very personal activity for executives. If your top team is lacking energy, you must act quickly; positive energy multiplies quickly *and* diffuses into the company. Yet, negative energy is even more infectious. While you are responsible for the energy of the entire company or large chunks of it, you first need to actively manage the energy of your own team and to act as role model for energetic action. Recall Hilti's Our Culture Journey program, in which the executive board members went through the culture camps *first,* to demonstrate their full engagement by managing their own energy, focus, and confidence. This personal involvement and proactive energy management at the highest levels at Hilti continuously contributes to the seriousness and effectiveness of culture development in the company as a whole. The box "How Well Do You Manage Your Organization's Energy?" asks three simple questions that you can use to quickly get a snapshot of your performance as a manager.

How Well Do You Manage Your Organization's Energy?

- Do you regularly assess the energy (the use of human potential) of your organization or unit and compare it against benchmarks or best practices?

- Do you set explicit ambitious goals in terms of leveraging your organization's energy?

- Do you actively manage the energy in your own management team?

Mobilizing Energy Around a Dragon or a Princess

The two mobilizing strategies to jump-start organizations we presented in this book—slaying the dragon and winning the princess—work by involving employees in either overcoming a threat or pursuing an outstanding opportunity. Both strategies rely on organizations' need to focus on a single pursuit for a period when they are trying to boost energy. The need to focus also means organizations need to decide consciously *not* to pursue other opportunities at the same level of priority and attention. Essentially, mobilizing energy requires that you don't opportunistically let your company become an unfocused punchball of external forces in the environment. Instead, you must channel the internal forces toward clear challenges, fully commit yourself, and fight for the chosen focus, whether that means coping with a threat or pursuing an exceptional opportunity.

As with managing energy, you need to mobilize energy first through the choices you make (in this case, by settling on either the dragon or the princess strategy) and the behaviors you exhibit in pursuit of your choice. If you choose to slay the dragon, for example, you must have the backbone to address difficult issues, and you will need to admit that the company faces a fierce challenge. You must be ready to show humility: to convincingly demonstrate that you are unable to fight the threat alone and that you count on your people's abilities to jointly solve the problem. In choosing to slay the dragon, you must admit that management is not omnipotent and does not have all the answers. Executives often struggle to acknowledge their limited influence and to simultaneously evoke the feeling that their people are needed. Yet at this time in particular, you need your people to be fully engaged and full of ideas and motivation if your organization is to overcome the imminent threat. When you are able to boost this motivation, people across the company tend to go far beyond expectations and invest their full potential to support the company, as we have seen at organizations such as Lufthansa, Lidl, and Sonova.

This strategy also requires that you resist the urge to pamper your people. Protecting employees from the true nature of a threat only prevents them from taking responsibility and becoming fully involved in the solution. Instead of taking on the full burden and delegating small activities into bite-sized pieces for your people—as executives so often do—you must trust your employees' ability to slay the dragon with the full force of their energy. This is the only way to create full involvement: to trust in the energy of your people.

The winning-the-princess strategy, on the other hand, requires that you focus your personal energy on an exceptional opportunity or vision—essentially, a dream with a due date. Creating a picture of a desired future is also a highly personal task for you as a leader, because it reveals your most closely held emotions and ambitions for the organization. Keeping in mind that there is no guarantee that the company will reach the desired princess or goal, you as a leader must nevertheless make your object of desire public to the company while demonstrating to your people the confidence that, together, you will succeed. We have seen leaders inspire their people in this way: Hubertus von Gruenberg at Continental AG, Gunther Olesch at Phoenix Contact, Tom Johnstone at SKF, and B. Muthuraman at Tata Steel.

While winning the princess implies committing to an object of desire and pursuing it with undivided effort, you should not become so narrowly focused as to miss the forest for the trees. Your commitment to the vision must be complemented by an openness to consider others' ideas, possible modifications, and other impulses. If you manage to accept these as enrichments, opportunities for further development of your own visions, then you will be able to involve others in the vision implementation and have the chance to grow personally (see "How Well Do You Mobilize Energy in Your Organization?"). Achim Badstübner, head of exterior design at Audi, described this interplay of his vision and external impulses as intense personal development. If you achieve this balance, you are on your way to a richer and more rewarding process; if you don't, you risk daydreaming, frustration, or reduced readiness for change. Badstübner explained the interplay: "The design process is similar to a love relationship. You may have an ideal idea, but you will only be able to develop an end result that you love even more than your original vision if you embrace the imperfect, the deviances, and the external impulses. This openness for the unexpected requires personal strength and courage—the courage to love. This courage is contagious—people in the team will also feel inspired to realize the vision and fight for it despite constraints, setbacks, and challenges of daily work."

How Well Do You Mobilize Energy in Your Organization?

- Do you mobilize the energy of your company or unit around a distinctive objective or priority that is clear to everyone—be it coping with a threat or pursuing an exceptional opportunity?

- In dealing with an overall threat or challenge, do your people understand that you count on them to conquer it?

- In pursuing a vision, do you balance full commitment and confidence with an openness to internal and external impulses?

Forcefully Cutting Corrosion

Effectively managing energy requires that you as a leader directly confront negativity and destructive forces. Again, this is a matter of choices you make and behaviors you exhibit. Yet many leaders isolate themselves from corrosive energy, to deny or even to actively ignore it. As in the fable of the emperor's new clothes, these leaders encourage an organizational environment that filters out negative signals, and they live in a world of artificial harmony. The problem is that as a rule, corrosive energy begins with minor issues, which when disregarded become stronger and more contagious until they start to dominate how people in your organization collaborate and do business. When you as a leader clearly exhibit passive behavior toward corrosion, you become part of the problem, allowing strong negative forces in the company to dominate and send the organization spiraling into the corrosion trap.

While you don't need to know every minor detail about conflicts and internal competition, you should become sensitive to weak signals and relevant misalignment within the company. Only then can you intervene quickly and prevent possible negative spirals that can damage performance and morale. To nip corrosive energy in the bud, demonstrate through your actions that your number one priority is to address corrosive acts directly. You can do this by taking the time to thoroughly analyze the sources of corrosive energy and then quickly and uncompromisingly remove them, as ABB, Lidl, and Otto Group did. Often, delicate issues such as a lack of integrity or power games in individual departments lie at the heart of the problem, and you may feel reticent to confront employees. But as a leader, you really have no choice but to get to the bottom of corrosion where it is brewing and act upon it.

Ultimately, you are a role model and should reflect this in your own behavior and integrity, staying ever mindful of your impact on others. When your personal behavior demonstrates that corrosive engagement is not accepted, you develop a culture where corrosive energy is dealt with in an uncompromising way. Therefore, don't shy away from taking strong measures when they are necessary, especially when employees spread corrosive energy, even if these individuals may be high performers.

Most important, you must start first with yourself and your own team when searching for signs of corrosion before looking at the organization as a whole. If there is distrust, aggression, misalignment, or other destructive energy in yourself or your management team, then you must be ready to do a thorough analysis of the sources of corrosive energy. You must be ready to admit your own mistakes and deal with the criticism, while forcefully removing the corrosive energy. As an executive, you ultimately lead by example and become a role model in dealing with negativity—for better or worse, and whether you realize it or not (see "How Good Are You at Cutting Corrosion?").

How Good Are You at Cutting Corrosion?

- Are you sensitive to weak signals of corrosive forces in your organization, and do you actively confront negativity?

- Is removing the sources of destructive energy a top priority for you?

- Do you regularly seek out feedback and reflect on your own behavior to find out whether you are part of the corrosive forces in your organization?

(continued)

- When finding signs of negativity, are you ready to confront destructive forces, deal with criticism, and admit possible mistakes to work off corrosive energy?

- Do you value the overall organizational purpose more than your own agenda?

Decelerating

As we mentioned earlier, about 50 percent of all companies fall victim to overacceleration: they lack focus and constantly operate at their limits, overtaxing employees, and driving the organization to collective burnout. Leaders must consciously reject the simplified interpretation of *Citius, altius, fortius.* Rather than constantly pushing the company beyond its capabilities, as a leader you can achieve your company's goals more effectively by focusing fully on fewer activities, but making them the *right* ones. Although this idea contradicts common leadership patterns of striving ever harder and higher, companies today need leaders who are willing to allow their organizations to "slow down to speed up." Curb the pace of your organization by stopping unnecessary activities and actively introducing a pit-stop culture.

Unfortunately, it is often the leaders themselves who generate overacceleration in their organizations because of their own lack of focus and their sense of busyness (to see whether you as a leader are part of your organization's overacceleration problem, answer the questions in "How Well Do You Decelerate Your and the Organization's Energy When It Is Needed?"). Yet only a small share of managers in organizations are highly energetic and focused; about 40 percent of all managers contribute to their company's lack of focus and overacceleration—busy managers.[2] Overenergetic leaders lack focus and enthusiastically produce a constant stream of ideas or initiatives and thus begins a vicious cycle, with leaders overwhelming their units or organizations, employees shutting down, executives increasing the pressure, and employees pushing back harder. When your employees start talking about the "new flavor of the month," you know they've hit their limit on new ideas.

How Well Do You Decelerate Your and the Organization's Energy When It Is Needed?

- Do you regularly check whether your company is showing signs of organizational burnout?

- Do you package initiatives with passion while establishing realistic, reachable goals?

- Do you regularly allow your company to slow down in order to speed up again?

- Do you personally take regular pit stops to recharge, refocus, and reflect on the top priorities of your company?

Again, leading by example is the best antidote. As a leader, you need to go beyond simply developing new ideas; your role must be instead to clarify for yourself and your employees where the organization or unit needs to concentrate its energy—and to make sure your people feel part of that process.

Moreover, in your daily life, you must become a role model, taking time-outs to show your troops that you take such a strategy seriously. As we mentioned earlier, Bill Gates takes a week off twice a year just to think, and recently, so have forty-three of his top teams at Microsoft. Only by slowing down and reflecting can you see beyond the daily business at hand and lead people deliberately toward your company's top priorities. Energetic managers with a clear sense of focus know what matters for the organization in the long term; taking regular pit stops sends a signal to the organization that decelerating is key for eventually speeding up again.

The Courage to Lead an Energized Company

As we saw in chapter 5, one of the greatest leadership challenges is sustaining energy—moving beyond number one. This is a fundamentally different challenge from *becoming* number one. When your company is in the lead, the biggest test you face as an executive is overcoming the fear of being unable to repeat success. Instead of moving beyond number one, you might sometimes be so focused on preserving the status quo that you can become paralyzed by a fear of the organization's decline. When this happens, you might tend to keep the status quo, stop questioning existing decisions and solutions, and cease trying new approaches. The result? Stagnation.

Instead, you need to be ready to switch from mobilizing energy to sustaining energy, which requires a fundamental shift in where that energy originates. Top leaders are the main source of energy in the mobilizing strategies of slaying the dragon and winning the princess, no matter how deeply they involve their teams in overcoming the challenge or taking advantage of the opportunity. But sustaining energy relies on many sources of energy, and that's why your main focus must switch from identifying opportunities or challenges and energizing the organization to building a management system that creates multiple energy sources.

To do so, one decisive step is to develop strong leaders on different levels and in different parts of the organization. These leaders work as energizers and generate a proactive sense of urgency in their various teams and units. Many executives have trouble learning this crucial skill; it's not laissez-faire leadership, but on the contrary, a highly demanding, active leadership that is based on two important actions: first, fully commit the organization to high performance, and second, develop the courage to let go. Yes, courage: the courage to accept no longer being the primary source of energy in the organization.

Love of Peak Performance

In a program called 21 grams, Audi explicitly strengthens its employees' love of peak performance—love of the product, the inner desire to improve even the smallest details, and the readiness to constantly go to the limit.[3] The program has several phases, during which the whole executive board experiences and reflects on Audi's unique, deeply internalized attitudes and behavioral patterns—the soul of Audi. In a further step, other groups of top executives participate in 21 grams to strengthen and spread the love of peak performance throughout the organization. At the end of the nineteenth century, Audi's founder, August Horch, left a previous employer because he felt the company had no visionary power. Instead of pursuing the "as good as necessary" principle practiced at his former employer, he founded his company on the principle of "as good as possible." It was his love of this philosophy that Audi's current leadership seeks to engender in its employees.

Other organizations share this love of achieving the best possible. As discussed in chapter 5, the German soccer club FC Bayern Munich, like only a few organizations, stands for ongoing, exceptional success. The whole club has uncompromisingly committed to peak performance. It has committed to the "philosophy of the number one," as Oliver Kahn, longtime goalie of FC Bayern Munich and the German National Team, described it. Similarly, you need to secure maximum effort from your company if you hope to internalize the love of peak performance. Kahn explained to us this shared love of peak performance: "In our club, the top management team and every member of the club, with a certain level of positive brutality, does everything to ensure maximum success and never gives in. They are never really satisfied . . . Who wants to rest must not join FC Bayern Munich. Everywhere and always, progress and success has to be visible. That is the philosophy of the number one."

As a leader, not only must you internalize this philosophy, but you need to help your entire company internalize this as well. Only when you create *many leaders throughout the organization* who are responsible for the enterprise's success will your people develop a sustained sense of urgency and productive energy in the organization and help the company rise above number one.

Courage to Develop Leaders

Executives are used to being in control and in charge. Yet such control from the top works against a proactive sense of urgency in organizations. Perhaps the biggest challenge for leaders with strong personalities is to have the courage to provide their people enough freedom for growth and to actively develop them and transform them into leaders. This often feels wrong to most executives, who have learned the opposite throughout most of their careers. But with their sheer force and presence, charismatic leaders often suffocate initiative and the strengths of their people. They must have the courage to resist well-meant care and masterminding all moves and processes in advance and instead must foster strong leaders and then step back and let go systematically and in a disciplined way.

If you do not manage to let go, you can become the bottleneck yourself. As discussed earlier, when three out of the four members of Hilti's executive board—including CEO Pius Baschera—had to be let go within a two-year period, the outgoing leaders quickly empowered the next level of leaders, demonstrating how independent Hilti truly was from its big leaders at the top.

During the 2006 world championship, Oliver Kahn experienced a special situation of letting go. He had long dreamed of winning the world championship with his German teammates in Germany, but he was not selected to start for the team and had to watch the game from the bench. He remembered this as the greatest challenge in his professional career: "I did not really know how to deal with it until I realized, this is exactly what life is expecting from you, from someone who wanted to become champion at all means." Often, making maximal effort is easier for strong leaders than letting go, but there is also another form of leadership: leading others to success. Kahn reflected: "I took on this challenge which led to this unbelievable result: I was not the great loser, but to the contrary, people were grateful and it was emotionally enormously rewarding. I had always believed that you can only win if you play yourself on the pitch and get the title. No, you can also win when not fighting on the pitch and getting the title yourself."

In order to sustain energy in your organization, you as a top executive must learn to let go like Kahn. You must learn that leading your company beyond number one does not imply that you must be the best performer yourself—but you must help others grow, win, and lead.

Such letting go is all the more difficult because many executives often enjoy the limelight. In our experience, there is a huge difference between leaders who intellectually grasp the potential of the energy concept but do not lead accordingly, and those who engage with energizing leadership and exploit the full potential of the tools and leadership strategies in practice. The latter develop one decisive, differentiating attribute: the courage to take on energizing activities and to overcome uncertainties, superficiality, and halfheartedness in dealing with the energy of their people.

To sustain energy, you must step back and have the courage to open the stage to your people—and to let them lead and create the next organizational win. Rather than making you less important, such a move allows you to make others strong and help them lead, instead of leading yourself. Especially in challenging times, that is, in times of crises, increased competition, accelerated innovation cycles, and intensified changes in organizations, we need strong and energizing leaders on all levels of the hierarchy—leaders with optimism and confidence.

Unleashing and maintaining a company's energy is your foremost task as a leader. You have many resources at your disposal, but ultimately, no organizational resource is as powerful as the energy of your people—the shared inspiration, mental agility, and concerted action in pursuit of joint goals. And as we move forward into the future, orchestrating energy is becoming *the* task of leaders everywhere, in every kind of organization across the globe. To ignite great performance, you must first take charge of your own love of peak performance, passion, and courage to lead an energized company.

How to Assess Your Organization's Energy

Throughout the book, we've discussed the importance of objectively assessing your company's energy state so that you have a solid insight to define leadership activities that boost your organization's performance. Often, the best way to make this assessment is through a standard survey of the parties involved. For work with organizations, we have extensively used the Organizational Energy Questionnaire 12 (OEQ 12), a short, standardized survey instrument that consists of twelve self-assessment questions. We have found that these self-assessments gave us an unbiased, accurate snapshot of the four energy states in an organization.

The OEQ 12

You, too, can use the OEQ 12 (Organizational Energy Questionnaire) as a self-assessment of your organization's energy (or unit's or team's energy).[1] It offers a way to quickly and systematically translate executives' and employees' experiences and thinking about the use of their companies' human potential into a transparent energy profile. Your organization's energy profile provides a precise picture of the distribution of the four energy states across the company, unit, or team. When you understand the strengths and possible weaknesses of your company's energy states, you can take certain actions to improve the energy situation. Then, as you read through this book, you will find a variety of leadership strategies to combat key energy challenges, for example, by mobilizing energy, overcoming corrosive energy, mastering the acceleration trap (avoiding the overabundance of energy), and sustaining productive energy.

Take the survey yourself now, using the OEQ 12, so that you will get the most from reading this book and will identify leadership activities you need to take in your organization, unit, or team. As you proceed, you should also invite your employees at all levels to complete the questions to gain a more complete picture about your unit. Eventually, you should use the OEQ 12 repeatedly, to start working with other executives to gain a shared understanding of the energy profile and energy issues in their entire teams, departments, and companies.

How to Complete the OEQ 12

1. Answer the twelve questions on the OEQ 12 using the appropriate answer column provided (table A-1). Keep your answers focused on your area of responsibility, for example, the whole company, division, unit, or department that you are responsible for. If you invite your employees to fill in the questionnaire, they should keep their answers focused on the unit or team to which they belong.

2. Avoid opting repeatedly for the middle-ground answer "Neutral."

3. Follow the instructions in table A-2 to calculate your energy scores for the four energy states.

4. Plot the scores from table A-2 into figure A-1, "Your Energy Profile." Connect the lines for a spider-web-like analysis. This is your organization's (division's, unit's or department's) energy profile (its OE Index). You can compare the values of your energy profile against the benchmark values in figure A-1 as a preliminary indicator. But we always tell clients that benchmark

TABLE A-1

The twelve-question Organizational Energy Questionnaire (OEQ 12)

No.	People in my _____ (please fill in "company," "department," "unit" or "team") . . .	Strongly disagree	Disagree	Neutral	Agree	Strongly agree
1	. . . like what they are doing.	0	25	50	75	100
2	. . . do not have much drive.	0	25	50	75	100
3	. . . feel relaxed in their jobs.	0	25	50	75	100
4	. . . are angry in their jobs.	0	25	50	75	100
5	. . . feel enthusiastic in their jobs.	0	25	50	75	100
6	. . . have no desire to make something happen.	0	25	50	75	100
7	. . . often speculate about the real intentions of our management.	0	25	50	75	100
8	. . . really care about the fate of this company.	0	25	50	75	100
9	. . . are efficient in how they conduct their work.	0	25	50	75	100
10	. . . often behave in a destructive manner.	0	25	50	75	100
11	. . . go out of their way to ensure that the company succeeds.	0	25	50	75	100
12	. . . feel discouraged in their jobs.	0	25	50	75	100

values have to be considered carefully. So far, we have not found differences according to industry, but size of the organization could usually play a role.

5. We have provided a few typical energy profiles that we have come across in our work with companies. Those and the profiles you have read at the end of chapter 1 will help you to identify strengths, potential weaknesses, and challenges in your own energy profile. Chapters 2 through 5 provide strategies and tools for how you can respond to your organization's particular challenges.

TABLE A-2

Calculating your energy scores

Productive energy score
Add up the numbers from questions 5, 8 and 11: _____ and divide by three: _____.
This is your self-assessed productive energy score: _____.

Comfortable energy score
Add up the numbers from questions 1, 3 and 9: _____ and divide by three: _____.
This is your self-assessed comfortable energy score: _____.

Resigned inertia score
Add up the numbers from questions 2, 6 and 12: _____ and divide by three: _____.
This is your self-assessed resigned inertia score: _____.

Corrosive energy score
Add up the numbers from questions 4, 7 and 10: _____ and divide by three: _____.
This is your self-assessed corrosive energy score: _____.

Interpreting Your OE Index

1. Look at your energy profile (OE Index), and identify the strongest energy state or states. Be aware that managers' self-evaluations are often significantly better than how employees evaluate the same organization, unit, or team. In other words, your results as a manager or leader may be positively biased by around 5–10 percent. Compare your unit's scores with the benchmark numbers in figure A-1, noting the following:

   - Productive energy should be around 75+ percent or higher (ideally around 80 percent).

   - Comfortable energy should not be dominant. A score around 70 percent and higher is very good if productive energy is at least as high. Resigned inertia should not be higher than 20–25 percent. Look closely at the resigned forces in the organization when resigned inertia is 25 percent or higher.

   - Corrosive energy should not be higher than 20–25 percent. Pay close attention to destructive forces in the organization when corrosive energy is 25 percent or higher.

FIGURE A-1

Your OE Index, or energy profile

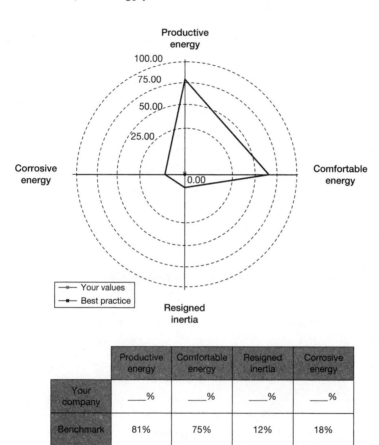

	Productive energy	Comfortable energy	Resigned inertia	Corrosive energy
Your company	___%	___%	___%	___%
Benchmark	81%	75%	12%	18%

Note: Benchmark data are from the top 10 percent of companies from a study with approximately 24,000 respondents in 187 German companies.

2. Write down the strengths and weaknesses in the energy profile of your company (division, unit, department). Write a detailed list of causes for each strength and weakness.

3. Take some further steps to deepen your understanding of the energy profile and the drivers of the results. Go back to the questions, think of typical behaviors and incidents that apply to the questions for the most critical energy state or states, and note

them on an additional sheet of paper. Then, identify root causes for the behaviors and incidents in your organization.

4. By now, you should have deeper insight into the energy of your unit of responsibility. Below we have listed some typical scenarios with potentially relevant leadership challenges and links back to the chapters in this book that you may want to read more closely.

5. You can begin sharing your results and analysis with your colleagues and your team. Also, you can invite them to undergo the same process in advance and then compare results and insights to start developing a shared understanding of the energy states in your company, the challenges it faces, and the actions needed to deal with these challenges.

Potential Energy Profiles from Your Self-Assessment

Although we cannot create here an exhaustive list of possible scenarios, this list should offer a starting point for helping you to determine possible actions to take.

Clearly productive energy: You are in the fortunate situation that your company (division, unit, or team) is predominantly in the productive energy zone—productive energy is high (above 75 percent), comfortable energy is not higher than productive energy, and both negative energy states are low, that is, below 25 percent. Jump-starting and mobilizing the positive forces of your company is not your core challenge. Rather, it is how to sustain the high productive energy in your unit. Chapter 5 offers help with sustaining energy and staying clear of the complacency trap, and chapter 4 offers tips on avoiding overacceleration.

Mixed bag of productive and comfortable energy: Your scores of productive energy are not particularly high, and comfortable energy is equally strong or even higher than the productive-energy score. Your main challenge is to mobilize productive energy. There are two alternative leadership strategies that you can use: mobilizing energy by involving people in overcoming a threat or negative challenge (slaying-the-dragon strategy) or involving people in achieving an exceptional opportunity (winning-the-princess strategy). Chapter 2 describes jump-starting the organization through both the princess and dragon strategies, and chapter 5 shows you how to prevent the complacency trap.

Corrosive energy with some productive energy: Corrosive energy is much higher than 25 percent and dominates your profile. The key challenge is to neutralize the destructive energy in your company. You cannot translate corrosive into productive energy—this attempt is a common mistake in management practice. Instead, you need to eliminate negativity; calm the organization down; and create room and openness for new trust, readiness to collaborate, and new interest in pursuing joint goals. Only when the corrosive energy is cleaned up can you begin to improve productive energy in the organization. See chapter 3 for actions you can begin to take now.

Mostly resigned inertia or comfortable energy: Unleashing productive energy should be your core concern and most important challenge. There are two alternative leadership strategies that you can use to mobilize energy: involving people in overcoming a threat or negative challenge (slaying the dragon) or involving people in achieving an exceptional opportunity (winning the princess). See chapter 2 on jump-starting the organization. In the case of strong resigned inertia, a lack of focus, and an overburdened organization, see chapter 4 on how to overcome the acceleration trap.

No energy whatsoever: Your company or unit doesn't score very high on any of the four energy states. Your unit has lost the ability to buzz with any kind of energy, positive or negative. People collectively have lost so much interest in the company, its purpose, and its activities that even on the negative side, people show little resignation, frustration, cynicism, or fighting spirit. Collective apathy prevails. Chapter 2 offers advice on mobilizing energy, and chapter 5 explains how to help change the mental habits, behavioral patterns, and emotional routines in your organization by developing a vitalizing management system.

Notes

Introduction

1. J. Dutton, *Energize Your Workplace* (New York: Jossey-Bass, 2003), 7.

2. A. Boesche, H. Bruch, and J. Kunz, "Die Kraft positiver Energien," *Personalwirtschaft* (December 2008): 54–56.

3. The Organizational Energy Questionnaire (OEQ) is copyrighted © 2010 by Institute for Leadership and Human Resource Management, University of St. Gallen, Switzerland. All rights reserved in all media.

4. Unless otherwise noted, quotations by executives are from interviews we have conducted.

5. H. Bruch and S. Ghoshal, "Unleashing Organizational Energy," *Sloan Management Review* 44 (2003): 45–51.

6. Similar to the idea of burnout and its emotional, cognitive, and physical dimension, the force of organizational energy consists of an interplay of emotional, cognitive, and physical characteristics of a company. See A. Pines, E. Aronson, and A. Aronson, *Career Burnout: Causes and Cures* (New York: Free Press, 1988).

7. For emotional energy, see Dutton, *Energize Your Workplace,* 7. For flow, see M. Csikszentmihalyi, *Finding Flow: The Psychology of Engagement with Everyday Life* (New York: Basic Books, 1997). For vitality, see R. M. Ryan and C. Frederick, "On Energy, Personality, and Health: Subjective Vitality as a Dynamic Reflection of Well-Being," *Journal of Personality* 65 (1997): 529–565. For thriving, see G. Spreitzer et al., "A Socially Embedded Model of Thriving at Work," *Organization Science* 16 (2005): 537–549. For vigor, see A. Shirom, "Feeling Vigorous at Work? The Construct of Vigor and the Study of Positive Affect in Organizations," in *Research in Organizational Stress and Well-Being,* ed. D. Ganster and P. L. Perrewe (Greenwich, CT: JAI Press, 2003), 135–165. For motivation, see E. A. Locke, "The Motivation Sequence, the Motivation Hub, and the Motivation Core," *Organizational Behavior and Human Decision Process* 50 (1991): 288–299; E. A. Locke, G. P. Latham, and M. Erez, "The Determinants of Goal Commitment," *Academy of Management Review* 13 (1988): 23–39. For positive arousal, see R. W. Quinn, and J. E. Dutton, "Coordination as Energy-in-Conversation," *Academy of Management Review* 30 (2005): 36–57. For engagement and vigor, see A. B. Bakker and E. Demerouti, "Towards a Model of Work Engagement," *Career Development International* 13, no. 3 (2008): 209–223.

8. S. G. Barsade, "The Ripple Effect: Emotional Contagion and Its Influence on Group Behavior," *Administrative Science Quarterly* 47 (2002): 644–675; E. Hatfield, J. T. Cacioppo, and R. L. Rapson, *Emotional Contagion* (New York: Cambridge University Press, 1994).

9. F. Walter and H. Bruch, "The Positive Group Affect Spiral: A Dynamic Model of the Emergence of Positive Affective Similarity in Work Groups," *Journal of Organizational Behavior* 29 (2008): 239–261.

10. E. H. Schein, *The Corporate Culture Survival Guide,* new and revised ed. (New York: John Wiley and Sons, 2009).

11. For our quantitative research, we developed the Organizational Energy Questionnaire (OEQ) as a survey tool for measuring and analyzing a company's energy state and assessing key drivers of energy such as leadership, strategic direction, and empowerment. We measured the energy in more than

seven hundred organizations, with more than 250,000 individuals participating in organizational energy assessments based on the OEQ. The responses cover fifty-five countries and twenty-five languages and include participants from the United States, Europe, and Asia. We found no significant differences among the energy profiles of organizations from different geographical regions. In some companies, we repeated the survey up to five times to assess energy over time. We also tested the impact of energy on performance. For our qualitative research, we conducted more than thirty case studies, for example, at ABB, Airbus, Alinghi, Alstom Power Service, Audi, Baloise Insurance, BMW, buw, Carlson Wagonlit Travel, Continental AG, Hilti, IBM, Lidl Switzerland, Lufthansa, Microsoft, Otto Group, Phoenix Contact, Sonova, Stryker, Sulzer, Swiss International Air Lines, Tata Steel, Tata Motors, and Unaxis. Within our extensive data collection over the years and in more than ninety workshops with top executives and line managers of various international companies, our energy-related leadership strategies and tools have proven to be practically relevant and effective.

12. H. Bruch and S. Ghoshal, "Unleashing Organizational Energy," *Sloan Management Review* 44 (2003): 45–51.

13. H. Bruch et al., "High Performance Work Systems and Firm Performance: The Mediating Role of Organizational Energy," paper presented at the Academy of Management Meeting, Chicago, 2009.

14. Data for energy states are based on a subsample of 3,773 respondents in 104 German companies in 2009; data for performance measures are based on a subsample of 225 top management team members in 104 German companies, also in 2009.

15. For a description of these consequences of collective energy in use, see A. Etzioni, *The Active Society* (New York: The Free Press, 1975).

16. Bruch et al., "High Performance Work Systems"; A. M. L. Raes and H. Bruch, "How Top Management Team Behavioral Integration Influences Organizational Energy and Employee Outcomes," working paper, 2010; H. Bruch, M. Cole, and B. Vogel, "Linking Productive Organizational Energy to Firm Performance and Individuals' Satisfaction," paper presented at the Academy of Management Meeting, Philadelphia, 2007.

17. H. Bruch and S. Poralla, "Sonova 2008: Orchestrating the Innovation Beat," Case Study (St. Gallen, Switzerland: University of St. Gallen, 2008).

Chapter 1

1. H. Bruch and S. Ghoshal, "Unleashing Organizational Energy," *Sloan Management Review* 44 (2003): 45–51.

2. R. Cross, W. Baker, and A. Parker, "What Creates Energy in Organizations?" *Sloan Management Review* 44 (2003): 51–56; and D. N. Sull, "Are You Ready to Rebound?" *Harvard Business Review*, March 2010, 70–74.

3. Q. N. Huy, "Emotional Balancing of Organizational Continuity and Radical Change: The Contribution of Middle Managers," *Administrative Science Quarterly*, 47, no. 1 (2002): 31–69; F. Walter and H. Bruch, "The Positive Group Affect Spiral: A Dynamic Model of the Emergence of Positive Affective Similarity in Work Groups," *Journal of Organizational Behavior* 29 (2008): 239–261.

4. H. Bruch and S. Poralla, "Sonova 2008: Orchestrating the Innovation Beat," Case Study (Gallen, Switzerland: University of St. Gallen, 2008).

5. H. Bruch, "Lufthansa 2003: Energising a Decade of Change," Case Study (St. Gallen, Switzerland: University of St. Gallen, in cooperation with Lufthansa School of Business, 2003).

6. Ibid.

7. J. Dutton, *Energize Your Workplace* (New York: Jossey-Bass, 2003). See also these articles on teams' positive emotions and performance: S. G. Barsade, "The Ripple Effect: Emotional Contagion and Its Influence on Group Behavior," *Administrative Science Quarterly* 47 (2002): 644–675; P. Totterdell, "Catching Moods and Hitting Runs: Mood Linkage and Subjective Performance in Professional Sport Teams," *Journal of Applied Psychology* 85 (2000): 848–859.

8. Data for energy states were based on a subsample of 3,773 respondents from 104 German companies in 2009; data for performance measures were based on a subsample of 225 top management team members from 104 German companies in 2009.

9. Data were based on a subsample of respondents from 104 German companies in 2009: 3,783 respondents for energy states, 3,886 respondents for commitment, and 3,893 respondents for satisfaction.

10. Data for employee energy states were based on a subsample of 3,783 respondents from 104 German companies in 2009. Data for top management team energy states were based on a subsample of 225 TMT members from 104 German companies in 2009.

11. This working hypothesis was based on the work of John Kotter, who observed that companies that are in the comfort zone have difficulties with change. For more information, see J. Kotter, *A Sense of Urgency* (Boston: Harvard Business School Press, 2008).

12. P. Cooke and J. Hastings,"New Industries: Imperative for Agriculture's Survival, Regional Australia Summit," October 27–29, 1999.

13. For Laura Ashley and IBM, see D. N. Sull, "Why Good Companies Go Bad," *Harvard Business Review,* July–August 1999. For Swissair, see W. Ruigrok, "A Tale of Strategic and Governance Errors," *European Business Forum* 17 (2004): 56–60. For Polaroid, see H. De Bodinat, M. Dougan, and C. Urdl, "Product Alignment: The Key Driver of Profit and Growth," *Prism* 1 (2004): 23–39.

14. D. N. Sull, *Why Good Companies Go Bad and How Great Managers Remake Them* (Boston: Harvard Business Press, 2005).

15. S. Raisch et al., "Organizational Ambidexterity: Balancing Exploitation and Exploration for Sustained Performance," *Organization Science* 20, no. 4 (2009): 685–695.

16. Sull, *Why Good Companies Go Bad.*

17. M. Tushman and C. A. O'Reilly III, "Ambidextrous Organizations: Managing Evolutionary and Revolutionary Change," *California Management Review* 38 (1996): 8–30.

18. Sull, *Why Good Companies Go Bad.*

19. F. Walter, and H. Bruch, "Structural Impacts on the Occurrence and Effectiveness of Transformational Leadership: An Empirical Study at the Organizational Level of Analysis," *Leadership Quarterly* 21(2010): 765–782.

20. E. H. Schein, *The Corporate Culture Survival Guide,* new and rev. ed. (New York: John Wiley and Sons, 2009).

21. P. Brandes, R. Dharwadkar, and J. W. Dean, "Does Organizational Cynicism Matter? Employee and Supervisor Perspectives on Work Outcomes," *Eastern Academy of Management Best Papers Proceedings* (1999): 150. See also M. S. Cole, H. Bruch, and B. Vogel, "Emotion as Mediators of the Relations Between Perceived Supervisor Support and Psychological Hardiness on Employee Cynicism," *Journal of Organizational Behavior* 27 (2006): 463–484.

22. Data were based on a subsample of respondents from 104 German companies in 2009: 3,783 respondents for energy states, 3,886 respondents for commitment, 3,893 respondents for satisfaction and 225 TMT members for performance measures.

23. H. Bruch and W. Jenewein, "ABB 2005: Rebuilding Focus, Identity, and Pride," Case Study (St. Gallen, Switzerland: University of St. Gallen, 2005).

24. K. Braham and C. Heimer, *A.B.B., the Dancing Giant: Creating the Globally Connected Corporation* (London: Pitman Publishing, 1998).

25. Bruch and Ghoshal, "Unleashing Organizational Energy."

26. T. A. Wright and D. G. Bonnett, "The Contribution of Burnout to Work Performance," *Journal of Organizational Behavior* 18 (1997): 491–499; T. A. Wright and R. Cropanzano, "Emotional Exhaustion as a Predictor of Job Performance and Voluntary Turnover," *Journal of Applied Psychology* (1998): 486–493; H. Bruch and I. J. Menges, "The Acceleration Trap," *Harvard Business Review,* April 2010, 80–86; J. W. Greenwood III and J. W. Greenwood Jr., *Managing Executive Stress* (New York: John Wiley & Sons, 1979).

27. G. Probst and S. Raisch, "Die Logik des Niedergangs," *Harvard Business Manager* 26 (2004): 37–45.

28. H. Bruch and S. Poralla, "Transformationale Führung bei Baloise Schweiz 2007," Case Study (St. Gallen, Switzerland: University St. Gallen, 2007).

29. Bruch, "Lufthansa 2003."

30. Q. N. Huy, "Emotional Balancing of Organizational Continuity and Radical Change," *Administrative Science Quarterly* 47(2002): 31–69.

31. A. C. Edmonson and D. Mclain Smith, "Too Hot to Handle? How to Manage Relationship Conflict," *California Management Review* 19 (2006): 6–27.

32. Data were based on a subsample of 5,904 respondents for trust and 409 TMT members for TMT energy states and performance measures (from 164 German companies, overall) in 2008.

33. Data were based on a subsample of 5,976 respondents for company energy states and 397 TMT members for TMT energy states (from 104 German companies, overall) in 2009.

34. M. Masuch, "Vicious Circles in Organizations," *Administrative Science Quarterly* 30 (1985): 14–33; H. L. Rausch, "Interaction Sequences," *Journal of Personality and Social Psychology* 2 (1965): 487–499.

35. S. Hareli and A. Rafaeli, "Emotion Cycles: On the Social Influence of Emotion in Organizations," *Research in Organizational Behavior* 28 (2008): 35–59; J. R. Kelly and R. Barsade, "Emotions in Small Groups and Work Teams," Organizational Behavior and Human Decision Processes 86 (2001): 99–130; B. Parkinson, "Emotions Are Social," *British Journal of Psychology* 87 (1996): 663–684.

36. S. G. Barsade and D. E. Gibson, "Why Does Affect Matter in Organizations?" *Academy of Management Perspectives* 21 (2007): 36–59; C. A. Bartel and R. Saavedra, "The Collective Construction of Work Group Moods," *Administrative Science Quarterly* 45 (2000): 197–232.

37. P. J. Frost, *Toxic Emotions at Work: How Compassionate Managers Handle Pain and Conflict* (Boston: Harvard Business School Press, 2003).

38. Data are based on a subsample of 104 German companies overall in 2009: 3,773 respondents for energy states, and 3,834 respondents for identity.

39. Data were based on ibid.

40. A. Boesche, H. Bruch, and J. Kunz, "Die Kraft positiver Energien," *Personalwirtschaft* 2 (2008): 54–56.

41. The OEQ 36 is copyrighted © 2010 by Institute for Leadership and Human Resource Management, University of St. Gallen, Switzerland. All rights reserved in all media.

42. The OEQ 12 is copyrighted © 2010 by Institute for Leadership and Human Resource Management, University of St. Gallen, Switzerland. All rights reserved in all media.

43. The Organizational Energy Index (OEI) is copyrighted © 2010 by Institute for Leadership and Human Resource Management, University of St. Gallen, Switzerland. All rights reserved in all media.

44. We categorized the participating companies in the top 10 percent, bottom 10 percent, and average, using the sample of 24,000 respondents in 187 German companies. We suggest the top 10 percent score as a benchmark.

45. Data were based on a subsample of 104 German companies overall in 2009: 3,783 respondents for energy states, 3,886 respondents for commitment, 3,673 respondents for turnover intention, and 225 TMT members for performance measures.

46. H. Bruch and B. Vogel, "Alstom Power Service 2005: Building a Service Identity," Case Study (St. Gallen, Switzerland: University of St. Gallen, 2004).

47. W. Graenicher, "Leadership und Identität. Untrennbar für Erfolg bei Alstom Power Service 2005," in *Leadership: Best Practices und Trends* ed. H. Bruch, S. Krummaker, and B. Vogel (Wiesbaden: Gabler), 219–230.

48. C. Bareil, A. Savoie, and S. Meunier, "Patterns of Discomfort with Organizational Change," *Journal of Change Management* 7 (2007): 12–24; S. Oreg, "Personality, Context, and Resistance to Organizational Change," *European Journal of Work and Organizational Psychology* 15 (2007): 73–101; S. K. Piderit, "Rethinking Resistance and Recognizing Ambivalence: A Multidimensional View of Attitudes Toward an Organizational Change," *Academy of Management Review* 25 (2000): 783–794; A. E. Rafferty and M. A. Griffin, "Perceptions of Organizational Change: A Stress and Coping Perspective," *Journal of Applied Psychology* 91 (2006): 1154–1162.

Chapter 2

1. H. Bruch and S. Ghoshal, "Unleashing Organizational Energy," *Sloan Management Review* 44 (fall 2003): 45–51 have vividly described these two strategies.

2. Ibid.

3. G. Hamel, and C. K. Prahalad, *Competing for the Future* (Boston: Harvard Business School Press, 1994).

4. R. S. Lazarus, *Emotion and Adaptation* (New York: Oxford University Press, 1991); N. H. Frijda, *The Emotions* (Cambridge: Cambridge University Press, 1986).

5. H. Bruch, "Lufthansa 2003: Energising a Decade of Change," Case Study (St. Gallen, Switzerland: University of St. Gallen, in cooperation with Lufthansa School of Business, 2003).

6. D. B. Bibeault, *Corporate Turnaround: How Managers Turn Losers into Winners* (New York: McGraw-Hill, 1982).

7. H. Bruch, B. Shamir, and G. Eilam-Shamir, "Managing Meanings in Times of Crises and Recovery: CEO Prevention-Oriented Leadership," in *Being There Even When You Are Not: Leading Through Strategy, Structures, and Systems,* ed. R. Hooijberg et al. (Oxford: JAI Press, 2007), 127–153.

8. R. A. Heifetz and D. L. Laurie, "The Work of Leadership," *Harvard Business Review,* January–February 1997, 132.

9. J. P. Kotter, *Leading Change* (Boston: Harvard Business Press, 1996).

10. R. S. Lazarus, *Emotion and Adaptation* (New York: Oxford University Press, 1991); N. H. Frijda, *The Emotions* (Cambridge: Cambridge University Press, 1986); J. M. George and J. Zhou, "Understanding When Bad Moods Foster Creativity and Good Ones Don't: The Role of Context and Clarity of Feelings," *Journal of Applied Psychology* 87(2002): 687–697.

11. J. E. Dutton and S. Jackson, "Categorizing Strategic Issues: Links to Organizational Action," *Academy of Management Review* (1987): 76–90.

12. The last four strategies are drawing on self-efficacy theory. See A. Bandura, *Self-Efficacy: The Exercise of Control* (New York: Freeman, 1997).

13. Dutton and Jackson, Categorizing Strategic Issues."

14. Bandura, *Self-Efficacy*; R. D. Goddard, W. K. Hoy, and A. Woolfolk Hoy, "Collective Efficacy Beliefs: Theoretical Developments, Empirical Evidence, and Future Directions," *Educational Researcher* 33 (2004): 3–13.

15. C. B. Watson, M. M. Chemers, and Preiser, "Collective Efficacy: A Multilevel Analysis," *Personality and Social Psychology Bulletin* 27 (2001): 1057–1068.

16. Friday letter no. 3, September 13, 2002.

17. G. Chen and P. D. Bliese, "The Role of Different Levels of Leadership in Predicting Self- and Collective Efficacy: Evidence for Discontinuity," *Journal of Applied Psychology* 87 (2002): 549–556.

18. H. Bruch and S. Ghoshal, "Unleashing Organizational Energy."

19. J. P. Kotter, "Leading Change: Why Transformation Efforts Fail," *Harvard Business Review* March–April 1995, 59–67.

20. P. C. Nutt and R. W. Backoff, "Transforming Organizations with Second-Order Change," *Research in Organizational Change and Development* 10 (1997): 229–274.

21. A. Wrzesniewski and J. E. Dutton, "Crafting a Job: Revisioning Employees as Active Crafters of Their Work," *Academy of Management Review* 26 (2001): 179–201.

22. J. P. Kotter and D. S. Cohen, *The Heart of Change: Real-Life Stories of How People Change Their Organizations* (Harvard Business Press: Boston, 2002).

23. Bruch and Ghoshal, "Unleashing Organizational Energy."

24. T. C. Davenport and J. C. Beck, *The Attention Economy: Understanding the New Currency of Business* (Boston: Harvard Business Press, 2001); N. M. Tichy and M. A. Devanna, *The Transformational Leader* (New York: John Wiley & Sons, 1986), 179–180. Our empirical research shows repeated, statistically significant connections between a strong vision and emotional, mental, and action-based mobilization.

25. N. M. Tichy and S. Sherman, *Control Your Destiny or Someone Else Will: How Jack Welch Is Making General Electric the World's Most Competitive Corporation* (New York: Doubleday Business, 1993).

26. Bruch and Ghoshal, "Unleashing Organizational Energy."

27. B. Shamir, R. J. House, and M. B. Arthur, "The Motivational Effects of Charismatic Leadership: A Self-Concept-Based Theory," *Organizational Science* 4 (1993): 577–594. University of Michigan professor Kim Cameron recommends that executives need to engage much more in emotionally positive communication than they should in negative statements (K. S. Cameron, *Positive Leadership* [San Francisco: Berrett-Koehler, 2008]).

28. H. Bruch and U. Frei, "Tata Steel 2005: The Vision of Harmonizing Profitable Growth and Social Responsibility," Case Study (St. Gallen, Switzerland: University of St. Gallen, 2004).

29. See http://www.vijaygovindarajan.com/2009/03/the_tata_nano_product_or_socia.htm.

30. See http://www.ft.com/cms/s/0/94b77e52-b563-11dc-896e-0000779fd2ac.html.

31. R. M. Kanter, B. A. Stein, and D. T. Jick, "The 'Big Three' Model of Change," in *The Challenge of Organizational Change: How Companies Experience It and Leaders Guide It,* ed. R. M. Kanter, B. A. Stein, and D. T. Jick (New York: Free Press, 1992), 3–19; Kotter, "Leading Change."

32. Kotter, *Leading Change.*

33. H. Bruch, D. Dolle, and C. Schudy, "Die besten Arbeitgeber im deutschen Mittelstand," in *Top Job,* ed. W. Clement and H. Bruch (Heidelberg: Redline Wirtschaft, 2010), 4–19.

34. L. E. Ginzel, R. M. Kramer, and R. I. Sutton, "Organizational Impression Management as a Reciprocal Influence Process: The Neglected Role of the Organizational Audience," *Research in Organizational Behavior* (ed. B. M. Staw and L. L. Cummings) 15 (1993): 227–266.

35. Kotter, "Leading Change"; J. C. Collins, *Good to Great: Why Some Companies Make the Leap and Others Don't* (New York: HarperBusiness, 2001).

36. B. M. Bass and R. Bass, *Bass Handbook of Leadership,* 4th ed. (New York: Free Press, 2008**).**

37. Bruch and Ghoshal, "Unleashing Organizational Energy."

Chapter 3

1. S. G. Barsade, "The Ripple Effect: Emotional Contagion and Its Influence on Group Behavior," *Administrative Science Quarterly* 47 (2002): 644–675; E. Hatfield, J. T. Cacioppo, and R. L. Rapson, *Emotional Contagion* (New York: Cambridge University Press, 1994).

2. Ibid.

3. H. Bruch, "Lufthansa 2003: Energizing a Decade of Change," Case Study (St. Gallen, Switzerland: University of St. Gallen, in cooperation with Lufthansa School of Business, 2003).

4. E. W. Morrison and F. J. Milliken, "Organizational Silence: A Barrier to Organizational Change and Development in a Pluralistic World," *Academy of Management Review* 25 (2000): 706–725.

5. Data were based on a subsample of 104 German companies overall in 2009: 3,783 respondents for energy states, 3,886 respondents for commitment, 3,845 respondents for trust, and 3,673 respondents for turnover intention. Data for performance measures are based on a subsample of 225 top management team members from 104 German companies in 2009.

6. This person's real name and other relevant identifying information have been disguised.

7. Q. N. Huy, "Emotional Balancing of Organizational Continuity and Radical Change," *Administrative Science Quarterly* 47 (2002): 31–69.

8. H. Bruch and W. Jenewein, "ABB 2005: Rebuilding Focus, Identity, and Pride," Case Study (St. Gallen, Switzerland: University of St. Gallen, 2008).

9. Ibid.

10. This person's real name and other relevant identifying information have been disguised.

11. This person's real name and other relevant identifying information have been disguised.

12. R.-G. Zuelsdorf, *Strukturelle Konflikte in Unternehmen. Strategien für das Erkennen, Lösen, Vorbeugen* (Wiesbaden, Germany: Gabler, 2007).

13. Ibid.

14. This person's real name and other relevant identifying information have been disguised.

15. Zuelsdorf, *Strukturelle Konflikte.*

16. P. J. Frost and S. Robinson, "The Toxic Handler," *Harvard Business Review,* July–August 1999, 96–106.

17. The real names of individuals and other relevant identifying information have been disguised.

18. Frost and Robinson, "The Toxic Handler"; for middle managers, Huy, "Emotional Balancing," also speaks of the role of the therapist.

19. Frost and Robinson, "The Toxic Handler."

20. Ibid.

21. Ibid.

22. S. Albert and D. A. Whetten, "Organizational Identity," *Research in Organizational Behavior* 7 (1985): 263–295; N. Ellemers, D. De Gilder, and S. A. Haslam, "Motivating Individuals and Groups at Work: A Social Identity Perspective on Leadership and Group Performance," *Academy of Management Review* 29 (2004): 459–478.

23. H. Bruch and S. A. Boehm, "Organizational Energy and the Role of Identity," *Human Factor* 1 (2005): 38–43.

24. Data were based on a subsample of 164 German companies overall in 2008: 5,976 respondents for energy states, 5,939 respondents for pride, and 5,873 respondents for identification.

25. Data were based on a subsample of 164 German companies overall in 2008: 5,976 respondents for energy states and 5,698 respondents for strong shared vision.

26. Bruch and Boehm, "Organizational Energy."

27. S. A. Boehm, "Die organisationale Identität von Unternehmen als Quelle starker positiver Emotionen," in *Erfolgsfaktor Emotionales Kapital—Menschen begeistern, Ziele erreichen,* ed. J. Menges, L. Ebersbach, and C. Welling (Bern, Switzerland: Haupt, 2008), 71–90; H. Bruch and S. A. Boehm,

"ABB 2005: Rebuilding Focus, Identity, and Pride," teaching note to Case Study (St. Gallen, Switzerland: University of St. Gallen, 2004); Bruch and Boehm, "Role of Identity."

28. Bruch and Boehm, "ABB 2005," teaching note.

29. Ibid.

30. R. Deshon et al., "A Multiple Goal, Multilevel Model of Feedback Effects on the Regulation of Individual and Team Performance," *Journal of Applied Psychology* 89 (2004): 1035–1056.

31. There is only a small body of literature on the concepts of collective goal commitment: R. P. Deshon et al., "A Multiple Goal, Multilevel Model of Feedback Effects on the Regulation of Individual and Team Performance," *Journal of Applied Psychology* 89 (2004): 1035–1056; H. Klein, and P. W. Mulvey, "Two Investigations of the Relationships Among Group Goals, Goal Commitment, Cohesion, and Performance," *Organizational Behavior and Human Decision Processes* 61 (1995): 44–53; H. Klein and P. W. Mulvey, "The Impact of Perceived Loafing and Collective Efficacy on Group Goal Processes and Group Performance," *Organizational Behavior and Human Decision Processes* 74 (1998): 62–87. These publications usually conceptualize commitment at the team level of analysis. No studies known to the authors deal with goal commitment on an organizational level.

32. H. Bruch and B. Vogel, "Continental 2001: Liberating Entrepreneurial Energy," Case Study (St. Gallen, Switzerland: University of St. Gallen, 2001).

33. For a similar strategy on the team level, see R. Hackman, The Design of Work Teams," in *Handbook of Organizational Behavior,* ed. J. W. Lorsch (Englewood Cliffs, NJ: Prentice-Hall, 1987) 315–342.

34. Hollenbeck, Williams, Klein (1989).

35. For an analogous strategy on the individual level, see E. A. Locke, K. N. Shaw, and L. M. Saari, "Goal Setting and Task Performance," *Psychological Bulletin* 90 (1981): 125–152; K. D. McCaul, V. B. Hinsz, and H. S. McCaul, "The Effects of Commitment to Performance Goals on Effort," *Journal of Applied Psychology* 17 (1987): 437–452; L. J. Millward and L. J. Hopkins, "Psychological Contracts, Organizational and Job Commitment," *Journal of Applied Social Psychology* 28 (1998): 1530–1556.

36. Bruch and Boehm, "ABB 2005."

37. Friday letter no. 7, October 11, 2002.

38. B. E. Ashforth and F. Mael, "Social Identity Theory and the Organization," *Academy of Management Review* 14 (1989): 20–39.

39. Friday letter no. 88, July 2, 2004.

Chapter 4

1. H. Bruch and I. J. Menges, "The Acceleration Trap," *Harvard Business Review,* April 2010, 80–86.

2. Data were based on a subsample of 104 German companies overall in 2009: 3,783 respondents for energy states, 3,555 respondents for emotional exhaustion, 3,893 respondents for satisfaction, and 3,673 respondents for turnover intention. Data for performance measures were based on a subsample of 225 top management team members from 104 German companies in 2009.

3. Data were based on a subsample of 3,777 respondents in 104 German companies in 2009.

4. Data as in ibid.

5. Data as in ibid.

6. H. Bruch and W. Jenewein, "ABB 2005: Rebuilding Focus, Identity, and Pride," Case Study (St. Gallen, Switzerland: University of St. Gallen, 2005).

7. Data were based on a subsample of 3,777 respondents from 104 German companies in 2009.

8. H. Bruch, "Lufthansa 2003: Energizing a Decade of Change," Case Study (St. Gallen, Switzerland: University of St. Gallen, in cooperation with Lufthansa School of Business, 2003).

9. This person's name and other relevant identifying information have been disguised.

10. F. Malik, *Managing Performing Living* (Frankfurt: Campus Verlag, 2006), 323.

11. For the concept of energy and focus, see H. Bruch and S. Ghoshal, *A Bias for Action: How Effective Managers Harness Their Willpower, Achieve Results, and Stop Wasting Their Time* (Boston: Harvard Business Press, 2004).

12. Friday letter no. 57, 31 October 2003.

13. R. J. Zaugg and N. Thom, "Excellence Through Implicit Competencies: Human Resource Management, Organizational Development, Knowledge Creation," *Journal of Change Management* 3 (2003): 1–21.

14. D. A. Nadler, and M. L. Tushman, "Types of Organizational Change: From Incremental Improvement to Discontinuous Transformation," in *Discontinuous Change: Leading Organizational Transformation,* ed. D. A. Nadler, R. B. Shaw, and A. E. Walton (San Francisco: Jossey-Bass, 1994), 15–34; P. C. Nutt and R. W. Backoff, "Transforming Organizations with Second-Order Change," *Research in Organizational Change and Development* 10 (1997): 229–274.

15. H. Bruch and S. Poralla, "Hilti 2008: Leadership with Energy and Focus," Case Study (St. Gallen, Switzerland: University of St. Gallen, 2008).

16. Bruch and Poralla, "Hilti 2008."

17. H. Bruch, J. I. Menges, and C. Schudy, "Die besten Arbeitgeber im deutschen Mittelstand," in *Top Job,* ed. W. Clement and H. Bruch (Heidelberg: Redline Wirtschaft, 2008), 6–27.

Chapter 5

1. The work of N. Nohria, W. Joyce, and B. Roberson, "What Really Works," *Harvard Business Review,* July 2003, 42–52, supports our suggested management systems. The researchers studied must-have management practices for high-performance organizations and referred to strategy, culture, and structure as the primary components of these organizations and leadership as a secondary component. We have found that to a lesser extent, the secondary areas of execution, mergers and partnerships, talent, and innovation are directly linked to sustaining energy, but we have categorized these secondary areas as parts of the three management systems we described in the text (strategy, leadership structures, and culture). Moreover, we include Nohria, Joyce, and Roberson's "structure" in what we call "leadership structures." See also E. E. Lawler III and C. G. Worley, *Built to Change: How to Achieve Sustained Organizational Effectiveness* (San Francisco: Jossey-Bass, 2006).

2. The debate took place at the Swiss Performance Academy trend talk on June 6, 2008, in Zurich. Participants were Valentin Chapero, CEO of Sonova Group; Oswald Gruebel, until 2007 CEO of Credit Suisse and since February 2009 CEO of UBS; Thomas Kubr, CEO of Capital Dynamics; and Thomas Christoph Brand, CEO of Sunrise Communications.

3. G. S. Day and P. J. Schoemaker, "Are You a Vigilant Leader?" *MIT Sloan Management Review* 49 (2008): 43–51.

4. N. J. Allen and J. P. Meyer, "Organizational Socialization Tactics: A Longitudinal Analysis of Links to Newcomers' Commitment and Role Orientation," *Academy of Management Journal* 33 (1990): 847–858.

5. G. Mueller-Stewens and C. Lechner, *Strategisches Management—wie strategische Initiativen zum Wandel fuehren,* 3rd ed. (Stuttgart: Schäffer-Poeschel, 2003).

6. H. I. Ansoff, "Managing Strategic Surprise by Response to Weak Signals," *California Management Review* 18 (1975): 21–33.

7. G. Probst and S. Raisch, "Die Logik des Niedergangs," *Harvard Business Manager,* 26 (2004): 37–45.

8. H. Bruch and S. Bieri, "Hilti 2003: Maintaining a Proactive Sense of Urgency," Case Study (St. Gallen, Switzerland: University of St. Gallen, 2003); H. Bruch and S. Bieri, "Hilti 2003: Maintaining a Proactive Sense of Urgency," teaching note in Case Study (St. Gallen, Switzerland: University of St. Gallen, 2003).

9. H. Bruch and S. Poralla, "Hilti 2008: Leadership with Energy and Focus," Case Study (St. Gallen, Switzerland: University of St. Gallen, 2008).

10. See C. Argyris and D. Schön, *Organizational Learning: A Theory of Action Perspective* (Reading, Mass.: Addison-Wesley, 1978).

11. Bruch and Bieri, "Hilti 2003"; Bruch and Bieri, "Hilti 2003," teaching note; Bruch and Poralla, "Hilti 2008."

12. G. M. Spreitzer and R. E. Quinn, "Empowering Middle Managers to Be Transformational Leaders," *Journal of Applied Behavioral Science* 32, no. 3 (1996): 237–261. Contrary to B. M. Bass's *Leadership and Performance Beyond Expectations* (New York, NY: Free Press, 1985) concept of transformational guidance discussed here, other approaches concentrate on the vision-oriented guidance on the company level, which tends to be limited to the behavior of top management and other high-level personnel. See B. W. Bennis and B. Nanus, *Leaders: Strategies for Taking Charge* (New York: Harper & Row, 1985); J. P. Kotter, *Leading Change* (Boston: Harvard Business Press, 1996); N. M. Tichy and M. A. Devanna, *The Transformational Leader* (New York, NY: John Wiley, 1986).

13. U. R. Dumdum, K. B. Lowe, and B. J. Avolio, "A Meta-analysis of Transformational and Transactional Leadership Correlates of Effectiveness and Satisfaction: An Update and Extension," in *Transformational and Charismatic Leadership: The Road Ahead,* ed. B. J. Avolio and F. J. Yammarino (Oxford: Elsevier, 2002), 35–66; F. Walter and H. Bruch, "Structural Impacts on the Occurrence and Effectiveness of Transformational Leadership: An Empirical Study at the Organizational Level of Analysis," *Leadership Quarterly* 21 (2010): 765–782.

14. Data were based on a subsample of 104 German companies overall in 2009: 3,758 respondents for inspirational leadership climate, 3,804 respondents for energy states, 234 respondents for performance measures.

15. B. M. Bass, and B. J. Avolio, *Improving Organizational Effectiveness Through Transformational Leadership* (Thousand Oaks, Calif.: Sage, 1994). For a review, see F. Walter and H. Bruch, "An Affective Events Model of Charismatic Leadership Behavior: A Review, Theoretical Integration, and Research Agenda," *Journal of Management* 6, no. 35 (2009): 1428–1452.

16. H. Bruch and S. Poralla, "Transformationale Führung bei Baloise Schweiz 2007," Case Study (St. Gallen: University of St. Gallen, 2007).

17. B. Shamir, R. J. House, and M. B. Arthur, "The Motivational Effects of Charismatic Leadership: A Self-Concept-Based Theory," *Organization Science* 4 (1993): 577–594.

18. Bruch, Shamir, and Eilam-Shamir, "Managing Meanings."

19. Data were based on a subsample of 104 German companies overall in 2009: 3,758 respondents for prevention-oriented leadership climate, 3,804 respondents for energy states, 234 respondents for performance measures.

20. Walter and Bruch, "Structural Impacts."

21. Data were based on the sample explained in the introduction: a sample of 14,300 respondents from 104 German companies in 2009.

22. H. Bruch, D. Dolle, and C. Schudy, "Die besten Arbeitgeber im deutschen Mittelstand," in *Top Job,* ed. W. Clement and H. Bruch (Heidelberg: Redline Wirtschaft, 2010), 4–19.

23. S. B. De Jong and H. Bruch, "The Importance of a Homogeneous Transformational Leadership Climate for Organizational Performance," working paper, University of St. Gallen, Switzerland, 2010.

24. D. A. Nadler and M. L. Tushman, "The Organization of the Future: Strategic Imperatives and Core Competencies for the 21st Century," *Organizational Dynamics* 28 (1999): 45–60. See also Gary Hamel, *The Future of Management* (Boston: Harvard Business School Press, 2008).

25. Walter and Bruch, "Structural Impacts"; J. I. Menges, F. Walter, B. Vogel., and H. Bruch, "Transformational Leadership Climate: Performance Linkages, Mechanisms, and Boundary Conditions at the Organizational Level," *The Leadership Quarterly,* forthcoming.

26. Ibid.

27. Bruch and Poralla, "Hilti 2008."

28. B. Vogel, "Linking for Change: Network Action as Collective, Focused and Energetic Behavior," *Long Range Planning* 38 (2005): 531–553.

29. H. Bruch and S. Ghoshal, "Lufthansa 2000: Maintaining the Change Momentum," Case Study (London: London Business School, 2000).

30. J. Dutton, *Energize Your Workplace* (New York: Jossey-Bass, 2003).

31. Ibid.

32. H. M. Weiss and R. Cropanzano, "Affective Events Theory: A Theoretical Discussion of the Structure, Causes and Consequences of Affective Experiences at Work," *Research in Organizational Behavior* 18 (1996): 1–74.

33. H. Bruch and S. Poralla, "Sonova 2008: Orchestrating the Innovation Beat," Case Study (St. Gallen, Switzerland: University of St. Gallen, 2008).

34. H. Bruch, J. I. Menges, and C. Schudy, "Die besten Arbeitgeber im deutschen Mittelstand," in *Top Job,* ed. W. Clement and H. Bruch (Heidelberg: Redline Wirtschaft, 2008), 6–27.

35. Ibid.

36. K. Blanchard and S. Bowles, *Raving Fans: A Revolutionary Approach to Customer Service* (New York: William Morrow, 1993).

37. E. H. Schein, *Corporate Culture Survival Guide* (San Francisco: Wiley, 2009).

38. G. Morgan, *Images of Organization,* 2nd ed. (Thousand Oaks, Calif.: Sage, 1997); E. Chein, *Corporate Culture Survival Guide* (San Francisco: Wiley, 2009).

39. Bruch and Bieri, "Hilti 2003"; Bruch and Bieri, "Hilti 2003," teaching note.

40. Bruch and Poralla, "Hilti 2008."

41. For strategies for company inertia, see chapter 2 as well as H. Bruch and S. Ghoshal, *A Bias for Action: How Effective Managers Harness Their Willpower, Achieve Results, and Stop Wasting Their Time* (Boston, Harvard Business Press, 2004).

42. S. Sohm, "Living Corporate Culture: A Case Study on Novo Facilitations and their Applicability in other Companies," Case Study (Gütersloh, Germany: Bertelsmann Stiftung, 2000).

43. C. Gibson and J. Birkinshaw, "Antecedents, Consequences, and Mediating Role of Organizational Ambidexterity," *Academy of Management Journal* 47 (2004): 209–226. For an overview, see S. Raisch et al., "Organizational Ambidexterity: Balancing Exploitation and Exploration for Sustained Performance," *Organization Science* 20, no. 4 (2009): 685–695; C. Schudy and H. Bruch, "Productively Energizing the Organization Through a High Performance Context: Contextual Ambidexterity and Its Performances Consequences," *Academy of Management Best Paper Proceedings,* 2001.

44. Data were based on a subsample from 104 German companies overall in 2009: 104 respondents for ambidexterity, 3,804 respondents for energy states, and 234 respondents for performance measures. See also Gibson and Birkinshaw, "Organizational Ambidexterity."

45. R. Charan, "How Networks Reshape Organizations—for Results," *Harvard Business Review,* September–October 1991, 104–115.

46. Data were based on a subsample of 104 German companies overall in 2009: 3,905 respondents for entrepreneurship and 234 respondents for energy states.

47. Bruch and Ghoshal, *Bias for Action.*

48. W. E. Morrison and F. J. Milliken, "Organizational Silence: A Barrier to Organizational Change and Development in a Pluralistic World," *Academy of Management Review* 25 (2000): 706–725.

49. L. Perlow and S. Williams, "Is Silence Killing Your Company?" *Harvard Business Review,* May 2003, 52–58.

50. Friday letter no. 7, October 11, 2002.

51. H. Bruch and B. Vogel, "Die Philosophie der 'Nummer 1,'" *Harvard Business Manager* 30 (2008): 32–42.

52. Bruch and Ghoshal, *Bias for Action*; E. H. Schein, *Organizational Culture and Leadership,* 2nd ed. (San Francisco: Jossey-Bass, 1992).

53. Bruch and Bieri, "Hilti 2003"; Bruch and Bieri, "Hilti 2003," teaching note; Bruch and Poralla, "Hilti 2008."

Chapter 6

1. R. Cross, W. Baker, and A. Parker, "What Creates Energy in Organizations?" *Sloan Management Review* 44 (2003): 51–56.

2. H. Bruch and S. Ghoshal, *A Bias for Action: How Effective Managers Harness Their Willpower, Achieve Results, and Stop Wasting Their Time* (Boston: Harvard Business Press, 2004).

3. The program's name, 21 grams, is drawn from the experiments of Duncan MacDougall (1866–1920), an early-twentieth-century physician in Massachusetts, who sought to measure the weight of the human soul (D. MacDougall, "Hypothesis Concerning Soul Substance, Together with Experimental Evidence of the Existence of Such Substance," *Journal of the American Society for Psychical Research* [1907]).

Appendix

Index

ABB, 8, 231
  CEO's charisma, 188
  dedicating to challenges, 102–103
  drastic reorganization, 146–147
  emotional encouragement, 81–83
  employees, 103, 114–115, 135
  excessive growth and incessant change, 34
  leadership development, 189
  Friday letters, 164–165
  identity, 137
  Leadership Challenge Program, 189
  multiloading, 146
  organizational exhaustion, 147
  overacceleration, 146
  pride, 136
  rapid growth, 36
  resigned inertia, 34–35
  strengths and past successes, 136
  sustainable identity, 137
acceleration culture, 171–172
acceleration trap, 16–17, 36–37, 139
  business trends, 149
  change, 153, 155, 157–167, 169–171
  corrosive energy, 140
  detecting, 143, 144–148
  early warning signs, 149
  escaping, 19, 139–172
  feedback systems, 157, 167, 169–170
  hamster wheel of activity and pressure, 142
  harming company, 140
  multiloading, 146–147, 149
  overloading, 144–146, 149
  performance, 140
  perpetual loading, 147–149
  pit-stop culture, 167
  refocusing management systems, 155, 157–161
  simultaneous activities, 140–142
  slowing down to speed up, 156–157, 165–167
  spring cleaning, 151–153
  stopping the action, 149–153
  symptoms, 140
  time-outs, 156, 161–165
accomplishments, explicitly recognizing, 135
aggression and acceleration trap, 140
airlines, drastic collapse after September 11, 23–24
ALSTOM, 8
Alstom Group, 55
Alstom Power Service. *See* APS
ambitious goals, 179
Appel, Egbert, 169, 197, 220
Apple, 28
APS (Alstom Power Service), 55
arrogance, 216
ASPIRE (ASPirational Initiatives to Retain Excellence), 93
assessing organizational energy, 14, 239–245
  applying the OEQ, 55–58
  benchmarks, 51–52
  business performance and, 12
  comfortable energy, 27–32
  common traps, 14–17
  corrosive energy, 38–45
  employee survey, 24–25, 27
  energy profile, 244–245
  instant energy check steps, 59
  OEQ Index, 48–54
  OEQ (Organizational Energy Questionnaire), 12, 13, 38, 47–49
  productive energy, 21–27
  pulse-check, 56–58
  questions to ask about, 8
  resigned inertia, 32–38
  self-assessment, 244
  self-concepts, 31
  strategies, 31
  in workshops, 58

AT&T, 90
Audéo, 167
Audi, 91–92
    creative disobedience, 213
    entrepreneurial spirit, 213
    intense personal development, 229
    love of peak performance, 234–235
    21 grams program, 234

Badstübner, Achim, 229
Baloise Group, 40, 199
Baloise Switzerland, 40, 81, 191–192
Balzers' goal agreement, 157–158
Barnevik, Percy, 34, 36, 114, 146, 188
Barsade, Sigal G., 7
Baschera, Pius, 71, 176, 182, 185, 197, 198,
    215–216, 236
behavioral potential, 5–6
Berg, Hans, 116, 117
Berlin Wall, fall of, 6–7
Bibeault, Donald B., 69
Birken, Alexander, 118
Black & Decker, 182
Bleicher, Knut, 101
blinders, overcoming, 177, 183–184
BMW, 178–179
Bolli, Thomas, 163
boosting energy, 20
Bosch, 182
Bosch-Siemens Haushaltsgeräte. See BSH
bottlenecks, identifying, 53–54
brainstorming, destructive, 120–123
branding, 95
Brooklyn Brewery, 206
BSH (Bosch-Siemens Haushaltsgeräte), 15–16,
    38–39
Buechner, Ton, 145
Busch-Jaeger, 77–78, 205
Bush, George H. W., 6
business-related issues, 194
busyness versus focus, 214
buw, 207

Carl Zeiss, 209, 221–222
Carlson Wagonlit Travel. See CWT
CAS, 80–81
celebrating successes, 163–164
Centerman, Jörgen, 35, 147
CEOs. See executives
Citius, altius, fortius (Olympic motto), 16
challenges, identifying, 61
challenging goals, 179
change
    clear beginning and end-point, 165
    monitoring, 54
    spring cleaning and, 153, 154
    unending or unsuccessful, 35–36, 95

change agents, identifying, 53–54
Chapero, Valentin, 16–17, 22, 166, 176
Church of St. Nicholas (Leipzig), 6
cleaning up corrosive energy, 112–125
cognitive potential, 5–6
collective commitment, 133–134
collective dynamic force, 7
collective energy, 6
collective goals, 89
comfortable energy, 9–10, 12, 27, 113,
    242–245
    change and, 31
    complacency trap, 28–29
    dominance, 28, 29–31, 51
    efficiency, 213
    employee inaction, 28
    entrepreneurship, 213
    innovation, 213
    inspirational leadership, 189
    Lufthansa, 30–31
    perceiving weak signals, 28
    positive qualities of, 33
    prevention-oriented leadership, 192
    questions to detect, 32
    reduced level of activity, 28
    score for, 51–52
    practical example for, 28
    without productive energy, 27
commitment to yourself. See COTOYO
common energy traps, 14–17
communication
    appealing to employees' emotions, 77–78
    awareness of, 75–78
    encouraging, 107
    leadership, 189
    polished communication versus real
        dialog, 110
    realistic and relevant danger, 75–77
    restoring lines of, 112
    spurring action, 75
communication technologies, excessive
    use of, 172
companies, 179
    change, 31, 165
    comfortable energy, 12, 29–31
    complacent identity, 28, 130
    corrosive energy, 11, 13
    customer feedback, 77–78
    doing more with less, 37
    drained identity, 129–130
    energy states, 48
    enthusiasm of customers, 206–207
    high corrosive energy, 44
    high productive energy, 11, 24
    identifying weak signals, 70
    inequalities among divisions, 40
    insufficiently channeling energy, 84

negative competition among internal
    units, 40
OE Index, 48
overacceleration, 140
productive energy, 24
pursuing goals, 11
refocusing management systems, 155,
    157–161
resigned inertia, 11, 13
rootless identity, 130
sources of ideas and inspiration, 176
sustainable identity, 131
sustaining energy, 170
taking on too much, 139
too-rapid growth, 145
unconnected and negative brainstorming,
    121–122
values, culture, and mutual support, 44
company-wide networks, 199–201
competition
    corrosive energy, 40
    energizing employees for, 76
    major threat, 73
complacency, 129–130
    avoiding, 69
    decentralized leadership structures, 197
    indicators for, 29
    leadership patterns, 31
complacency trap, 15, 28, 173
    escaping, 18–19
    identifying threat, 62
    moving companies out of, 85–86
    primary tools for combating, 61
    slaying the dragon, 15
    winning the princess, 15
compulsory values, 220
ConocoPhillips, 8
consistent culture, 220–222
contextual ambidexterity, 212–213
Continental AG, 98–99, 100, 229
    automotive industry, 103
    company-wide networks, 199
    division between groups, 179
    identifying princess, 98
    RDE (research-development-engineering)
        meetings, 134, 179
    shared goals and strong collective
        commitment, 134
continuity, 179
corporate identity, 130–133
corrosion
    forcefully cutting, 230–232
    preventing, 125, 127–131, 133–137
corrosion trap, 15–16
    alignment, 110–111
    cleaning up, 112–125
    conflict, 108–109

denial of versus proactive dealing with
    corrosive tendencies, 110
early warning signs, 110–11
escaping, 19, 105–137
looking for, 107–108
measuring corrosion, 109, 111–112
polished communication versus real
    dialog, 110
trust, 111
weak organizational identity, 111
corrosive cultures, chronic nature of, 118
corrosive energy, 3–4, 9–11, 13, 38–45, 242–245
    acceleration trap, 140
    acting quickly against, 105–106
    aggression and destructive forces, 53
    anger and fury, 39
    bad feelings from, 125
    bureaucratic and administrative issues, 44
    burnout, 44
    clear picture of, 106–107
    collective commitment, 133–134
    confronting organization about, 119–120
    corporate productivity, 44
    damaging companies, 106
    dangers of, 43–45
    denying evidence of, 108
    destructive energy, 39
    destructive power, 106
    directly addressing, 230–231
    downward spiral of, 43
    dramatic wake-up call, 118–123
    early detection, 108–109
    efficiency, 213
    egoistic behaviors and, 41–42, 113
    emotional exhaustion, 44
    emotional shake-ups, 118–123
    entrepreneurship, 213
    escalating rapidly, 43–44
    fighting, 44
    growth of companies, 43
    harming and weakening others, 39
    high versus low, 38, 43, 45, 107–108
    infighting, 105
    innovation, 213
    internal coordination and process
        improvement, 44
    internal rivalries, 105
    internal struggles, 39
    interpersonal aggression, 105
    letting off steam, 114–118
    long-term effects, 42
    management and, 107
    negative competition, 40
    negative emotions, 42
    passive behavior toward, 230
    perceived unfairness, 113
    benchmarks percentages, 52–53

corrosive energy (*continued*)
    performance rates, 43
    playful way of dealing with, 117–118
    power struggle, 113
    preventing or reducing, 56
    prevention-oriented leadership, 192
    questions to detect, 46
    quickly and forcefully removing, 53
    reasons for, 39–43
    redirecting, 112
    searching for signs of, 231
    top management, 42–43
    toxic handlers, 123–125
corrosive forces
    detecting, 106–112
    diffusing underlying, 115
COTOYO (commitment to yourself), 211
courage
    to develop leaders, 235–237
    to lead energized company, 233–237
    versus uncertainty, 216–217
crisis management and stop the action, 154
cultural change, 222
cultures
    acceleration, 153, 155, 157–167, 169–171
    analyzing current, 218
    changing and influencing, 217
    comfortable energy and, 212
    complacency, 29, 30
    consistent, 220–222
    corrosive energy, 212, 231
    courage versus uncertainty, 216–217
    defining, 207
    developing, 217–223
    entrepreneurial initiative versus obedience,
        213
    feedback, 107
    focus versus busyness, 214
    innovation versus routine, 212–213
    integrity versus opportunism, 213–214
    management system, 219
    need for excellence versus need for manda-
        tory performance levels, 215–216
    open feedback versus overtolerance,
        214–215
    preferred, 218–219
    resigned inertia, 212
    spring cleaning, 152
    strategically reviewing, 222
    values, 219
    vitalizing, 175, 207–223
customer feedback, 202, 204–206
customer touch points
    creation, 202
    customer feedback, 204–206
    customers' enthusiasm, 206–207
    employee recognition, 204–206

    employees developing sense for market,
        202–203
    energizing, 201–207
    positive energy and, 201
CWT (Carlson Wagonlit Travel), 2–5, 7–8,
    12–13
CWT Netherlands, 2–5, 10, 47

DAIG (Deutsche Annington Immobilien
    Group), 57
Day, George, 176
decelerating, 232–233
decentralized leadership structures, 196, 197–199
defensive avoidance, 69–70
Dekker, Jan Willem, 2–5, 7–8, 47
demands, exploding, 145
denial of versus proactive dealing with corrosive
    tendencies, 110
destructive brainstorming, 120–123
detecting corrosive forces, 106–112
Deutsche Annington Immobilien Group. *See*
    DAIG
direct customer service, 202
direction, lack of, 36
discipline, lack of, 171
dominant comfortable energy, 29–31
Domino's Pizza, 90
Dormann, Juergen, 81, 102, 133, 164–165, 174,
    188
    communication culture, 215
    emphasizing commonalities, 136
    Friday letters, 135–137
Drack, Silja, 63, 126
dragons, 72–73
    mobilizing energy around, 226–228
    sequencing with princess, 102–103
drained identity, 129–130
Dutton, Jane, 24

e-mail, excessive use of, 172
early warning system, 181–183
Edmonson, Amy C., 42
Eisert, Klaus, 82
emotional encouragement, 81–83
emotional engagement, 66
emotional shakeups, 119–123
emotions, appealing to employees', 77–78
employee opinion surveys, 56
employee satisfaction surveys, 51–52
employee surveys, OEQ as, 54–56
employees
    absenteeism, 32
    apathy, 32–33
    attributing success to, 80
    burnout, 44
    collective goals, 89
    comfortable energy, 28

confidence in company, 78–81
corrosive energy, 3–4
creative thinking about problem, 72
customer-promotion focus, 191
customers, 3, 202–203, 204–206
dealing with threats, 79–80
destructive behavior and aggressiveness, 42
detachment from threat, 74–75
deviating from norm, 194
egoistic behavior, 41–42
emotionally appealing visions, 90–93
emotions of, 21, 38, 44, 77–78,
       114–115, 124
feedback, 54, 169
highly destructive energy, 4
identifying weak signals, 70
keeping problems away from, 75
lack of commitment, 34
lack of communication, 3
lack of motivation, 2–3
lack of resources, 142
messengers and catalyzers, 82
peak performance, excellence, and
       enthusiasm, 3
problem solving, 75–78
productive energy, 4
questioning status quo, 188
realistic and relevant danger, 75–77
recognition of, 202, 204–206
reduced sense of identity among, 44
resigned inertia, 3–4, 33–34
shared perspective, 128
sharing negative experiences, 124
strongly committed, 25
threats and, 76
time-outs, 163
trusting in energy of, 229
vision and strategy, 4
watching for weak signals, 183
what can we stop doing, 150–151
end-of-the-dragon period, 102
energetic refocusing, 113
energizing leaders, 225–237
energy
       boosting, 2, 20
       collective, 6
       contagious, 7
       destructive, 39
       entrepreneurship, 213
       Hilti, 175
       misdirected and misused, 106
       none, 245
       orchestrating, 1–20
       organization definition, 1, 5
       positive and negative, 9–10
       proactively managing, 226–227
       productive, 21–27

rated by employees, 11
self-reinforcing spirals, 7
spillover effect, 7
energy matrix, 18, 21
       comfortable energy, 27
       corrosive energy, 38–45
       productive energy, 21–27
       resigned inertia, 32–38
energy profiles, 3, 47, 186, 239–240, 243
       lack of communication combined with
              deep uncertainty, 111–112
       self-assessment, 244
energy states, 50–52, 242
       dominant, 48
       picture of, 48
       sugarcoating bad news about, 107
Enron, 29, 37
enthusiasm for visions, 90–93
entrepreneurial initiative versus
       obedience, 213
escaping corrosion trap, 105–137
eustress, 77
executives
       addressing negativity, 53
       corrosive energy, 108, 123
       emotional shake-ups, 123
       handling conflicts, 108
       hot topics, 42
       negative forces, 107–108
       organizational pride, 131
       overaccelerated mode and, 154
       staff members and, 75
       state of energy, 46–47
external threats and stress triggers, 65

facing conflict head-on, 108–109
false sense of security, 181
FC Bayern Munich, 216, 235
feedback
       customer, 204–206
       descriptive rather than accusatory, 116
       employees, 169
       open, 214–215
       strategies and, 183
feedback systems, 157, 167, 169–170
financial crisis, 103
Fischer, 182
FME (Fujitsu Microelectronics Europe), 194
focus
       lack of, 171
       organizational energy, 19, 139–172
Ford, 90
Frerks, Martin, 119–120
Fritsche, Christian, 92
Frost, Peter, 44, 123
future, clear, vivid, and unique picture of, 88–89
future-oriented activities, 100

Gates, Bill, 162–163, 233
Genscher, Hans-Dietrich, 41
global financial crisis and Swiss CEOs, 176
goal-agreement system, 157–159
goals, 179
    appreciation and celebration of, 164–165
    Balzers, 157–158
    common, 22
    personal connection to, 191
    time-outs, 163
Gorbachev, Mikhail, 6
Grünes, Thomas, 152

Happy Gate, 118
Hätty, Holger, 24, 148
Heifetz, Ronald A., 75
high corrosive energy and performance, 44–45
high-energy companies, 26
high productive energy, 11, 12
Hilti, Michael, 168, 198, 211, 220
Hilti Group, 8, 174, 191, 212
    behavioral norms, 214
    board members departure, 197
    circle of habits, 210, 216
    company-wide networks, 199
    Competition Radar, 181–182, 185
    competitors, 182
    continually evolving, 185
    COTOYO (commitment to yourself), 211
    courage, 216
    cultural development, 198, 222
    cultural training program, 159
    culture, 207–208, 211–212, 219–220, 222
    customer satisfaction surveys, 182
    customer surveys, 185
    customer touch points, 203
    decentralized structure, 197, 211
    developing leaders, 236
    direct sales, 197, 203
    EMG (executive management group), 185,
        197–198
    employees, 182, 185, 197, 211
    EMT (executive management team), 198
    energy, 175, 181
    executive board, 198
    fairness, 220
    feedback, 215
    Foundation camp, 212
    freedom of choice, 210
    identifying roots of problem, 72
    INNO training, 207–208, 210, 211
    innovation-oriented culture, 211
    integrity, 214
    misaligned incentives, 72
    need for excellence, 216
    Our Culture Journey, 168, 208, 212,
        214, 227
    performance, 175
    Pit Stop camp, 168–169, 212
    principles, 210–211
    promotions, 220
    questioning activities, 159
    role models, 80
    Rubicon camp, 212
    Rule 56, 197
    rules, 210
    salespeople and competitors, 182
    stop-doing lists, 159
    strategic goals, 71
    strategies, 185
    success and, 71
    swing of life, 210–211
    systematic market orientation, 182
    time-outs, 168
    values, 210, 212, 220
    vitalizing management, 175
    weak signals in environment, 182
Holtz, Ulrich, 163
Horch, August, 234
Huber, Heinrich, 77
Hubschneider, Martin, 80–81
human potential, organization use of, 47
hurry-up culture, 161

IBM, 28, 100, 212
    company-wide networks, 199
    jam events, 183–184
iF Product Design award, 205
infighting, 105
individual energy and organizational
        energy, 6–7
individual leaders, 20
individualized support, 192
inert companies, mobilizing, 84
informal relationships, 197–201
innovation, 209
    versus routine, 212–213
input versus output orientation, 171
inspirational leadership, 189–194, 197
inspirational motivation, 191
instant customer feedback, 204–206
instant energy check, 58–59
intensity, 21
internal competition, 40, 105–106
interpersonal aggression, 105
Itemis, 204–205

John Paul II (pope), 6
Johnstone, Tom, 76–77, 229
joint goals, refocusing, 133

Kahn, Oliver, 216, 235, 236
Kawi, Ryoichi, 73
Kennedy, John F., 90

key phases, defining, 165
Kohl, Helmut, 6
Komatsu, 73, 76
Kössler, Peter, 91, 92
Krabbe, Hans-Georg, 77–78
Krüger, Harald, 178
Kurz, Dieter, 221

Laura Ashley, 28
Laurie, Donald L., 75
leaders
    activities, 152
    attacking only symptoms, 70
    bonuses, 98
    corrosive energy, 230
    courage to develop, 235–237
    defensive avoidance, 69–70
    desired future or special opportunity, 88–89
    downplaying or ignoring problems, 69
    emotionally shaking up company, 118–123
    employees letting off steam, 117
    energizing, 188–196, 225–237
    failure to communicate threat, 75
    focusing on threat, 72
    illustration of challenge, 73
    idealized influence
    individualized support, 192
    inspirational motivation, 191
    intellectually stimulated, 191
    lacking frameworks and tools, 8
    less dependence on, 186
    organizational energy, 6, 7–8
    overacceleration, 232
    pausing and regrouping, 154
    peak performance, 234–235
    positive approach, 85
    pushing companies to edge of abilities,
        147–148
    setting focus, 73
    simultaneous activities, 16
    slaying the dragon, 66
    states of energy, 1, 52–54, 242
    stopping the action, 150
    time-outs, 162
    time pressure, 70
    vitalizing management system, 174–175
leadership
    climax, 193–194
    communication, 189
    complacency, 29, 30
    complacency and inertia, 15
    continuity of, 100–101
    continuous feedback, 188–189
    core capability of organization, 186
    formal development, 188–189
    general climax of, 193–194
    inspirational, 189–192

    inspiring and energizing teams, 187
    management structures, 194–196
    orchestrating energy, 1–20
    organizational energy, 188. See also
        organizational energy.
    prevention-oriented, 192–193
    principles clashing with incentives, 194
    productive energy, 187. See also productive
        energy.
    sharing, 186
    vitalizing, 175
leadership structures
    communicating autonomy, 199
    company-wide networks, 199–201
    customer touch points, 201–207
    decentralized, 196, 197–199
    energizing leaders, 188–196
    informal relationships, 197–201
    vitalizing, 185–196, 197–207
leading by example, 227, 233
Lehnhardt, Silke, 148
letting off steam, 114–118
Lidl Switzerland, 161, 226, 231
    company-wide project ban, 161
    corporate principles and mission statement,
        126
    entering Swiss market, 62–65, 126–127
    growth opportunities, 69
    management contact point for, 126
    massive growth, 161
    motivation and positive atmosphere, 126
    negative energy, 127
    slaying the dragon, 62–65
    social workers handling toxicity, 126–127
Lindahl, Göran, 35, 146
logos, overusing, 94
long-term opportunity, overfocusing on, 99–100
Loos, Christoph, 168
low-energy companies, 26
low intensity, 8–9
low positive or negative energy, 10
low productive energy, 25
Ludwig-Ehrhard Award, 205
Lufthansa, 2, 8, 174, 212, 226
    actions to overcome threats, 79
    burnout, 148
    C-Experience, 200
    comfortable energy, 30–31
    company-wide networks, 199
    complacent leadership patterns, 31
    cost control, 148
    costs of conflict, 41
    culture, 30
    D-Check Acute program, 23, 24
    D-Check program, 23, 68, 71, 180
    damage to, 41–42
    defensive avoidance, 69–70

Lufthansa (*continued*)
    drastic collapse after 9/11, 23–24
    executive board and managers, 24
    Explorers 21, 199–200
    financial crisis in 1990s, 30
    formalization, bureaucracy, standardization,
        and centralization, 30
    identifying dragon, 68
    junior managers development program,
        199–200
    leadership, 30
    long-term change process, 148
    milestones, 180
    Operational Excellence, 180
    organizational culture, 209
    Passenger Transportation, 148
    passengers, 30
    pilots' strike (2001), 41–42, 106
    preventing complacency, 17
    problem-solving strategies, 79
    productive energy, 23
    Program 15, 179, 180
    Program 93, 180
    reducing human resources costs, 23–24
    School of Business, 148, 199
    shifting focus, 148
    slaying the dragon, 68
    STEP, 200
    strategic initiatives, 179–180
    strategy, 30
    target goals, 23–24
    Team Lufthansa, 200
    Upgrade, 180
    worst-case scenario, 68

major threats, identifying, 61
Makita, 182
Malik, Fredmund, 151
Malkowich, Philipp, 96
management
    integrating culture into, 219
    lack of clarity and mutual agreement, 73
    slaying the dragon involvement, 73–75
    structures aligning with leadership
        principles, 194–196
    vitalizing, 174–175
management-by-objective system. *See* MBO
    system
managers
    defensive avoidance, 69–70
    deviating from leadership norm, 194–196
    doubting abilities of, 186
    downplaying or ignoring problems, 69
    egoistic behavior, 41–42
    goals, 135, 179

    instant energy check, 58
    MBO (management-by-objective) system,
        158
    overly rules-oriented, 31
    ranking projects, 154
mandatory performance levels need versus need
        for excellence, 215–216
Marcano, Gabriel, 115
Maru-C approach at Komatsu, 76
Mauerer, Florian, 221
Mayrhuber, Wolfgang, 148
MBO (management-by-objective) system, 158
McDonald's, 90
measuring organizational energy. *See also*
        assessing organizational energy
    analyzing and visualizing with OE Index,
        49–54
    assessments, 239–245
    OEQ (Organizational Energy Question-
        naire), 47–49, 54–58
    reasons for, 46–47
mental alertness, 66
Microsoft, 162–163, 233
milestones, 180–181
Miller, David, 111–112
Milliken, Frances J., 107
Mobility Technologics. *See* MT
mobilizing
    companies, 85–101
    energy, 226–228
    inert companies, 84
mobilizing organizational energy, 61–104
    slaying the dragon, 61, 62–85
    winning the princess, 61
Morrison, Elizabeth Wolfe, 107
Moser, Peter, 151
MT (Mobility Technologics), 97–98
multiloading, 146–147, 149
Muthuraman, B., 93, 229
mystery shoppers, 204

negative brainstorming, 121–122
negative energy, 9
    confronting, 108
    measuring, 107
    proactively involving managers, 74
negativity
    phasing down, 113–118
    release valves for, 114–118
    role-playing, 118
Nike, 90
Nokia, 90, 184
Novo Nordisk, 207, 212
Number ONE on Tour, 178–179
Number ONE strategy, 178

obedience versus entrepreneurial initiative, 213
objectives
    limiting, 157–159
    most important, 179
O'Connell, David, 123–124
OE Index, 48
    analyzing and visualizing organizational
        energy, 49–54
    comfortable energy score, 51
    corrosive energy, 38–45
    dominant energy states, 48
    energy states, 50, 51
    good-practice benchmark, 51
    interpreting, 242–244
    negative energy states, 52
    productive energy, 51
    resigned inertia, 32–38
OEQ (Organizational Energy Questionnaire),
        12, 47–49, 109, 186, 226
    applying, 54–58
    APS (Alstom Power Service), 55
    CWT (Carlson Wagonlit Travel), 3, 10, 12
    as employee survey, 54–56
    energy states, 54
    how to complete, 240–241
    as instant energy check, 58
    organizational energy pulse-check, 56–58
    organizational energy quality, 55–56
    participation in, 48
    productive and counterproductive forces, 48
    questions, 49
    relevant drivers of energy, 54
    resigned inertia, 13
    self-assessment of organization's energy,
        239–240
    usage, 54–58
Olesch, Gunther, 82, 154, 226–227, 229
on-hold activities, 155
open feedback, 209
    versus overtolerance, 214–215
opportunism versus integrity, 213–214
opportunities
    abstract nature, 87–88
    aligning reward systems with, 97–99
    challenges, 175
    defining, 87–89
    employees, 89
    focusing energy on, 229
    identifying, 87–989, 175
    interpreting, 87–89
    long-term, 99–100
    mobilizing companies, 85–101
    passionately communicating, 90–95
    pursuing, 85–101
    strengthening confidence in, 95–99

time limitation of, 101
    vivid and unique picture of, 88–89
orchestrating energy, 1–20
O'Reilly, Charles, 29
organizational culture, 7. See also cultures
organizational energy, 6–7, 20. See also energy
    analyzing and visualizing, 49–54
    assessing, 14, 239–245
    attractive opportunities and, 86
    best strategy for, 14
    comfortable energy, 9–10
    common traps, 14–17
    components of, 5–6
    corporate vitality, 2
    corrosive energy, 9–10
    current state of, 7
    defining, 1, 5
    emotional, cognitive, and behavioral
        potential, 5–6
    energy matrix, 8–10
    focusing, 19, 139–172
    getting most from, 14–18
    independence of states, 10
    individual energy and, 6–7
    intensity of, 8–9, 21
    leaders and, 6, 7–8
    malleable, 5, 7–8
    measuring, 46–59, 186
    mobilizing, 18–19, 61–104
    most relevant drivers, 54
    performance and, 11–13
    poor use of, 11
    proactively managing, 226–227
    productive energy, 9–10
    pulse-check, 56–58
    quality, 9, 21
    resigned inertia, 9–10
    sustaining, 17–20, 173–223
    systematic and sustained destruction, 186
    types of, 5
Organizational Energy Questionnaire. See OEQ
organizational identity, 113
    complacent identity, 129
    drained identity, 129–130
    organizational pride, 128
    preventing corrosion, 125, 127–131,
        133–137
    rootless identity, 129
    shared perspective, 128–129
    sustainable identity, 129
    visible and credible investments in, 136
organizational pride, 128, 131, 135–137
organizational silence, 214–215
organizations
    burnout of, 37

organizations (*continued*)
    confidence dealing with threat, 78–81
    contextual ambidexterity, 212–213
    corrosive energy, 119–120
    degree of negativity, 52
    emotion, thoughts, and actions in, 7
    emotional, cognitive, and behavioral
        potential, 5–6
    energy profiles coexisting in, 53
    leadership core capability, 186
    measuring corrosion, 109, 111–112
    overloading resources and humans, 36
    quasi-crisis and, 65
    sharing radar information, 183
    worst-case scenarios for, 120–121
OTTO Group, 117–118, 152, 231
Our Culture Journey, 168
outside challenges and mobilizing company,
    62–85
outside role models, 81
overacceleration, 36–37, 165, 167, 232
overcoming blinders, 177
overfocusing on long-term opportunity,
    99–100
overloading, 144–146, 149
overtolerance versus open feedback, 214–215
overwhelming companies, 83–84

Palmisano, Sam, 184
PCA (personal communication assistant), 167
peak performance, 234–235
people
    collective force of, 6–7
performance
    acceleration trap, 140
    comfortable energy, 27–28, 32–33
    corrosive energy, 44–45
    CWT (Carlson Wagonlit Travel), 13
    elevated crucial indicators, 90
    Hilti, 175
    indicators, 90
    key informants and, 11
    organizational energy affecting, 11–13
    productive energy, 24, 26, 28
    resigned inertia , 34–38
perpetual loading, 147–149
personal communication assistant. *See* PCA
personal initiative, 209
Phoenix Contact, 207, 212, 229
    ABC program, 154–155
    annual best-practice workshop, 83
    board of executives wage reduction, 82–83
    clear and simple goals, 179
    collecting success stories, 81
    commitment, 179
    communicating openly, 82–83
    confidence in, 83

    cost reduction activities of employees,
        82–83
    developing leaders, 195
    dismissals, 82
    fiscal crisis of 2008-2009, 154
    leadership principles, 195
    milestones, 180
    new strategic ambition, 195
    proactively managing energy, 226–227
    ranking projects, 154
    recession and, 82– 83
    short-time work, 82
    spring cleaning, 154–155
    Strategy 2020, 180
Pit Stop, 168
Pit Stop culture, 167
    Hilti, 168–169
Pohl, Andreas, 62–64, 161
Polaroid, 28
polished communication versus real
    dialog, 110
positive energy, 9, 19, 27, 105–137
positive spirals, 22
preferred culture, 218–219
Premium Sprint vision, 103–104
preserving status quo, 234
prevention-oriented leadership, 192–193
princess
    mobilizing energy around, 226–228
    period, 102
    sequencing dragon with, 102–103
priorities, confusion about, 102
proactive sense of urgency, 174
proactively managing energy, 226–227
Probst, Gilbert, 37
productive energy, 4, 9–10, 21–27, 50, 213,
    242–245
    building up, 56
    channeling, 84
    comfortable energy without, 27
    common goals, 22
    company potential, 84
    constructive discussions, 42
    customer experiences, 201
    decentralized leadership structures, 197
    decreasing energy back to, 143–144
    degree of, 51
    diminishing rapidly, 84
    distribution of, 25–26
    as dominant state, 29
    efficiency, 213
    entrepreneurship, 213
    focus, 214
    goals, tasks, and shared initiatives, 113
    hierarchical levels and, 26–27
    high versus low, 12, 24, 28, 52
    innovation, 213

leadership, 187, 189
Lufthansa, 23
positive energy, 105–137
positive performance effects, 44
positive spirals, 22
preserving, 56
prevention-oriented leadership, 192
productive urgency, 22
questions to detect, 26
shared enthusiasm, alertness, and effort, 24
shift away from, 16
success-critical core activities, 21
progress dashboard, 180–181
Progressive Insurance, 190, 191
project burying, 160
project management system, 159–160
projects, pursuing strategically important, 161
pulse-checks, 56–58

quality, 21

radar for weak signals, 177, 181–183
Raisch, Sebastian, 37
Reagan, Ronald, 6
rebuilding positive energy, 105–137
refocusing
    joint goals, 133
    management systems, 155–161
regeneration
    lack of, 172
    no possibilities for, 147
    time-outs, 162
regularly reviewing strategy, 177
relationships, building high-quality, 200–201
release valves for negativity, 114–118
resignations and acceleration trap, 140
resigned inertia, 3, 9–11, 32–38, 245
    ABB, 34–35
    affects on employees, 33–34
    apathy, 32–33
    attributes, 33
    change and, 33, 35–37
    collective stress, 65
    efficiency, 213
    entrepreneurship, 213
    excessive growth, 37
    goals, 33
    high versus low, 33
    identifying threat, 62
    innovation, 213
    inspirational leadership, 189
    internal dissociation and frustration, 85–86
    lack of clear-cut or positive direction, 36
    low activity levels, 33
    moving companies out of, 85–86
    negativity created by, 33
    OEQ results from, 13

overacceleration, 36–37
percentages, 52–53
preventing or reducing, 56
prevention-oriented leadership, 192–193
questions to detect, 38
reasons for, 34–38
reduced communication, 33
removing, 53
satisfaction and, 34
slaying the dragon, 66
spread of, 53
top management changes, 35–36
winning the princess, 66
Risberg, Bo, 80, 174
Robinson, Sandra, 123
role models based on past successes, 80–81
rootless identity, 129, 130, 137
routine versus innovation, 212–213

Schneider, Georg, VI, 74, 206
Schneider & Brooklyner
        Hopfen-Weisse, 206
Schneider Weisse brewery, 74, 206
Schoemaker, Paul, 176
Schulz, Hans, 157–158
Securetec, 203
sequencing dragon with princess, 102–103
Serview GmbH
    customer feedback, 204
    high-energy environment, 169–170
    SMART feedback system, 170
shared commitment, 134
shared goals, 213
shared leadership, 186
shared perspective, 128–129, 131
    collective commitment, 133–134
    company's future, 131, 133–135
shared strategy, 177, 178–181
Sigrist, Beat, 145
SKF Group, 76–77, 229
Slaaen, Eivind, 168
slaying the dragon, 15, 18–19, 61, 62–85
    authentic threats, 65
    communication, 75–78
    effectiveness, 83–84
    emotional encouragement, 81–83
    emotional engagement, 66
    imaginary dragons, 65
    increasing energy in crisis, 62
    involving employees, 66
    Komatsu, 76
    leaders, 66
    Lidl, 62–65
    Lufthansa, 68
    management team involvement, 73–75
    mastering challenge, 66
    mental alertness, 66

slaying the dragon (*continued*)
  mobilizing energy around, 76, 101–102, 226–228
  orchestrating use, 101–104
  prevention-oriented leadership, 192–193
  prior to, 83–84
  resigned inertia, 66
  role models based on past successes, 80–81
  summary of tasks, 67
  tasks, 67–83
  threats, 67, 69–75, 78–81
  vivid picture of dragon, 72–73
  winning the princess, 103–104
slowing down to speed up, 165–167, 232–233
Smith, Diana McLain, 42
social workers at Lidl, 126–127
solution based on mutual agreement, 115–117
Sonova Group, 176, 226
  Audéo, 167
  employees interacting with customers, 202
  hearing devices, 167
  high-energy and regeneration phases, 17, 166–167
  innovation as key activity, 22–23
  new product generations yearly, 16–17
  product information events, 202
  Verve Steinway Edition, 166–167
sports and customer feedback, 205–206
spring cleaning, 151–155
stagnation, 234
staying number one, 233–234
Steel, Gary, 188
Steinway & Sons, 166
stop-doing goals, 158
stop the action, 155
  crisis management, 154
  psychological employee benefits, 154
  spring cleaning, 151–153
  What should we stop doing?, 150–151
Strategic Corporate Development, 221
strategies
  complacency, 29, 30
  continuity, 179
  continuously developing, 185
  decentralized, 183
  decisions and current information, 183
  discussing issues, 71
  feedback and, 183
  flexibility, 181
  focused and realistic, 183
  milestones, 180–181
  monitoring implementation, 54
  regularly reviewing, 177
  shared, 178–181
  slaying the dragon, 65
  winning the princess, 101–104

strategy processes
  homing radar for weak signals, 177, 181–183
  involving people, 178
  overcoming blinders, 177, 183–184
  regularly reviewing strategies, 177, 184–185
  shared strategy, 177, 178–181
  vitalizing, 175, 177–185
Strobel, Martin, 40, 81
Stryker GmbH & Co. KG, 203, 206–207
successes
  celebrating, 163–164
  explicitly recognizing, 135
successful companies and threats, 69
Sulzer, 145–146
sustainable identity, 129, 131, 137
sustaining organizational energy, 17–20, 170, 173–224
Swedish Asea Group, 34
swing of life, 210–211
Swiss Aviation Training, 163
Swiss Brown Boveri Group, 34
Swiss CEOs and global financial crisis, 176
Swiss International Air Lines, 163
Swiss Re company-wide innovation sessions, 184
Swissair, 28–29
Swisscom company-wide networks, 199

Tata, Ratan, 94, 101
Tata Group, 94
Tata Motors, 90, 94, 101
Tata Steel, 8, 93–94, 229
TeamBank, 95
threats
  adopting radar process, 182
  authentic, 65
  awareness of, 62
  communicating to employees, 75–77
  competitors, 69
  confidence in dealing with, 78–81
  defensive avoidance, 69–70
  discussing, 71
  emotional concern for, 77
  employee detachment from, 74–75
  external, 65
  focusing on, 72
  following through, 78
  identifying, 62, 69–70
  imaginary, 65
  interpreting, 70–72
  mobilizing employees, 84
  as positive challenge, 78–80
  pressure of, 70–71
  protecting employees from, 226
  quantitative and qualitative, 182
  roots of, 70–72

successful companies, 69
tangible actions to overcome, 79
understanding, 70–72
time-outs, 156, 161–165
    Bill Gates, 162–163
    Hilti, 168
Tomasi, Markus, 22
top management, 42–43
    boosting confidence in vision, 97
    filtering or polishing bad news, 107
    frequent changes of, 35–36
    good leadership, 189
top priority activities, 155
Toxic Emotions at Work (Frost), 44
toxic handlers, 123–125, 127
travel industry, 2
trust
    lack of, 111
    toxic handlers, 124
turnaround processes, 54
Tushman, Michael, 29
Tyco, 37

UBS, 191
Unaxis, 8
uncertainty versus courage, 216–217
University of St. Gallen, 101

values
    compulsory, 220
    promoting desired, 219
    substantive and vitalizing, 208–217
    testing, 211
Verve Steinway Edition, 166–167
visions
    abandoning pursuit of, 103
    abstract nature, 87–88
    awareness of, 90
    clear branding, 94–95
    commitment, 229
    desired, 88
    employees, 90–93
    enthusiasm for, 90–93
    famous effective, 90
    focusing energy on, 229
    interpreting and understanding, 92
    investing energy toward, 191
    long-term, 100, 103
    monitoring pursuit of, 95

    not supporting, 97
    participating personally and visibly, 97
    positive imagery, 88–89
    reward systems and, 97–99
    Tata Steel, 93–94
vitalizing
    culture, 207–223
    leadership structures, 185–196, 197–207
    management system, 174–175, 222–223
Volkswagen, 100
von Gruenberg, Hubertus, 98–99, 103, 134,
    179, 229
von Weizsaecker, Richard, 6

weak organizational identity, 111
weaknesses, identifying, 10
Weber, Juergen, 2, 17, 23, 30, 68–71, 174
Wells Fargo, 191
winning the princess, 18–19, 61, 85–101
    aligning rewards with vision, 97–99
    clear branding of vision, 94–95
    confidence in opportunity, 95–99
    continuity, 100–101
    cynicism, frustration or negative stress, 86
    employees not supporting vision, 97
    inspirational leadership, 189–192
    leveraging positive tension, 86
    long-term pursuit, 100–101
    mobilizing energy around, 226–228
    monitoring vision progress, 95
    opportunities, 87–89
    orchestrating use, 101–104
    prior steps, 99–101
    productive energy, 86
    pursuit of joint vision, 102
    resigned inertia, 66, 85–86
    slaying small dragons on way to, 103–104
    summary of tasks, 87
    tasks, 87–99
    time limitation of opportunity, 101
Wolter, Sieglinde, 91
Work@Home project, 12
WORLDCOM, 29, 37
Würth Group, 182

yes-men, 31

Zimmermann, Rudolf, 203
Zschokke, Alexander, 22

About the Authors

Heike Bruch is a Senior Professor and Director of the Institute for Leadership and Human Resources Management at the University of St. Gallen (Switzerland). She is the founder and Research Director of the Organizational Energy Program (OEP) and the energy factory St. Gallen AG and she is a member of the McKinsey Academic Sounding Board, the Management Board of the German Association for Leadership (DGFP), as well as the Academic Committee of the Demographic Network (ddn).

Earlier roles include Senior Research Fellow at the London Business School and Lecturer at the University of Hannover. She received her PhD in Management from the Leibniz University of Hannover, Germany and her habilitation in Leadership from the University of St. Gallen.

Heike Bruch's research interests include organizational energy, leadership in high-performance organizations, and leaders' emotion, volition, and action. She has received numerous academic awards, written six books, edited another six, and published in international top-tier journals. She is a coach and consultant to companies in Europe, the United States, and Asia.

Bernd Vogel is Assistant Professor of Leadership and Organizational Behavior at the Henley Business School, University of Reading, United Kingdom. Earlier roles include project leader in the Organizational Energy Program (OEP) at the University of St. Gallen, Switzerland and Visiting Scholar at the University of Southern California's Marshall School of Business. He received his PhD in Management from the Leibniz University of Hannover, Germany.

His research focuses on organizational energy, leadership, change, and followership. Bernd has written several books and published in international top-tier journals. He is teaching and consulting internationally based on his expertise in both unleashing leadership and generating organizational energy.